ROOM USE ONLY

Popular Music in a Digital Music Economy

In the late 1990s, the MP3 became the *de facto* standard for digital audio files and the networked computer began to claim a significant place in the lives of more and more listeners. The dovetailing of these two circumstances is the basis of a new mode of musical production and distribution where new practices emerge. This book is not a definitive statement about what the new music industry *is*. Rather, it is devoted to examing what this new industry is becoming by examining these practices as experiments, dedicated to replacing an "object based" industry that had been oriented around the production and exchange of physical recordings. In this new economy, constant attention is paid to the production and licensing of intellectual property and the rise of the "social musician" who has been encouraged to become more entrepreneurial. Finally, every element of the industry now must consider a new type of audience, the "end user", and their productive and distributive capacities around which services and musicians must orient their practices and investments.

Tim J. Anderson is an Assistant Professor in the Department of Communication and Theater Arts at Old Dominion University, USA.

Routledge Research in Music

Popular Music in a Digital Music Economy

Problems and Practices for an Emerging Service Industry

Tim J. Anderson

Routledge
Taylor & Francis Group

NEW YORK   LONDON

First published 2014
by Routledge
711 Third Avenue, New York, NY 10017

and by Routledge
2 Park Square, Milton Park, Abingdon, Oxon OX14 4RN

*Routledge is an imprint of the Taylor & Francis Group,
an informa business*

Library of Congress Cataloging-in-Publication Data
Anderson, Tim J.
    Popular music in a digital music economy : problems and practices for
an emerging service industry / by Tim J. Anderson.
        pages cm. — (Routledge research in music ; 8)
    Includes bibliographical references and index.
    1. Music trade.   2. Music and the Internet—Economic
aspects.   I. Title.
    ML3790.A64 2014
    338.4'778—dc23
    2013026245

ISBN13: 978-0-415-89063-2 (hbk)
ISBN13: 978-1-315-85094-8 (ebk)

Typeset in Sabon
by IBT Global.

This book is dedicated to . . .

. . . the family who raised me. My father showed me what love is when he nursed my mother into her passing. It was the bravest thing I have ever seen and the best lesson a son could learn from his parents.

. . . the family who has changed me and challenged me to change. Robert, Mary Alice and Kathleen, I am lucky to be in your life.

. . . my wife, Katie: I can't imagine not having you in my life. You've given me more than I can ever give back. Because of you I have another parent, another sister, two brothers, cousins, a son and two daughters to love. Most importantly, I have you to wake up to. You're so cute. I love you. Let's dance!

Contents

Acknowledgments

First the friends that contributed to the manuscript: Susan Greenhow, Frank Denier, Levi Stahl, Joe Germuska, Brian Gaddie, Dave Gilbert, Marc Giordano, Saylor Breckenridge, Chelsey Crago, Tim Lucas, Yury Khidekel, Leila Marsh, Bob Frantz, Tim Porges, Annie Taylor, Cary Johnston, Nora Stickney, Marcia Germ, Mike Marunowski, and Mike Butcher. None of you know it, but in some way or another you said or did something that helped. Thanks. If I forgot a name, apologies.

The manuscript began as a book proposal that was funded by a grant provided by the Old Dominion University Research Foundation. The research was supported by my department, my peers, and students at Old Dominion University. Thanks to Gary Edgerton, Avi Santo, Fran Hassencahl, Tom Socha, Bob Arnett, Burton St. John, Alison Lietzenmeyer, Joleen Westerdale, Alfredo Torres, TuanAhn Vu, Jonathan Leib, Warren "Chip" Russell, Satasha Maricruz, Amy Adcock, Jeffrey Jones, Dana Heller, Yi Fan Chen, Jinsun Lee, Jim Baesler, Andrea Battle, and Jennifer Barksdale for making this process much smoother than it could have been.

In the world of the academy, good thoughts and conversations have come from Judd Ruggill, Jonathan Gray, Paul Theberge, Jonathan Sterne, Kathleen Battles, Daniel Marcus, Charles McGovern, Arthur Knight, Erin Copple-Smith, Kay Dickinson, Danielle Stern, Ben Aslinger, Jason Mittell, Chuck Tryon, Mimi White, Jim Schwoch, Mark Williams, Mary Beth Haralovich, Norma Coates, Eileen Meehan, Jackie Byars, Sarah Hill, Debra White-Stanley, and Kathleen Fitzpatrick; they all contributed their ears and voices to the cause. They may not know it, but they helped. The example and support of Derek Kompare provided me a model of scholarly perseverance and friendship. One would have been enough, but Derek's generosity is only matched by his ability. His friends are lucky to know him. I am lucky to count myself as one of his friends.

Quite a bit of much-needed encouragement was offered to me by the wonderful one-day conference in Bristol, England at the first annual Severn Pop Music Conference in 2013. Dedicated to examining the small economies of the new music industry, it was exactly the type of collegial support that I needed to remind me why I was working so hard to finish this manuscript. Much thanks to Lee Marshall of the University of Bristol for organizing and hosting the event. Without it finishing this work would have been much more difficult.

While the contents of this book may not directly reflect it, it has its basis in discussions and interviews that I was fortunate to have with David De Busk, Peter Jenner, Ariel Hyatt, Bryan Calhoun, Tim Westergren, Brian Zisk, Maura Johnston, Nelson Jacobsen, Robert Kaye, Michael Petricone, Charles McEnerney, and the staff at the United States Copyright Office in The Library of Congress. All of these people and their institutions are in the "thick of it," as one might put it. Their time is valuable, their insights even more so. This book would not have been possible without both.

There is no way to truly estimate how important the Future of Music Coalition has been for this work. They assemble innovators, educators, politicians, and industry actors for open debate about where the music industry is going and how it should get there. The organization goes out of its way to bring both its supporters and detractors together to discuss and argue about business and governmental policy. They have also allowed me to come to their meetings, provided me with opportunities to ask questions, and offered answers when they have had them. Most important to this process has been Casey Rae, the Interim Executive Director of the Future of Music Coalition. He has been a knowledgeable interlocutor and as good a guide through this beautiful but tangled mess of a business.

Introduction

Just occasionally we find ourselves watching on the sidelines as an order comes crashing down. Organisations or systems which we had always taken for granted—the Union of Soviet Socialist Republics, or Continental Illinois—are swallowed up. Commissars, moguls and captains of industry disappear from view. These dangerous moments offer more than political promise. For when the hidden trapdoors of the social spring open we suddenly learn that the masters of the universe may also have feet of clay

—John Law (2003, p. 379)

Record is a word that does not exist in the vocabulary of a 15-year old.

—Leoni-Sceti (Ashton, 2009, p. 7)

Throughout its 40-year existence Virgin has always associated the brand with youth and alternative, progressive lifestyles. In the 1990s and 2000s Richard Branson would push his Virgin brand into the digital realm as his labels and retail stores established web presences and, eventually, mobile telephone services in territories such as the UK, Australia, South Africa, India, and the United States ("Virgin looks at money services and marijuana," 1994). Yet Virgin's longest association has been with recorded music. Beginning as a mail-order music business in 1970, Virgin became a London record retailer in 1971. Two years later the Virgin label released Mike Oldfield's *Tubular Bells*, which would go on to become a gold-selling record. Thus, when Virgin relinquished control of its famous megastore retail chain in 2007 it came as a shock to the music world. Selling the 125 Virgin Megastores not located in North America, including the one at the end of London's Oxford Street, to the Zavvi Entertainment Group effectively signaled the beginning of the end of the company's involvement with brick and mortar music retail ("Branson sells British Virgin Megastores," 2007). The North American megastores, which at one time claimed 23 locations, were bought by real estate companies who "made it clear that the chain's true value was not in its sales but in the real estate that its stores occupied." Two years later the remaining stores, including the megastore in Times Square, liquidated their stock and shuttered their doors. As one former Virgin employee noted, "Unfortunately the large retail music store is a dinosaur" (Sisario, 2009).

Retailers fold all the time. Yet this situation was particularly interesting: the establishment, expansion, celebration, and contraction of Virgin's North American retail chain is an interesting piece of music history that finds a comfortable home in the boom/greed/bust narrative of the 1990s. Taking place less than 15 years before the chain's sale, at one time Virgin's investment in a global music seemed like a sure bet. The 1996 opening of the Times Square store, a 75,000-square foot, three-story "entertainment retail complex" stocked with compact discs, DVDs, books, and magazines, was positioned as a beachhead for expanding the Virgin brand into North America markets. Richard Branson told *The New York Times* that he "felt if we could create a really special store in New York, there'd be a market for it" (Elliot, 1996). Branson's more-than-significant extension of his retail chain could not be ignored and it exuded his all-but-trademarked "I believe in what I'm doing" bravado. The key to these spaces would be atmosphere, not size. In 1996 the initial manager of the Times Square Megastore, Christos Garkinos, stated, "We think we offer a great environment with huge selection that's fun to hang out in. It's a way to experience pop culture all in one setting" (Elliot, 1996). At its height Virgin's North American investment grew to 24 Megastores, each of which included multiple listening stations and connections to a real-time data warehouse that analyzed purchases and customer traffic so managers could identify trends in a just-in-time fashion. Commenting on his Times Square store, Branson noted that "if you create the best in anything, there's usually a market for it, and my Times Square store is the best" (Winship, 1996). The publicity surrounding Virgin Megastores hit a peak when Virgin proposed to open a store in Vancouver, Canada and the retailer's then-president, Ian Duffel, claimed that the Paris Megastore was the city's "second largest tourist attraction, generating $120 million US a year" (Constantineau, 1996). Established in the 1990s, Virgin's Megastores were stocked with compact discs and DVDs that promised consumers a rich digital media experience and labels wide margins. The profits garnered from remastering and reissuing decades of content in the early 1990s combined with labels' legacy holdings of master tapes drove global investors to acquire and fold them into larger media conglomerates.[1] It also drove an expansion in retail, which Virgin's investment was part of and included the growth of so-called "Big Box Stores" such as Walmart, Circuit City, Best Buy, and Borders. Throughout the 1990s each of these chains invested so quickly and significantly in space and expertise for music retail that there seemed to be only one logical outcome: self consumption. *The Washington Post* reported in 1995 that "every time word gets out that another music chain is considering expanding in the Washington area, local music retailers shudder." The compulsion to expand even befuddled those managing some of Washington, D.C.'s Tower Records, a chain that had opened two more locations in the area. Then-regional manager for Tower Records, Kevin Ferreter, quipped, "I don't understand why people are still opening stores. The pie is just way too thin. It's terrible— there's just not enough room for all these retailers" (Webb Pressler, 1995b, p. C01).[2] Like Virgin, Tower Records shrugged off the threats of inflated competition, expanded, and then promptly collapsed. In 2004 Tower

Records, arguably the most storied record retailer in U.S. history, would file for bankruptcy. By 2006 the chain could no longer secure their assets, shuttered each of its 89 national spaces, and laid off 3,000 of its employees (Knopper, 2009, p. 213). Even more than Virgin's collapse, in the United States Tower's fall from greatness would come to symbolize "for many the bankruptcy of bricks and mortar music retailing" (Laurson & Pieler, 2006). Tower had seen the handwriting on the wall and tried to adjust to online environments. In 2000, "[Tower's] Web site was ranked No. 1 for online music sales" (Laurson & Pieler, 2006).

So what happened? As wide-scale record retail practically vanished from its brick and mortar domains, a conventional narrative emerged: the combination of significantly compressed, relatively high-fidelity digital formats with the proliferation of seemingly ubiquitous broadband networks and personalized information control technologies through which music would now be distributed killed the music industry. Forbes.com would report that "with the music buying experience evolving by the moment, old-fashioned record stores with leases, staff and high inventory costs (tying up millions in capital), needed a drastic overhaul" and too many managers "slept through the revolution, making gestures toward the new music retailing landscape but too little, too late" (Laurson & Pieler, 2006). For anyone who has lived in North America in the last 15 years this narrative makes sense. From Napster to Kazaa to BitTorrents, from dial-up to DSLs, from desktops to smart phones to digital tablets, from MySpace to Facebook, etc., in little over a decade more of the world began to engage an unimaginable ecosystem of digital networks and tools. Yet this destruction by digital is only one part of the story. The other part is the story with which this book is concerned: how an industry has and continues to undergo multiple experiments to create a viable set of practices to replace those that have been lost. The trouble with writing this book is that these practices are still being discovered and are not completely understood, even by those participating in the experiments. So let's be clear for a moment: those of us who are interested in music as a business stand together in a moment of great challenge, change, and new organizing forces. We are now in the midst of a set of actors, structures, and authorities that in 1991 many longtime music fans, professionals, and institutions simply would not have recognized nor been able to envision. This book is about how institutions and actors are negotiating the effects that these actors have exerted on music industry practices, particularly those involving pricing, sales, radio, publishing, and finance.

The popular imagination has paid most attention to the significant loss of control that elements such as major labels, radio, and retail have negotiated as they have wrestled with the effects of ubiquitous networks of exchange. Yet, what has occurred is so much more than a loss of control. It is the loss of standard practices. From the late-1900s to the late-1990s the U.S. music industry had been built around the production, distribution, and sale of mass produced and mass distributed objects. Whether these objects came as sheet music or recordings, the major income streams derived from the sale of these objects. Not that recordings or sheet music required the *same* practices. Elsewhere I argue that the shift from a music industry economy based on performances to one based on recordings in the period after World War II occurred through conflicts with labor, labels adapting practices from publishers, and the negotiation of recording and playback techniques as new technologies entered the marketplace. The difficulty of the transition involved new formats, new networks, new audiences, new playback systems, and even new genres (Anderson, 2006). Indeed, the music industry continued to engage the challenges from new technologies, audiences, and genres from the end of World War II to the beginning of the 21st century through moments of growth and recession. However, what is different is that the changes over the last 15 years have moved us into a paradigm involving the exchange and transformation of networked information by users. This has involved numerous experiments that have begat technological mutations (in the 1990s did you ever think your phone could become a portable jukebox?) and new, important musical agents, many of which are not human. In this world algorithms and end users coexist together as new and important actors. This book is an attempt to better understand some of the new actors and practices that are creating a new music industry.

Please note that one problem that this book will avoid is the future. I have opinions about what will and won't work in the future, but they are not for this volume. Instead, I remain focused on new practices and new actors and their evolving relationships in a new and somewhat disorienting ecosystem. This shift has made industry workers that were once minor considerations such as "music supervisors" into stars in their own right; it has littered our language with a litany of neologisms such as "the cloud" and services such as Pandora and Spotify; it has forced the industry to rethink long-established principles and practices of pricing and financing. And, of course, it has made the industry rethink how it brings goods to market. For someone who spent years working and shopping in record retailers the collapse of this ecosystem was profound. Retail is much more than the final gate of the marketplace or simple spaces of exchange. In truth, all retail spaces are composed of complex sets of practices that involve relationships between managers, buyers, floor employees, customers, and goods. From independently-owned shops, to local, regional, and national chains, retailers establish their own cultures and their own ways of relating to distributors, customers, music, and managers. Retailers often purposely employed local musicians, disc jockeys, tastemakers, and people who had spent years as part of local music scenes. These employees were integral to the environment often suggesting, promoting, and holding records and CDs for specific customers. Many shops retained the same employees for decades and were spaces for friendship and debate. As one former Virgin employee noted, shuttering the chain mattered because even the large store "was a social gathering space, and that's one thing that buying music online lacks" (Sisario, 2009).

This isn't to say that the social aspect of retail has gone the way of the dodo. As I will argue, a large part of the experimentation by many new parties has been devoted to making online retail more social. Yet these new parties, many of which have come in the form of Internet start-ups, have not been able to completely disrupt an entire industry. They, too, have had to negotiate with legacies upon which the music industry operates. Indeed, when I began this manuscript I toyed with the idea of subtitling it "The Internet did not destroy the music industry no matter how much you wanted it to." The liberatory rhetoric that has accompanied much of the popular press regarding the collapse of the older, object-based music industry, the record industry in particular, would have one think that somehow all the injustices that capitalism has delivered to musicians, genres, and scenes could be crushed by Sweden's Pirate Party and a number of Apache-enabled servers. Perhaps what has been most problematic is the misunderstanding of the term "music industry," a term that is all too often misused in everyday parlance and scholarship to describe a centralization of capital assets that simply isn't the case. For those interested in media studies this can lead to some interesting problems. It is tempting to believe that major labels connected to large media conglomerates easily controlled the industry from some sort of commanding height. However, this is no easy task and it simply ignores the many years that these companies have invested in solving those problems of labor coordination and networking that are particularly acute in the music industry. It is one of the reasons that the record industry and music publishers must rely on a number of "third parties," intermediaries who initiate and lubricate specific media exchanges and placements. These third parties can never truly be captured, but they can work together with the proper incentivizes.

Viewing the music industry as a series of interlocking networks of workers and traditions is key to this book. There are a number of ways to envision these fields but for now I would like to use Dave Hesmondhalgh's delineation of "core and peripheral" cultural industries. For Hesmondhalgh the core industries involve "broadcasting," "film industries," "the content aspects of the Internet industry," "music industries," "print and electronic publishing," "video and computer games," and "advertising and marketing." The peripheral industries are the "creative arts" and tend to use semi-industrial or artisanal means of production such as theater and many of the visual arts like painting and sculpting (Hesmondhalgh, 2007, pp. 12–13). There are three issues at work here that involve the music industry. First, technically Hesmondhalgh is correct about the core industries of recording and publishing. They are core cultural industries because their primary orientation involves the "industrial production and circulation of texts" (Hesmondhalgh, 2007, p. 12). Second, Hesmondhalgh also correctly understands that the issue of culture is a key term for the music industry and draws from Raymond Williams' understanding as a "whole way of life" for a distinct people or another social group (Hesmondhalgh, 2007, p. 11). However, there is a third issue: the continual invocation of constantly changing third parties that are necessary for labels and publishers to square the circles between organizational principles and cultural demands. What this means for publishers and labels is that they must understand and respect that these cultural demands can only be met with cultural practices that can change from group to group, city to city, and time to time. Keith Negus points out the importance that intermediaries play when organizing these industries that "the activities involved in producing popular music should be thought of as meaningful practices" (Negus, 1999, p. 20). This emphasis on "meaningful practices" is one of the reasons that Negus and others have focused on the issue of "genre" as a longstanding key for publishers and labels to help them distribute their commodities. However, the only means through which these products can find their place within meaningful genre worlds is in the passage through numerous social and cultural spaces and functionaries such as disc jockeys, clubs, performers, and radio and television stations. These elements are part of what Simon Frith calls a "genre world": "a complex interplay of musicians, listeners, and mediating ideologues" and "is much more confused" than typical marketing processes because genre in popular music is as much a sociological issue as it is a formal issue (Frith, 1996, p. 88). For Negus this means that "record companies are not unified businesses, but collections of units organized according to a musical genre" (Negus, 1999, p. 49). As such, genre is a driving, meaningful force through which A & R, marketing, and, in some cases, entire record labels and publishers are organized. Furthermore, as genres change so do their actors in the organization.

In a similar fashion this book conceives of the "music industry" as a complex and always-unfinished set of institutions and actors. I am not alone in this conception. John Williamson and Martin Cloonan argue that the term, while often employed in a totalizing manner, can never fully comprehend the multiple actors and organizations that compromise those systems that make and market music. Instead, there are "music industries rather than an industry" and this requires "a considerable shift in thinking" (Williamson & Cloonan, 2007, pp. 312–313). For Williamson and Cloonan, "[the problem with] most academic studies of the popular music industries [is they] have continued to privilege the recording industry as being the music industry" (Williamson & Cloonan, 2007, p. 312). Williamson and Cloonan are not alone. In his 2009 book *The Music Industry: Music in The Cloud*, Patrik Wikström draws from Andrew Leyshon's conception of the music industry as a set of overlapping networks (creativity, reproduction, distribution, and consumption) with great benefit and provides a definition that he uses throughout his book: "The music industry consists of those companies concerned with developing musical content and personalities, which can be communicated across multiple media" (Wikstrom, 2009, p. 49). Finally, Simon Frith notes that the industry is best understood as a strategic amalgam of sometimes interlocking actors that tactically change depending on specific cultural trends, shifts in economic forces and new technologies (See Frith, 1988, pp. 12–13). Again, this is not the result of sloppy organization. Rather, the relative independence of these actors allows for the most efficient formation and dissolution of networks, systems, and practices. It allows for a creative flexibility so that all actors involved may negotiate numerous cultural, technological, communication, and financial institutions as they change. In a sense, this arrangement allows these arrangements to be plastic, ever-changing, and often reactionary. In this manner the term "music industry" is less a singular noun but an ever-shifting plurality that describes an intersection of relationships that at any given time temporarily solidify or destabilize as conditions change. The instability that the industry is undergoing is the result of losing the sale of a mass reproduced physical good as the center around which actors and industries could be organized. This has meant that the network of record companies and music publishers, unions, rights organizations, consumer electronic companies, live venues, booking networks, television, film, radio programmers, disc jockeys, copy writers, distributors, and retailers that have been primarily oriented to the sale of things have found their practices lacking a purchase they once could claim.

As an industry based on the sale of objects has stumbled, the question of what actors and practices are needed to make music profitable looms unanswered, although numerous answers have been offered. Writing for his blog, Alexander Osterwalder notes that "Today's music industry is a business model playground—and to a certain extent battleground." For Osterwalder the "battleground" is not about competing companies. Given that "85% of the recording industry, the most important subset of the music industry, is controlled by only four players, Sony Music Entertainment, Universal Music Group, Warner Music Group, and EMI," issues of competition reside elsewhere (Osterwalder, 2010a). Instead, while past versions of the music industry seemed to be "characterized by one dominant business model design (the one of the major recording companies), the future will be characterized by multiple competing business models" (Osterwalder, 2010b). No doubt there seems to be no lack of models. For example, music consultant and occasional investor Bruce Warila identifies three competing music industry models: "The Lottery Model," "The Free Culture Model," and "The Click Control Model," each of which come with significant problems and benefits for labels and publishers alike (Warila, 2009). Derek Sivers, founder of the independent online music store CD Baby, holds that while the present is changing, the future is unknown and far too often predictions made about which future business models will succeed stem from specific vested interests. In 2009 Sivers' answer to the question about the future of the music industry was "Nobody knows the future. Anyone who pretends is full of shit and not to be trusted" and that he just didn't know how it would pan out (Sivers, 2009). This unpredictability has made it difficult for any major investor to finance major music business propositions. Musicians, promoters, and financiers are simply exasperated by spending hours building profiles, learning social media skills, producing records, and working with services and business models that never gain traction. Indeed, we exist in a pre-paradigmatic period where no agreed upon model and sets of practices exist.

This is the reason that this book begins with the demise of brick and mortar music retail. The widespread contraction of these national chains may be the most physical reaction to digital networks and ubiquitous computing that all media forms have met with in the last decade and a half. In the United States CDs can still be bought in larger retail spaces such as Best Buy, Target, and Walmart, where the discs are a very minor part of their business and they invest little to nothing in catalogue sales. However, at the moment of this writing there is only one significant chain with a music retail legacy in the United States. Purchased by Trans World Entertainment in 2006, the chain is partially composed of older mall spaces occupied by Sam Goody stores, a record store chain with roots reaching back to the 1940s. By the end of 2000 the Sam Goody chain could claim 986 stores and boast that music accounted for around 75% of their sales. However, by the end of fiscal year 2009, the same company held 565 stores with only 37% of their sales coming from music (Christman, 2010). Like other retailers, Trans World Entertainment was forced to close locations and rethink the way their stores thought about what goods they stocked. However, in 2009, while other retailers vied for exclusive music merchandise and other marketplace advantages, Trans World began to work with EMI, Universal, Sony, and numerous independent labels to experiment with a wholesale $6.50–$7.50 per disc pricing for their FYE chains. Trans World also worked with 118 stores in 30 different markets to eliminate variable pricing and make the $9.99 CD a standard price. The pricing experiments were not limited to physical retailers. Both iTunes and Amazon began variable pricing practices in the same year (Christman, 2009). Over the past decade or so music retailers have simply existed in a prolongated moment of widespread commercial failure and their only option has been to experiment to discover what models will work in this quickly evolving atmosphere. In a 2009 interview, the author of *Appetite for Destruction: The Spectacular Crash of the Record Industry in the Digital Age*, Steve Knopper, was asked if along with iTunes whether there was a possible model for retail "in an era of digital distribution." Knopper's answer summarized the belief held by many in the industry, that what pervades is a "less-than-unified" set of practices:

> You know, I interview a lot of record executives for my job as a reporter at *Rolling Stone*, and the thing I hear over and over again from record executives is it's not just one thing. We used to be trapped in this model of we're going to sell CDs and that's it. Now it's everything. You've got

social networking services like Facebook, you've got subscription services like Rhapsody. You've got—LPs are coming back, they're making a very unexpected comeback among hipster college students. So, we're going to sell those to you. (Gross, 2009)

As exciting as multiple opportunities may sound, such indeterminacy comes with great wariness. For every new way of getting to know your audience and bringing your musical wares to market, there are multiple fears about not knowing what is the best way for your art and your investments. Lest we forget that even in eras of relative stability most commercial recordings and pieces of sheet music failed to find profits. And until very recently the music industry employed a strategy where they made multiple investments knowing that the great majority of them would be financial losers but that a few would hit so significantly that the sheer scale of these sales would result in a profit. This strategy is no longer employed and what we have stepped into is a period where precedents are being scrapped and new practices being examined, discarded, established, and learned by loosely affiliated communities of practitioners. In a sense, the music industry is evolving as a new environment of users and third parties discover what works and what doesn't in a post-object economy of file sharing and streaming. As is always the case evolution is about adaptation. Evolution, as one of my former philosophy professors put it, isn't about being strong and surviving. It means, what you do have today hasn't killed you, yet. Sometimes these adaptations are planned, but more often than not they are discovered through mistakes and unexpected moments. Evolution isn't always clear when it is happening, but often only after the process has occurred. And sometimes what lasts and mutates comes from places and organizations that for years were ignored as small potatoes. Such is the case of musicians directly selling their records, their band merchandise, and developing their brand.

This sentiment is best expressed by Gerald Casale, longtime member of the band Devo. Beginning in the 1970s, the band has had a five-decade career replete with numerous hiatuses and active periods. In 2009 the band began to record their first studio album since the 1990. As a band Devo has always been experimental both in terms of style and instrumentation. Less acknowledged was the band's considerable entrepreneurial spirit, one that included the self-production of independent releases and merchandise well before these activities were the norm. As Casale noted in 2009,

When we started out we released a self-pressed single through independent record stores and used our live shows to spread the word about the band. Before we even got signed we'd already successfully distributed and marketed ourselves. That was considered weird at the time—like we weren't really rock'n'roll because we didn't follow the usual cliché of the wasted musician who is basically an attention-seeking fucked-up child. Now all bands are having to do what we did. At least they used to give you big advances back then. Now unless you're Beyonce or Diddy labels can't do much for you. (Long, 2009)

In the 1980s, when other bands sold only albums, Devo sold albums that included sleeves with a mail order form so their fans cold buy their plastic energy domes and reproductions of the many uniforms they wore onstage and in their videos. The band actively sold their merchandise and brand before branding and merchandising were widely practiced. However, those major labels that once scoffed at this income as little more than ancillary, now require a percentage of this income stream in most of their new contracts. As records sell less and record retail has collapsed, labels have scrambled for these once-dismissed income streams. Labels, along with every other factor of the business, are experimenting. To quote Casale, "The music business has imploded and the old models are gone and there's no new paradigm to replace the old one. There are no rules" (Long, 2009).

This book begins with a look at the figure of the end user and throughout it examines how the construction of a ubiquitously networked user has affected the practices of pricing, streaming, radio, publishing, and finance. The combination of user communities and pre-existing institutions have created new ways to associate in things business and social. The means of association, these networks, are formed through a number of practices that are also known as protocol. As Alexander R. Galloway points out, networks do not allow a "free for all" of information production and association (Galloway, 2004, p. xv). Galloway is adamant: "every network is a network because it is constituted by a protocol." Part of this is constituted as a "political economy," wherein "protocol modulates, regulates, and manages the interrelationality between vital systems" (p. xviii). This is a book dedicated to understanding those experiments to revitalize a music industry that feels shaken as some parts of it atrophy and others are consumed without the promise of remission. The music industry will continue. What it will look like, what will remain, and what will emerge is hardly a sure bet. And while the contents of this book studiously avoid predictions, the models it documents are placing their bets on a future where they materialize from the ruins of record stores.

BIBLIOGRAPHY

Anderson, T. J. (2006). *Making Easy Listening: Material Culture and Postwar Recording*. Minneapolis, MN: University of Minnesota Press.
Ashton, J. (2009, March 8). EMI Has a New Spin on Record Market; New Chief Elio Leoni-Sceti Is Devising a Fresh Business Model, Writes James Ashton. *The Sunday Times*, 7.
Branson sells British Virgin Megastores. (2007). *UPI*.
Christman, E. (2009, December 19). Stayin' Alive. *Billboard*.

Christman, E. (2010, January 23). Solutions for Sale. *Billboard.*

Constantineau, B. (1996, February 3). Regulators frown on Virgin Records, *The Vancouver Sun.*

Elliot, S. (1996, April 17). For the Debut of a Virgin Megastore, Everything's on a Grand Scale. *The New York Times.*

Frith, S. (1988). *Music For Pleasure: Essays in the Sociology of Pop.* New York: Pantheon.

Frith, S. (1996). *Performing Rites: On the Value of Popular Music.* Cambridge, MA: Harvard University Press.

Galloway, A. (2004). *Protocol: How Control Exists After Decentralization.* Cambridge, MA: The MIT Press.

Gross, T. (2009). The Rise and Fall of the Music Industry. *Fresh Air.* Philadelphia, PA: National Public Radio.

Hesmondhalgh, D. (2007). *The Culture Industries* (2nd ed.). Los Angeles: Sage Publications.

Knopper, S. (2009). *Appetite for Self-Destruction: The Spectacular Crash of the Record Industry in the Digital Age.* New York: Free Press.

Laurson, J. F., & Pieler, G. A. (2006). The Tower That Fell. *Forbes.com.* Retrieved from http://www.forbes.com/2006/11/15/tower-music-bankruptcy-oped-cx_jfl_1115tower.html

Law, J. (1992). Notes on the Theory of the Actor Network: Ordering, Strategy and Heterogeneity *Systems Practice, 5* (4), 379–393. Doi: 10.1007/BF01059830

Long, P. (2009, May 2). The Guide: We Are Legend: New Wave Oddballs Devo Used to Warn That Consumerism Was Crumbling. Now They're Back to Say We Told You So. *The Guardian, 14.*

Negus, K. (1999). *Music Genres and Corporate Cultures.* New York: Routledge.

Osterwalder, A. (2010a). The Music Industry (Part I)—What's Broken. Retrieved from http://www.businessmodelalchemist.com/2010/01/the-music-industry-business-model-innovation-part-i.html

Osterwalder, A. (2010b). The Music Industry (Part II)—Two of the New Models. Retrieved from http://www.businessmodelalchemist.com/2010/01/the-music-industry-part-ii-two-of-the-new-models.html

Sisario, B. (2009, June 15). Retailing Era Closes With Music Megastore. *The New York Times,* C1.

Sivers, D. (2009). Unlearning. Retrieved from http://www.musicthinktank.com/blog/unlearning.html

Virgin Looks at Money Services and Marijuana. (1994, October 14). *The Financial Post,* 8.

Warila, B. (2009). The Lottery Model, The Free Culture Model, The Click Control Model. Retrieved from http://www.musicthinktank.com/blog/the-lottery-model-the-free-culture-model-the-click-control-m.html

Webb Pressler, M. (1995a, April 25). Best Buy's D.C. Rivals Find Some Benefits in the Battle. *The Washington Post.*

Webb Pressler, M. (1995b, April 29). The Unsound of Music; The Hills Are Alive With Record Stores Whose Abundance Is Erasing Profit Margins. *The Washington Post,* C01.

Wikstrom, P. (2009). *The Music Industry: Music in the Cloud.* Cambridge, MA: Polity Press.

Williamson, J., & Cloonan, M. (2007). Rethinking the Music Industry. *Popular Music, 26*(2), 305–322. doi: 10.1017/S0261143007001262

Winship, F. M. (1996, April 16). Times Square Gets Huge Record Store. *United Press International.*

1 Enter the End User
A New Audience for a New Media

> We look first at the audience concept itself, since it can appear under different names or with different meanings for the same name. These different versions of the audience sometimes stand for different ways of perceiving the same thing and sometimes for different realities.
>
> —Denis McQuail in *Mass Communication Theory: An Introduction* (1984, p. 149)

> The media industries are undergoing another paradigm shift. It happens from time to time.
>
> —Henry Jenkins in *Convergence Culture* (2006, p. 5)

Among the more celebrated and embraced sectors of the new music economy in the United States has been the growth of online radio, Pandora in particular. Describing their service, Pandora claims that it is a "new kind of radio—stations that play only music you like" ("Pandora," 2010). Each Pandora user can pick from a continually-growing library of songs (well over 700,000 in early 2010) that are hand coded by trained employees to identify upwards of 400 possible musical traits, aka "genes." Upon choosing the song, the user can either apply a "thumbs-up" or "thumbs-down" tag, or simply let it play, and the service will choose a song with similar "genetic qualities." The combination of an artisanal attention to detail with the organization's willingness to engage listeners' specific demands through detailed correspondence and gatherings has generated a potent musical service. On more than one occasion, Tim Westergren, the service's cofounder, has gone on tours throughout the U.S. to meet Pandora users at "Town Hall" meetings and discover what they like, love, and loathe about the service. Paying such attention to its users has served Pandora well. In April 2010, Pandora announced that it had "passed the 50 million-user mark" (Ha, 2010). By July of the same year another report noted that the user base had grown to 60 million (Greer, 2010). As the numbers grew it was clear that by 2010 Pandora was among the most successful in a long line of new music services that were based around new principles of online media. These services are many and originate from a variety of cultural and regulatory contexts. They come in the forms of competing webcasters (Last.FM, Slacker, etc.) as well as on-demand streaming services (Spotify, Rhapsody, Mog, Grooveshark, we7, Deezer, etc.). Each of these have their own ambitions and models, yet each have one aspect in common:

they nichecast music through ubiquitous digital networks to service each specific user's needs while framing their stock in trade as sets of quantifiable relationships rich with associative probabilities. Unlike the past 90 years of American broadcasting where stations traded access to somewhat anonymous audiences, in comparison users are far more discrete and with allegiances and preferences much more clearly understood due to their constant monitoring.

One would think that the value in this data would be clear for advertisers. However, as will be addressed in later chapters that focus on Pandora and Spotify, these new services have had to labor mightily to establish new pathways of trust to assuage investors' nerves about a new ecosystem, a new set of practices, practitioners, technologies, and terms. Lest we forget that moving from one media system to another is rarely smooth. For example, in the case of programmers moving from radio to television James Schwoch points out that despite the efforts of many network sales staffs in the U.S., the transition was filled with anxieties and "throughout World War II, broadcasters worked toward overcoming those anxieties and wooing the agency and the advertiser over to the new medium. For every radio sponsor in 1941 ready and willing to jump into television, twenty to thirty other sponsors and agencies remained wary" (Schwoch, 1990, p. 57). Like other forms of social capital the establishment of trust, the resource that remedies wariness and eliminates numerous transactional costs, can only be developed over long stretches of time. Indeed, the rapid pace of change has provided little time to establish the foundations upon which many elements of the music industry have felt comfortable mooring themselves. Their move into digital media structures, like those in television and film, has been marked with significant amounts of distrust and confusion. Through this turmoil one term among media practitioners, "convergence," has gained substantial traction as multiple forces take on digital paradigms. As a term, convergence is used to describe the conflation of television, radio, and film in a digital ecosystem. Henry Jenkins places the term "media convergence" alongside "participatory culture" and "collective intelligence" as key terms that are defining this new era of digitally networked media. For Jenkins, "media convergence" describes "the flow of content across multiple media platforms, the cooperation between multiple media industries, and the migratory behavior of media audiences who will go almost anywhere in search of the kinds of entertainment experiences they want"; furthermore, Jenkins explains that the term "manages to describe technological, industrial, cultural, and social changes depending in who's speaking and what they are talking about" (Jenkins, 2006, pp. 2–3). Jenkins' identification of the contingent nature of "media convergence," primarily its ever-shifting placement in media discourse, is extremely helpful. It highlights the contingent nature of convergence culture, a culture that is in perpetual beta, prefers innovation over stability, and seems to feed the anxieties of an industry that, although it continually chased aesthetic and cultural trends, had established a way of doing business that was quickly dissolving. These digital music services seemed to display a protean nature and gaining any kind of strategic foothold, discursive or economic, on systems that seemingly mutate as they pass throughout layers of "digital clouds" is, to say the least, difficult. Worse, much of this difficulty is due to the fact that these applications are designed, adopted, rejected, and remodified by users, a category that has only recently claimed a vital importance for media industries whose practices have for decades been modeled with audiences in mind.

The question of the user is key for Jenkins' attempt to understand how media industries are adjusting to their new digital environs. Jenkins is clear about this facet: "media convergence is more than simply a technological shift. Convergence alters the relationship between existing technologies, industries, markets, genres, and audiences. Convergence alters the logic by which media industries operate and by which media consumers process news and entertainment" (2006, pp. 15–16). For media firms such as Pandora and Spotify their interest in users is not too surprising. As media companies, the value of these services rest upon the features that they provide to their user bases. The emphasis on a developed, activated user base rather than an audience presents new opportunities and problems. Reckoning with this turn, a turn where audiences have seemed to acquire powers far beyond those they had before, is something that both academics and industry have had to confront. Jenkins' emphasis on active consumers in digital realms places his work alongside other scholars that are processing the development of this ecosystem. Throughout the research and musings of many writers digital audiences are positioned as part of a large-scale generational rift (Tapscott, 1998, 2008; Palfrey, 2008); a newly-enabled collective workforce and a transformed set of workplaces (Lessig, 2008; Surowiecki, 2005; Shirky, 2008; Howe, 2008; Benkler, 2006; Li & Bernoff, 2008; Locke, Levine, Searls, & Weinberger, 2001; Poster, 2006, pp. 231–249); and a population with special talents (Johnson, 2005) and/or significant detriments (Bauerline, 2008). Unstated but perpetually pronounced by comparison with previous media formations is that what has emerged is a new type of audience, a media public that has been enabled as part of a large-scale technological upheaval. Yochai Benkler is most explicit:

> We are seeing the emergence of the user as a new category of relationship to information production and exchange. Users are individuals who are sometimes consumers and sometimes producers. They are substantially more engaged participants, both in defining the terms of their productive activity and in defining what they consume and how they consume it. (Benkler, 2006, p. 138)

This new category is part of the social circumstances that Stuart Hall would label as the "whole communicative process." This process includes not only technologies but those "'social relations' of the communicative process" and "various kinds of 'competences' (at the production and receiving end)" (Hall, 1973, p. 1).

Unlike other chapters in this book, this one is the most concerned with media theory as it analyzes a basic proposition that not only affects how the music industry is configured in an era of digital convergence, but media in general. Specifically, this chapter claims that we need to radically rethink how media audiences are positioned in our new media ecosystems. Put simply, what we once called the audience has been replaced with a new actor called the end user, an actor that is essential to the formation, operation and sustenance of digital information networks. Because of this, the end user cannot be thought of as simply "audience plus." The end user is not an *ad hoc* neologism empowered with new tools or "extra powers." Instead, what media industries have encountered is an altogether new actor that is explicitly positioned as an essential part of the design and architecture behind the production, distribution, and exhibition of information that circulates throughout new media ecosystems. Furthermore, this has fundamentally altered the music business from an economy based on the sale of physical goods to a service-based economy. To understand this new model and the consequences it has for a new music industry, we have to recognize the following: (1) how these new media users operate in database-driven systems; (2) how the end user is surveyed and measured; (3) the significance of monitoring and measuring what the end user produces and shares; and (4) how the end user is often contractually obliged and limited by a legal contract that has become a staple of our daily lives, the End User License Agreement (EULA). These practices of definition, discrete monitoring, measurement, and contractual agreement have found their way into debates about privacy, media responsibilities, and our investments in new media ecosystems. Thus, understanding the value of the end user has consequences for every aspect of this ecosystem, from online radio, to cloud-streaming services, to Internet retail, brand management, and financing. Without recognizing this facet we cannot adequately understand the many tactical and strategic decisions made by the players in this environment, particularly those discussed in this book.

For the moment let us assume a clean break and the general dominance of a digital infrastructure in our media lives, even though we know so many us are and will continue to exist in an analogue media universe. Let us indulge the prospect that new media audiences are not the traditional audiences of the 20th century, but something else entirely. The scholar who most closely articulates this sentiment is P. David Marshall. Marshall argues that "If we can characterize broadcast media as continually producing an 'audience-subjectivity,' that is, an experience that can be collectively organized and sold as a coherent-commodity, new media forms such as the Internet produce what I would call a 'user-subjectivity'. The user-subject hails the individual to see themselves *producing* their cultural activity" (Marshall, 2009, p. 84). New media services and applications enable a solid sense of "user-subjectivity" where "users fabricate their own stories, their own connections, and their own social networks" (Marshall, 2009, p. 85). Marshall argues that there are three conditions that facilitate the user: (1) an architecture of interactive usage where data about use is recirculated into a contained system; (2) as "interactivity" is developed, it is labeled as "smartness" and the system better anticipates and assists the user with his or her needs; and (3) interactivity is designed to create and facilitate connections with other humans through an expansion of expression and communication (pp. 85–86).

Marshall's comments dovetail with those information architectural conceptions that allow interactivity to proliferate. These are scalability (the ability for a network or system to grow in an eloquent manner), interoperability (the ability to have multiple networking and computing systems to work together, in concert), and open architecture (a system architecture that is "open," seeable by the user who can add on and/or alter parts of the system as they need). The importance of these concepts is key to any successful implementation of digital media. In his 1995 book *Being Digital*, Nicholas Negroponte notes that early attempts at "digitizing TV" went awry because early digital television engineers ignored these principles:

> When video engineers approached digital television they took no lessons from computer network design. They ignored the flexibility of heterogenous systems and information-packed headers. Instead, they argued among themselves about resolution, frame rate, aspect ratio, and interlace, rather than let those be variables. Broadcast TV doctrine has all the dogma of the analog world and is almost devoid of digital principles, like open architecture, scalability, and interoperability. This will change, but change has so far been very slow in coming. (Negroponte, 1995, p. 181)

After 15 years of experiments Negroponte's points have been addressed as digital cable and satellite packages, DSL lines, and third-party devices connect to multiple screens and a variety of digital services. Indeed, this has become the norm in a culture of digital convergence: increasingly everyday devices such as televisions, phones, laptops, and tablets host digital applications that are explicitly designed for flexible user interactions to produce unique, individuated experiences. This ecosystem devoted to capturing user interactions and feeding them back into systems dedicated to optimizing user experiences are the key to social networks, search engines, and the numerous digital media streaming services that are emergent. This includes the likes of iTunes, Spotify, and Pandora as they make their services much more flexible and attentive to specific user needs and desires.

Fundamental to making these open, scalable, and interoperable systems work is the end user, an actor that is not independent of these systems. Instead, the end user is a key component for media production that is decentralized, micro in focus, and mediated through ever-multiplying and ever-flexible networks. Thus, successful media programmers and producers must envision how end users are able to access and use media in a manner that produces new products and new information. This involves more than envisioning an audience who engages increasingly niche media. The end user is an essential component: it is both the productive laborer and consumer that these database-driven systems require. The idea of the user has a history of conceptions and application. For example, in economics and business the term "end user" is often differentiated from a consumer and employed to refer to a person who uses a product. In this conception a parent may buy a toy for a child and would be identified as the consumer, however the "end user" would be the child. Both computer and information sciences mobilize a similar understanding for the "end user" as the person who will use and operate a piece of software to access, manipulate, and produce information. As Repenning and Ioannidou point out, part of the design process for any new piece of software, substantial testing is administered to ensure its "usability." The fundamental aim of the process "is to empower users to gain more control over their computers by engaging in a development process. The users we have in mind, called end-users, are typically not professional software developers" (Repenning & Ioannidou, 2006, p. 51). To succeed programmers must adapt to the end user's specific needs. As such, "the need to enable these more complex forms of adaptation is quickly increasing for various reasons. Only the end-users of an application, not the developers of that application, can decide on how to deal with all this information." The result is that systems are in "perpetual beta" since, "application developers can no longer anticipate all the needs of end-users. This discrepancy between what application developers can build and what individual end-users really need can be addressed with [end-user development]" (Repenning & Ioannidou, 2006, pp. 51–52).

The ability to design services for flexible adaptation is necessary because the many needs and platforms that affect the end user can never be fully anticipated. For example, in the case of information managers, Wood, Brassil Horak, and Snow note that, "Many converging environmental forces have influenced the trend toward end user searching. These include: technological developments of 'user-friendly' systems and front ends; increased sales of microcomputers and modems; and aggressive marketing by database vendors directly to the end user" (Wood, Brassil Horak, & Snow, 1986, p. 1). The path between servers to modems, computers, and the user is also known as the information chain and throughout the end user is envisioned as an essential part of the structure. Bryan Pfaffenberger explains:

> In information science, the term end user refers to the place this person occupies in the information chain, which begins with information creators and includes primary publishers, secondary publishers, librarians, and finally end users, who are the information consumers. An

end user, in other words, is the person who actually uses for decision making or   analytical purposes the information that an information-retrieval system makes available. The information chain is a true chain, it should be noted, because end users can become information creators themselves, thereby closing the loop. (Pfaffenberger, 1990, p. 4)

In the field of knowledge management developing for the end user is key for the refined production of data and tools. Raymond Panko suggests that "perhaps the best way to think of knowledge management is as *knowl-edge plus process*" (Panko, 1988, pp. 164–165, italics mine).[1] Throughout it helps us to envision the process as one where data as content flowing to and from databases, users, distributors, and exhibitors in a continual feed-back loop. In this loop the data is accessed, altered, added to, and related to other processes through which it becomes "content plus." "Content plus" could be any number of items including "mashed-up" contents, content plus metadata, content plus comments/reviews, and so on. The key is that the data moved through this process becomes, by design, informative.

This concept of the information chain is fundamental for understanding how value is generated and extracted in digital media systems. The chain

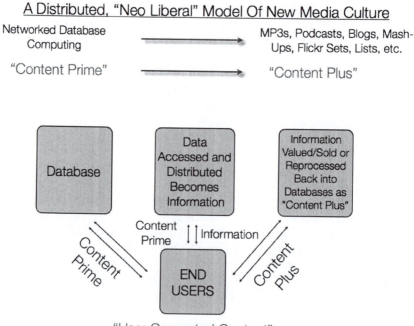

A Distributed, "Neo Liberal" Model Of New Media Culture

Networked Database Computing ——————→ MP3s, Podcasts, Blogs, Mash-Ups, Flickr Sets, Lists, etc.

"Content Prime" ——————→ "Content Plus"

| Database | Data Accessed and Distributed Becomes Information | Information Valued/Sold or Reprocessed Back into Databases as "Content Plus" |

Content Prime | Information

Content Prime

END USERS

Content Plus

"User Generated Content"

Figure 1.1   A model where media content flows to become "content plus." Key to this flow of information is the agency of the "end user" who is the key to its circulation.

is where data establishes numerous relationships, finds value, and becomes "informative." In this sense information has a distinct social dimension. As Bryan Pfaffenberger argues in his work on online databases and end-user searchability, "information is not a thing. For this reason, databases cannot be said to represent a valuable social resource in the absence of skilled decoders" (Pfaffenberger, 1990, p. 55). The social dimension of networked communication, as Ned Rossiter reminds us, "is about *relational processes* not representational procedures" (Rossiter, 2006, p. 13). Making information "accessible" and "relatable" is the fundamental role of the database, the key textual object of the new media age. Determining what information needs to be obtained from and deposited into the database, and when, is the role of the end user. Thus, prominent processes of relevance and differentiation *must be* clearly available to and/or generated by the end user rather than the database's author(s). As Pfaffenberger argues, "to discover whether an information retrieval system really retrieves information, we must ask if among all the tens of thousands of potentially meaningful differences that are retrieved there are any differences that make a difference to the user. The answer to this question is, simply, that everything depends on the user's subject expertise" (Pfaffenberger, 1990, pp. 62–63). Finally, the data generated about how data *is* related to other data through searches and choices is yet another source of valuable data for services that have embraced an explicitly social component. Much of this data is created in an unwitting manner by end users' everyday interactions with computers and the programs they engage.

For services such as iTunes, Pandora, and Spotify, the ability to generate recommendations for both users and providers is an essential part of their business strategy, one that includes the creation of a "quality user experience" that involves recommendations, interfaces, and information discovery. The information needed to create quality user experiences depends on building a stable information chain that creates "content plus." Of the many examples we could draw from one that involves three separate services, Spotify, Facebook, and ReverbNation illustrates the importance of the user in the information chain. Spotify, a service I will discuss in depth in Chapter 2, is a service that allows listeners to stream and listen to music in an on-demand fashion from an online database to a number of devices. Arriving in the United States in 2011, three years after the service launched in Sweden, Spotify worked closely with Facebook for its U.S. launch. Integrating "Facebook Connect" into its service, Spotify's relationship is so close that upon arrival to the U.S. it initially required all new users to acquire a Facebook account. Preliminary reports were that both services got something they wanted: Facebook received a tightly integrated music service that could keep listeners and users engaged on its platform while Spotify received access to an immense user base that they could access to sell their service and connect with for advertising (Olson, 2011). However, the real value in the relationship between Spotify and Facebook rests in the manner in which the services could leverage their databases to create both more valuable user experiences and data that they could exchange with other third parties. In June 2012 ReverbNation, a web-based service created in 2006 to cater to those in the independent music industry who wish to collaborate and network with each other, announced that it would be launching a Facebook advertising system called "Promote It." The service would allow ReverbNation users to "target potential fans on the music they're actually listening to by advertising to fans that have recently listened to similar artists on streaming music services like Spotify." The platform would allow advertisers to select "five similar artists or groups" and cross-compare them with geographic location, Facebook interest, and "likes". Once these were selected the Promote It platform allows advertisers to create ad copy or have their platform automatically generate it. The ads would come in one of three options that allowed users to either promote a song, a Facebook page, or a show. Finally, advertisers could view the effectiveness of their campaigns that showed how many "plays, downloads, shares, likes, and recommendations the platform has generated" and musicians could "connect and thank fans who have shared and downloaded their music" (Mickens, 2012).

Throughout the above example data about music and users flow back and forth between three distinct services. As data about the flow of data is gathered and processed services are able to generate more information, more value. And as is always the case, the ability of these services to track and record the online activities of users is by design. However, what this means for media that existed well before the time of the Internet has taken more time to digest as this paradigm shift from audience to end user occurred. This is the case of all paradigm shifts that occur when communities cooperate by embracing new sets of practices. Thomas Kuhn is clear on this point:

> Close historical investigation of a given specialty at a given time discloses a set of recurrent and quasi-standard illustrations of various theories in their conceptual, observational, and instrumental applications. These are the community's paradigms, revealed in textbooks, lectures, and laboratory exercises. By studying them and by practicing with them, the members of the corresponding community learn their trade. (1996, p. 43)

In the world of media researchers have begun to turn toward questions regarding users as media products have been systematically engulfed by digital media platforms. None of this has been easy. Indeed, this change has been the cause of substantial amounts of concern and anxiety about what to monitor and measure. One cannot underestimate the impact media have undergone as they have moved from measuring audiences to measuring users. Jon Gertner of *The New York Times Magazine* succinctly notes in his article "Our Ratings, Ourselves," "Change the way you measure America's culture consumption and you change America's culture business. And maybe even the culture itself" (Quoted in Lotz, 2007, p. 193). Drawing from Gertner, Amanda Lotz underscores this point: "Any one change in the measurement environment represents an enormous challenge to audience research norms and requires exceptional resources in response" (Lotz, 2007, p. 198). The parties that comprise the media measurement industry are organizations that continually searched for institutional longevity by establishing sets of standard (and often proprietary) measuring techniques and questions. Although a number of academic and profit-driven researchers have tried to research how media is "used," only recently as digital intermediaries have arrived *en masse* have questions about media use begun to emerge as a mainstream practice for these and other firms. In the case of television, technologies such as digital video recorders (DVRs), modern cable boxes, and other recent systems provide connections to central computing servers that often push, survey, and sample data flows to and from specific sets. James Webster, Lawrence Lichty, and Patricia Phalen note that these developments have created an opportunity for the U.S. media ratings company Nielsen to partner with companies such as TiVo and "create a large sample of DVR users to provide solid evidence of how these devices are being used" (2008, p. 110). The importance of this for television is that as it has adapted to digital networks throughout the 2000s and has begun to be pushed through cross-platform media delivery systems such as the Internet and onto computer screens, mobile phones, etc., television-only measurement technologies were made obsolete (Webster et al., 2008, p. 198). Further problems proliferated because, as Lotz comments, "the intermediary nature of new technologies and distribution systems" do not have the relative uniformity of content services or technologies that broadcast television did (2007, p. 197).

The result of this uneven terrain is that each service could no longer operate off of one mode of measurement. In some cases, intermediaries in the form of cable boxes were closed systems that refused to share proprietary data with others. In other cases, such as video-on-demand, services "desperately needed to establish measurement matrices to prove [their] economic viability" but had a difficult time finding "shared and consistent information" to make its case (Lotz, 2007, p. 197). These are not minor matters for media that trade on audience measures. The concerns about audience measurement methods, technologies, and data have been difficult to resolve for researchers since digitally networked media demand new relationships and new business practices. These new sources of information have caused confusion for broadcasters and advertisers who were used to a somewhat stable set of audience measures. However, as television has had a difficult time adjusting, advertisers have found in these technologies a once-in-a-generation opportunity to rethink what they should measure, what they want to know has also changed as they have moved to studying the analytics offered to them by the likes of Google, Facebook, and others. Lotz notes this opportunity when she points out that "replacing the sample-based data gathering methods that had figured audience behavior since radio with actual data of real set use represents the most significant advance in audience measurement to result from the introduction of digital technologies" (Lotz, 2007, p. 209). Furthermore, "Data about the use of these new technologies and effectiveness of commercial messages transmitted through them was vital to engender the confidence of advertisers to leave legacy models of commercial message delivery" (Lotz, 2007, p. 198). As the president of one media buying agency, Omnicon, explains, "We're developing more customized and proprietary measures on a client-by-client, case-by-case, and even medium-by-medium basis. We're less focused on comparing media choices than ever before and more interested in what consumers are doing and how we can use proprietary insights to help drive our clients' business" (Quoted in Lotz, 2007, p. 203).

While television and radio industries have adjusted to measuring users, the same sources of change have substantially shaken a music industry whose primary unit of measurement for success, "units sold," has very little in common with these techniques of audience and user measurement. For the music industry, the desire to understand "what consumers are doing" and derive predictions ended once a disc was sold. For the most part, the music industry simply did not care what happened once an object was first exchanged. However, as it has been overwhelmed by a paradigm where the "first sale" is no longer the only option, usage can be monitored by networked intermediaries, and streaming is becoming increasingly popular, the music industry is reorienting itself around reams of end user data. Recording the interactions of user and data on smart phones, laptops, desktops, MP3 players, etc., once unanswerable questions about where, when, how, and by whom music is used can be asked. But just as more data does not necessarily mean more information, more information does not necessarily mean more intelligent media (Lotz, 2007, p. 203). Only a better understanding of how to use this information and when is what will allow new music services to become "more intelligent." Because these decisions are focused on the user and not the audience the field has undergone a paradigm shift in the strict "Kuhnian" sense of the term. While the following may feel somewhat of a remedial note, it is all too often forgotten that for Kuhn the structure of scientific paradigms is contingent on the historical needs of those research communities who define what problems need to be solved. Thomas Kuhn explains that "Paradigms gain their status because they are more successful than their competitors in solving a few problems that the group of practitioners has come to recognize as acute" (1996, p. 23):

> one of the things a scientific community acquires with a paradigm is a criterion for choosing problems that, while the paradigm is taken for granted, can be assumed to have solutions. To a great extent these

are the only problems that the community will admit as scientific or encourage its members to undertake. Other problems, including many that had previously been standard, are rejected as metaphysical, as the concern of another discipline, or sometimes as just too problematic to be worth the time. (1996, p. 37)

In all cases, changes in paradigms are highlighted by great controversy and tumult within their communities. These communities have previously practiced longstanding sets of activities that Kuhn labels "normal science" and paradigm shifts result from moments of "crisis" that "are a necessary precondition for the emergence of novel theories" (1996, p. 77).[2] As new theories bring forth both new sets of questions they also bring with them sweeping changes to the research practices they address. For Kuhn, "the emergence of new theories is generally preceded by a period of pronounced professional insecurity" (1996, pp. 67–68).

The moment of crisis has been driven by the fact that media industries are engaged with the new actors such as the database-enabled user. Ubiquitously networked databases allow institutions to record and profile users and their interactions. As a result, legacy media have had to negotiate all the contingencies that come with these new technologies. New hires, practices, services, applications, and machines all come with suspicion and resistance to longstanding institutions. For example, broadcasters have long been interested in measuring audiences who engage in programming varieties of narrative texts. Whether they present songs, films, or television shows, the history of media programming is that broadcasters assume audiences are interested in narrative media and that various forms of storytelling are media's primary purpose. As Lev Manovich argues, forms such as the novel and cinema "privileged narrative as the key form of cultural expression in the modern age." However, the "computer age" has introduced a correlate form, the-database (Manovich, 1999, p. 80). Manovich notes that,

> many new media objects do not tell stories; they don't have a beginning or an end; in fact they don't have any development, thematically, formally or otherwise, which would organise their elements into a sequence. Instead, they are collections of individual items, where every item has the same significance as any database. (Manovich, 1999, p. 80)

As such, narratives are not *less important* than databases. However, their position has shifted through the significant efforts and negotiations of many actors. Thus, narrative texts now rest upon an infrastructure that prioritizes a logic of indexicality that turns them into specific, relatable data points. As Manovich notes, "data does not just exist—it has to be generated. Data creators have to collect data and to organise it, or create it from scratch. Texts need to written, photographs need to be taken, video and audio need to be recorded—or they need to be digitised from already existing media" (Manovich, 1999, p. 84). Indeed, the key to this struggle has not been the dematerialization of theses texts. Rather, it has been the labors of a massive, decentralized user base that has illustrated how easy the task of transferring millions of LPs, singles, and CDs into code is. However, the majority of the struggle has incurred around issues of legitimacy and discovery. The former issue has no easy solution and is well-documented throughout the remaining chapters.

The latter issue of discovery involves a number of programs that rest upon proprietary indices and algorithms dedicated to not only collect data, but are also designed to allow users to find, deposit, retrieve, and relate data to other data. In the case of music, this has meant the production of a variety of competing services that have tried to legitimately collect and refer musical entities to specific users. As a media culture we are only beginning to explore how audiences relate, create, and use data. The same holds true for the services discussed in this book, most of which are in their infancy and whose long-term success are dependent on structural factors that have yet to be resolved such as legislative issues and enticing reluctant actors to adopt these services. As databases, networks, and processors have become essential to our everyday lives, those "living systems" that were once the province of governments and corporations are now ready for our manipulation and reconfiguration. Within the rise of so-called "Web 2.0" media in the last decade a basic model as developed: systems are developed that encourage the user to use media, the user's interactions are recorded, and their relationship to data and these systems reconfigure both the data and the data's position within databases to continually generate new relationships between data and users.

The emphasis on *poeisis* as part of end user interactions and databases is key to understanding the nature of digital composition.[3] In the case of databases users are always writing whether or not they intentionally present themselves as writers. Take the example of the search engine. As each user accesses a search engine these programs are designed to decouple and associate user inputs to provide each user with retrieval of information that is algorithmically determined as most relevant.[4] John Battelle, writing on Google and search engines in general, notes, "link by link, click by click, search is building possibly the most lasting, ponderous, and significant cultural artifact in the history of humankind: the Database of Intentions" (Battelle, 2005, p. 6). In other words, the design of the database enables both the active and passive reader/writer/actor to feel empowered by his or her end user status, a status that is necessary both for reasons of productivity and knowledge management. Drawing directly from Foucault, Mark Poster argues that networked databases act as "circuits of communication" and "constitute a Superpanopticon, a system of surveillance without walls, windows, towers or guards" (Poster, 1990, p. 93). Indeed, this "database of intentions" has, as one astute blogger put it, "obvious unwanted social implications" as it "extend[s] to surveillance and impersonation" ("Swarming Media: Projected Identity, The Database, and Deleuze & Guattari in Web 2.0," 2006). Our digitized culture is, whether we like it or not, "creating selves outside ourselves" ("Swarming Media: Projected Identity, The Database, and Deleuze & Guattari in Web 2.0," 2006).

These "selves outside ourselves," also known as user profiles, are created by what Poster calls "quantitative advances in the technologies of surveillance [that have resulted] in a qualitative change in the microphysics of power" (Poster, 1990, p. 93). For Poster, "the populace has been disciplined to surveillance and are participating in the process" (Poster, 1990, p. 93). This acceptance is more than the acceptance of government identification and credit cards. It also means the acceptance of online profiles in exchange for access to search engines, online retail sites, and social media services. As such the surveyed and exchanged end user has become the basic unit of analysis, of the many sites and services that are part of the new music business ecosystem. In the U.S. Grooveshark, Spotify, Rhapsody, Google Music, Pandora, and Last.FM collect information about our "click throughs," ratings, purchases, "listens," and lists. Many of the items that are recorded users would not categorize as intentional jots. Other scrawls such as "wish lists," "queues," "shopping carts," "stations," and "scribbles" are less discrete, but just as key to producing the reminders and recommendations that make these systems more usable. Both explicit "likes" and purchases make impressions in databases that rely on intentional and unintentional sources of writing to produce effective services. Databases rely on both of these authored and surveyed markings. The new relationships that the end user produces are dependent on their scribbles. Without these relationships the data lacks relevancy, is not informative, and the index remains sterile. In fact, it is these relationships that have produced the most fecund, celebrated product of this technological evolution, "user generated content." Intended or not, this content is the key for these service's economic vitality. It is part of a larger political economic change from manufacturing economies centered on the production and distribution of "things" to economies based around service and information where more and more work is digital (and digitized). Elizabeth Regan and Bridget O'Connor argue that in the new digital economy, "collaboration is no longer an option. Collaboration will be an essential ingredient for success in the years ahead. It is the key to unleashing the energy in people, bringing the benefits of diverse thinking to solving problems and fostering a culture of innovation" (Regan & O'Connor, 2002, p. 44).

For most media, designing for this kind of large-scale networked collaboration between technologies and users is still relatively new. As mentioned earlier, both logistical and legal issues have yet to be worked out enough to reduce the anxieties of those players who are involved and those who would like to become stakeholders. In an object-oriented world of records, musicians, publishers, managers, and labels operated under a set of rules and restrictions that populated the systems with various levels of risk, reward, and disproportionate amounts of disadvantages, the rules of the game were at least somewhat clear. This new digital ecosystem may offer substantial opportunities for once impoverished players, but without the guarantee of some set of standard practices, entry into this marketplace comes with it the threat of "substantially wasted capital." In other words because there have been very few "textbook examples" of how to succeed in the new music industry, there are very few models that can be extracted by other players who wish to enter the game.[5] Systemic change brings with it substantial problems to those organizations and cultures, many of which are unforeseeable. For example, take the investments of end users to network, organize, and circulate information in an ever-shifting, decentralized fashion. The most infamous example of this kind of investment arrived in the late 1990s with the case of Napster. The importance of Napster is conveniently illustrated by the fact that this case quickly became synonymous with the problem of illegitimate peer-to-peer media sharing writ large. What is less recognized by the general public and scholars alike is the fact that Napster's founder, Shawn Fanning, was an independent, skilled end user who created what was essentially a very flexible and continually-updated database of networked music listings. Fanning's idea "was to have a real-time index that reflect[ed] all sites that are up and available to others on the network at that moment. [And] anyone who disconnected from the server would be immediately dropped from our index" (Menn, 2003, p. 34). To be sure, what was problematic for U.S. courts wasn't the activities of the end users, but rather the centralized directory that enabled and encouraged file exchanges. Even though Napster did not host these MP3 files, the Napster servers expressly facilitated peer-to-peer communication and file transferring. Thus the court decided "that Napster users are not fair users" ("A&M Records V Napster," 2001, p. 12).

The legal issue of fair use is a complex one that will not be adequately addressed in this book. What can and should be addressed is the issue of legitimate, contractual use. The most dominant, mainstream expression of contractual legitimation is the End User License Agreement (EULA). Also expressed as a "software license," a "shrink-wrap license," a "terms of service agreement," and a "click-wrap license," the EULA are all common contracts for this new ecosystem. To join or employ applications and services such iTunes, Pandora, Spotify, eMusic, etc., the user must "agree to" these contracts before they can be utilized. In each case these are legally-binding contracts between the producer and user of the software and/or service that are designed to protect "both [producer and user] from liability if the software is used in a way not intended by the manufacturer or author" (EULA). As agreeable as this may seem, Annalee Newitz argues that, "there are countless terms written into EULAs that could potentially harm consumers, or that may be downright unlawful":

EULAs are ubiquitous in software and consumer electronics—millions of people are clicking buttons that purport to bind them to agreements that they never read and that often run contrary to federal and state laws. These dubious "contracts" are, in theory, one-on-one agreements between manufacturers and each of their customers. Yet because almost every computer user in the world has been subjected to the same take-it-or-leave-it terms at one time or another, EULAs are more like legal mandates than consumer choices. (Newitz)

These contracts act as gatekeepers not only for the new media user, but they are key to understanding specifically how the music industry is remediating its assets. To listen to music through new services such as iTunes, eMusic, Spotify, and Pandora the user is required to "agree" to their contracts. This new development is the result of a paradigm shift that applies to all media. In past formations of the audience, whether they be mass, citizen, consumer, or commodity, the active and continual solicitation of a liberal, contractually-bound interlocutor has been the exception rather than the rule. In the case of the music industry licenses to listen have most often been "compulsory" in their status and administered by third parties authorized by the State. This practice has enabled mass audiences to legitimately access music without their consent and, more often than not, knowledge. With compulsory licenses sold to venues and broadcasters, listeners could enjoy recordings and performances and artists and investors could receive proportional royalty payments. By comparison EULAs and "terms of service agreements" are "optional" since one does not have to use these services and applications. Furthermore, they are written by private parties, and come with none of the progressivist impulses designed to address national audiences. They are decidedly neo-liberal in their formation and each contract is dependent on one moment of independent consent after another. These contracts do not address audiences, they address users and not every person will or can be a legitimate user who plays and replays, manipulates, stores, and relates data. As we will see throughout the remainder of this book, in many cases the contractual consent given to these services by involves soliciting consent to extract value to mine data from users to spur numerous exchanges.

It is important to continually remind ourselves what differentiates so many music services in the new paradigm from the older one is the reliance on end user data. As mentioned earlier, the history of the music industry has been oriented around the sale of music-related commodities. While this objective has not been completely abandoned, nor will it be anytime soon, what has crept in and will continue to challenge the music industry at every level is a new type of engagement between producers and listeners. It helps explain why services such as Pandora, Spotify, and iTunes, each with a distinctly different philosophies and different types of offerings, have rested a considerable amount of their financial future on collecting, organizing, and leveraging user data. For Pandora the collection of user data is a somewhat understandable move given the fact that it provides an online commercial radio service. Like terrestrial commercial radio services, Pandora sells commercial time and targets listeners based on specific amalgamations of data. Whereas commercial radio has looked at formats to find audiences that are based on estimates and projections, Pandora delivers specific user categories to advertisers as the listener listens. Pandora's aim is to generate an understanding of the user's activities on multiple computing platforms such as mobile phones. In 2011 Veracode, a Massachusetts-based software security firm, published a report titled "Mobile Apps Invading Your Privacy" where they noted that Pandora's Android mobile app "tracked users' age, sex, zip code and precise geographic location, which in many cases was updated in a continuous loop. The app then sent such information to servers operated by advertising services including AdMarvel and AdMob. Other information that was shared included the phone's device ID and the user's birth date." Furthermore, the report noted that in addition to hosting code libraries for AdMarvel and AdMob, the app also came bundled with code libraries for comScore, Google.Ads, and Medialets (Goodin, 2011).

Although many listeners understand that they are being exchanged with advertisers, the scale of how much data about a user's activities had been gathered and how they had been leveraged was still surprising. Issues of privacy abound and could be addressed at length here. I would like to focus on the aforementioned ad networks. As third-party brokers, these networks that purchase and digest the information captured by these tools and services are key to structuring a significant portion of the new music industry. For example, in summer 2010, nine years after the release of the iTunes app and service, Apple announced that iAd would be their in-house mobile advertising platform. After the acquisition of the mobile advertising firm Quattro Wireless in spring 2010, iAd would act as a firm that placed ads on applications sold through Apple's iTunes store and onto iOS-enabled products. In a way, this is not surprisong. Initially offered as a space to sell music, the iTunes service and app is a Trojan horse that has never limited itself to one kind of media sale, whether it be movies or data. Even though Steve Jobs had spoken out against the intrusive tracking of applications "that want to take a lot of your personal data and suck it up," iAd began placing ads into iOS apps (Thurm & Kane, 2010). The iAd service used data that the company could gather through its iTunes based App Store and iTunes music service that would use targeting criteria such as "the types of songs, videos and apps a person downloads" that included "103 targeting categories" (Thurm & Kane, 2010) Furthermore, Apple filed patent applications in May 2010 to produce a system that could place and price ads based on a user's web history, search history, and "the contents of a media library." For example, iAd could provide a service that targeted users who downloaded specific songs or playlists. Additionally, the patent application listed an ability to mine data by analyzing the contents of iTune media libraries used by a user's friends through "known connections on one or more social-networking websites" or "publicly available information or private databases describing purchasing decisions, brand preferences" (Thurm & Kane, 2010). For significant campaigns that have finished, iAd offers "a wrap-up report [that] provides key insights into user engagement, performance and best practices based on overall network results. By understanding how users are engaging with your ad, you can learn new things about your audience to hone your marketing strategy" (Anon., 2012).

The user is clearly not "the audience" in this paradigm. The most significant difference is that while media audiences were sampled and sometimes investigated, in a use-based paradigm media users are continually monitored and engaged in a dialogue with servers and services that provide discrete, micro-oriented portions of personalized media. It is along these lines that we end where we began and rethink what Pandora's Music Genome Project provides media users. The "personalized" radio stations Pandora helps produce, as I will discuss more in-depth later, comes from a rich mix of user decisions, friends' playlists, and already-encoded music. As a result, Pandora's initial design relies on the continual exchange of music service for information. It is precisely this design philosophy that a Michigan resident questioned in a lawsuit. Peter Deacon filed suit against the service in April 2010 claiming that Pandora's recent integration with the social network service Facebook resulted in an illegal disclosure of "sensitive listening records," a violation of Michigan's Video Rental Privacy Act. Michigan's law prohibits a company "that offer books, music or videos from disclosing customers' identities without their consent" (Davis, 2011). Passed in 1989, one year after the U.S. Congress enacted the Video Privacy Protection Act of 1988, federal legislation which was passed as a reaction to the nonconsensual publication of then-Supreme Court nominee Robert Bork's video rental records, the Michigan statute was much broader (Anon.). Deacon alleged in his complaint, filed in U.S. District Court for the Northern District of California, that "at no time did Pandora ever receive consent to disclose its users' protected information to their Facebook contact" (Davis, 2011). While Deacon's complaint is about an invasion of privacy, it is also about something unanticipated. As an audience member, my consumption of music was presumably private and communicated only to those peers and loved ones whom I trust. However, the creation of the continually-monitored user that is served is a critical object for the new music economy that heralds what Attali described as "the advent of a radically new form of the insertion of music into communication." For Attali, what is happening is we are entering a new period, one "that is overturning all of the concepts of political economy," one that he dubs a period of "composition" (Attali, 1985, p. 134). Attali's understanding of composition steps away from a political order based on the mass reproduction of time-based objects that are somewhat controllable. In "composition," Attali argues, we begin to see new practices and activities where "the listener is the operator" and "to listen to music in the network of composition is to rewrite it." Attali's assertions are not only theoretically thick, but are also provocative and prescient. Without a severe theoretical digression, Attali's proposition of a new music economy is one that begins when the "excess of repetition heralds a crisis of proliferation." The result of the crisis is a "confusion on the part of creators" who search for ways to wrestle with mutating structures and a new set of "relations between people and between men and commodities" (p. 135). The emergence of the user ushers in a set of relations between actors such as networked computers and databases that are being explored but have yet to be adequately understood. This understanding begins with the most basic aspect of the music business: the value of an exchange.

BIBLIOGRAPHY

A&M Records v. Napster. (2001). United States Court of Appeals for the Ninth Circuit.

Anon. (2012). iAd Network. Retrieved June 22, 2012 from http://advertising. apple.com/brands/

Anon. Video Privacy Protection Act. Retrieved from http://epic.org/privacy/vppa/

Attali, J. (1985). *Noise: The Political Economy of Music* (B. Massumi, Trans.). Minneapolis, MN: University of Minnesota Press.

Battelle, J. (2005). *The Search: How Google and Its Rivals Rewrote the Rules of Business and Transformed Our Culture.* New York: Portfolio Trade.

Bauerline, M. (2008). *The Dumbest Generation: How the Digital Age Stupefies Young Americans and Jeopardizes Our Future (Or, Don't Trust Anyone Under 30).* New York: Tarcher.

Benkler, Y. (2006). *The Wealth of Networks: How Social Production Transforms Markets and Freedom.* New Haven, CT: Yale University Press.

Davis, W. (2011). Sour Note: Pandora Sued For Violating Privacy, Via Facebook Integration. *MediaPost News.* Retrieved from http://www.mediapost.com/publications/article/159707/

Deleuze, G., & Guattari, F. (1987). *A Thousand Plateaus: Capitalism and Schizophrenia* (B. Massumi, Trans.). Minneapolis, MN: University of Minnesota Press.

EULA. Retrieved July 30, 2009, from http://www.webopedia.com/TERM/E/EULA.html

Goodin, D. (2011). Pandora's Mobile App Transmits 'Mass Quantities' of User Data: From Android's Lips to Advertisers' Ears. *The Register.* Retrieved from http://www.theregister.co.uk/2011/04/06/pandora_smartphone_privacy/

Greer, M. (2010). Is Pandora a Sirius Threat? *The Motley Fool.* Retrieved from http://www.fool.com/investing/general/2010/07/23/is-pandora-a-sirius-threat.aspx

Ha, A. (2010). Internet Radio Service Pandora Raises More Funding. *MobileBeat.* Retrieved from http://mobile.venturebeat.com/2010/06/02/pandora-funding/

Hall, S. (1973). *Encoding and Decoding in the Television Discourse.* Paper presented at The Council of Europe Colloquy on "Training in The Critical Reading of Televisual Language," Council and The Centre for Mass Communication Research, University of Leicester.

Howe, J. (2008). *Crowdsourcing: Why the Power of the Crowd is Driving the Future of Business.* New York: Crown Business.

Jenkins, H. (2006). *Convergence Culture: Where Old and New Media Collide.* New York: New York University Press.

Johnson, S. (2005). *Everything Bad Is Good for You: How Today's Popular Culture Is Actually Making Us Smarter.* New York: Riverhead Books.

Kuhn, T. S. (1977). *The Essential Tension: Selected Studies in Scientific Tradition and Change.* Chicago: The University of Chicago Press.

Kuhn, T. S. (1996). *The Structure of Scientific Revolutions* (3rd ed.). Chicago: The University of Chicago Press.

Lessig, L. (2008). *Remix: Making Art and Commerce Thrive in the Hybrid Economy.* New York: The Penguin Press HC.

Li, C., & Bernoff, J. (2008). *Groundswell: Winning in a World Transformed by Social Technologies.* Cambridge, MA: Harvard Business School Press.

Locke, C., Levine, R., Searls, D., & Weinberger, D. (2001). *The Cluetrain Manifesto: The End of Business As Usual.* New York: Basic Books.

Lotz, A. (2007). *The Television Will Be Revolutionized.* New York: New York University Press.

Manovich, L. (1999). Database As Symbolic Form. *Convergence: The International Journal of Research Into New Media Technologies, 5*(2), 80–98. doi: 10.1177/135485659900500206

Marshall, P. D. (2009). New Media As Transformed Media Industry. In J. Holt & A. Perren (Eds.), *Media Industries: History, Theory, and Method* (pp. 81–89). Malden, MA: Wiley-Blackwell.

McQuail, D. (1984). *Mass Communication Theory: An Introduction.* Beverly Hills, CA: Sage Publications.

Menn, J. (2003). *All The Rave: The Rise and Fall of Shawn Fanning's Napster.* New York: Crown Business.

Mickens, D. (2012). Spotify Listens Inform Facebook Targeting for Musicians. *ClickZ: Marketing News & Expert Advice.* Retrieved from http://www.clickz.com/clickz/news/2184197/spotify-listens-inform-facebook-targeting-musicians

Negroponte, N. (1995). *Being Digital.* New York: Vintage Books.

Newitz, A. Dangerous Terms: A User's Guide to EULAs. *Electronic Frontier Foundation.* Retrieved from http://w2.eff.org/wp/eula.php

Olson, P. (2011). Facebook to Launch Music Service With Spotify. *Forbes.com.* Retrieved from http://www.forbes.com/sites/parmyolson/2011/05/25/facebook-to-launch-music-service-with-spotify/2/

Palfrey, J. (2008). *Born Digital: Understanding the First Generation of Digital Natives.* New York: Basic Books.

Pandora. (2010). Retrieved June 2, 2010 from http://www.pandora.com/

Panko, R. R. (1988). *End User Computing: Management, Applications, and Technology.* New York: John Wiley & Sons.

Pfaffenberger, B. (1990). *Democratizing Information: Online Databases and the Rise of End-User Searching.* Boston, MA: G. K. Hall & Co.

Poster, M. (1990). *The Mode of Information: Poststructuralism and Social Context.* Chicago: University of Chicago Press.

Poster, M. (2006). *Information Please: Courage and Politics in the Age of Digital Machines.* Durham, NC: Duke University Press.

Regan, E. A., & O'Connor, B. N. (2002). *End-User Information Systems: Implementing Individual and Work Group Technologies* (2nd ed.). Upper Saddle River, NJ: Prentice Hall.

Repenning, A., & Ioannidou, A. (2006). What Makes End-User Development Tick? 13 Design Guidelines. In H. Lieberman, F. Paterno & V. Wulf (Eds.), *End User Development* (pp. 51–85). Dordrecht, The Netherlands: Springer.

Rossiter, N. (2006). *Organized Networks: Media Theory, Creative Labour, New Institutions.* Rotterdam, Netherlands: Eelco Van Welie, NAi Publishers.

Schwoch, J. (1990). Selling the Sight/Site of Sound: Broadcast Advertising and the Transition from Radio to Television. *Cinema Journal, 30*(1), 55–66.

Shirky, C. (2008). *Here Comes Everybody: The Power of Organizing Without Organizations.* New York: The Penguin Press HC.

Surowiecki, J. (2005). *The Wisdom of Crowds.* New York: Anchor.

Swarming Media: Projected Identity, The Database, and Deleuze & Guattari in Web 2.0. (2006). Retrieved July 12, 2009 from http://www.swarmingmedia. com/2006/02/projected_identity_the_databas.html

Tapscott, D. (1998). *Growing Up Digital: The Rise of the Net Generation.* New York: McGraw Hill.

Tapscott, D. (2008). *Grown Up Digital: How the Net Generation Is Changing Your World.* New York: McGraw-Hill.

Thurm, S., & Kane, Y. I. (2010). Your Apps Are Watching You: A WSJ Investigation Finds That iPhone and Android Apps Are Breaching the Privacy of Smartphone Users. *The Wall Street Journal.* Retrieved from http://online.wsj.com/ article/SB10001424052748704694004576020083703574602.html

Webster, J. G., Lichty, L. W., & Phalen, P. F. (2008). *Ratings Analysis: The Theory and Practice of Audience Research* (3rd ed.). Mahwah, NJ: Lawrence Erlbaum Associates.

Wood, S. M., Brassil Horak, E., & Snow, B. (1986). The Environment of End User Searching. In S. M. Wood, E. Brassil Horak, & B. Snow (Eds.), *End User Searching in the Health Sciences* (pp. 1–2). New York: The Haworth Press.

2 Why Don't We Give it Away?
The Value of Free for a New Music Industry

A gift consists not in what is done or given, but in the intention of the giver or doer.

—Seneca

In January 2011 *Billboard* reported a new low for the record industry. Cake, the successful American alternative rock band that had been active for almost 20 years, debuted their latest record. By some measures *Showroom of Compassion* could be considered a smash success. Appearing at the top of the *Billboard* 200 charts has always been an achievement of distinction while an album achieving the number one position in its debut week is something to be celebrated. Yet not this time. Unlike other number one debut albums, the 44,000 units sold made this moment remarkable: *Showroom of Compassion* had officially become the lowest-selling No. 1 album since the inception of Nielsen's Soundscan service in 1991. As painful as this may have been for Cake, this ignominious honor was not entirely their fault. Rather the low numbers were indicative of a much more important trend. The week before Cake's album topped the "Top 200," the chart was led by the sale of one the most successful popular artists in the last six years, Taylor Swift. Swift's CD, *Speak Now*, followed the release of her 2008 release, *Fearless*, a disc that had been certified six-tuple platinum, i.e., moving over 6 million units. *Speak Now*, which would go on to sell 4 million units, also debuted as a No. 1 album. However, *Speak Now* sold only "52,000 copies according to Nielsen SoundScan" in its initial week (Smith, 2011). These paltry numbers from a blockbuster artist were a convenient reminder that the music industry was going through another crisis. It was the kind of crisis that would lead David Geffen, one of the more storied record executives of the final quarter of the 20th century, to answer a question of what he would do if he were to enter the music business in 2012 as a producer or executive with the deadpan answer of "I'd kill myself" (Rose, 2012).

As is often the case, the problems that Geffen feared others envisioned as opportunities. In this case, as the material conditions and cultural practices of the listener rapidly changed there arrived a chance for some innovative as well as nascent practices and services to emerge. For example, in 2009 Warner Music's senior vice president of commercial strategy, Eric Daugan, noted that while the industry did not "immediately embrace the possibilities created by new technology, we've developed an increasingly sophisticated understanding of the opportunity." This included finding "new ways for people to interact with entertainment content" while focusing on "the relationship between artist and fan." For Daugan this relationship would remain "at the heart of the music business" (Forde, 2009a). Daugan's quote underscores two particular issues at the heart of this chapter: (1) the need for industrywide learning and experimentation; and (2) the understanding that artists continue to find new ways to emphasize the "relational aspects" of their career. However, the quote also obscures two rather distinct problems. First, the industry did more than simply avoid these new technologies: for much of the first decade of the 21st century they actively prosecuted many innovative practices that developers and users began to employ. Secondly, the nature of relationships between artists and fans have substantially changed as networking has become increasingly ubiquitous. This chapter reviews trade and popular business literature where theorists, artists, and leaders of many new music services are rethinking their most fundamental value proposition: the price at which services and goods are exchanged. Throughout these discussions, "free music" is positioned as a practice that is essential to establishing gift economies of exchange. As such the chapter includes the many opportunities as problems that the practice entails and explains why artists and investors must consider every aspect of the practice as they reposition themselves in a new music industry.

It is in this framework that we begin to understand David Geffen's remarks as something more than the grumblings of a media mogul. They were also the musings of an executive familiar with the practices needed to produce, distribute, and promote the sale of recorded objects in a large-scale manner. By the time Geffen had entered the industry in the 1960s the basic rules of this game were well-known. Simon Frith reminds us that by the end of 1945, "the basic structure of the modern music industry was in place. Pop music meant pop records, commodities, a technological and commercial process under the control of a small number of large companies." Controlling this process would depend "on the ownership of the means of record production and distribution." Furthermore, the record industry, just like the music publishing business before it, "had been organized around the manufacture and distribution of songs," and would be "organized around the marketing of stars and star performances." While live music performance would continue to be an important portion of this industry, "its organization and profits were increasingly dependent on the exigencies of record making" (Frith, 1988a, p. 19). By the mid-1950s one facet of this new economy, tape, would be "the technological change which allowed new, independent producers into the market—the costs of recording fell dramatically even if the problems of large-scale distribution remained" (p. 21). For independent producers the problem of how to distribute their product at scale would remain for almost 50 years, only to be partially solved with the rise of the Internet. However, as everyone understands, the solution that the Internet provided was also the source of a considerable problem. The combined presence of cheap computer processors and the acceptance of MP3 as an audio format obliterated the problem of mass production and, thereby, created another source of concern by eliminating scarcity. These crises are part of all capitalist systems: investments into new production and communication technologies often drive economies to critical moments of surplus where problems of overproduction. All technologies of scale disrupt capitalist economies as they always involve that most fundamental practice: pricing.

Discussions about pricing have long been the province of economists. It is a domain in which artists often turn to trusted third parties to help them negotiate. One such third party is the famous entertainment manager, Peter Jenner. An economist who taught at the London School of Economics as a lecturer in his early 20s, Jenner left behind his academic position of four years to manage an early iteration of Pink Floyd. Jenner's career would have been notable if it had simply ended after his time with one of the most important rock acts in history. However, Jenner continued to manage a set of clients that reads like a list of rock royalty: Syd Barrett, T-Rex, Ian Dury, The Clash, Robyn Hitchcock, and Billy Bragg have all employed his guidance. Throughout his years of management Jenner's aim has been the same as all entertainment managers: to better the careers of his clients in a manner that both strategically and tactically increases their revenues. Furthermore, as both a manager and an economist Jenner understands that the most basic principle of economics, supply and demand, will always dictate pricing practices. It was with this training in economics and time spent in the music industry that the longtime British pop and rock act manager addressed the International Association of Entertainment Lawyers in a 2010 blog post titled "The Challenges of Digital Music: An Ex-Economist's View." Like Geffen, Jenner both remembers and understands how the "product based world" worked. In this world multinational record companies with significant capital investments benefitted from economies of scale that "allowed them to reduce unit costs as volume increased, driving prices down." As Jenner explains, "By being the manufacturer, promoter, investor and owner of the rights in the product, record companies became the prime investors in music, and also the default route to the market for anyone who wanted to invest in music." In addition, because copyright law granted "quasi monopoly rights" to these investors, "the profitability of unit sales increased as marginal costs declined" as long as "the rights owners could maintain their quasi monopoly price." The end result meant that, "if an artist wanted to be really big, nationally or internationally, you had to deal directly or indirectly with these quasi monopolies, and if you managed to get big without them as an artist or independent label they would make an offer that could not be refused, as they could nearly always make more money out of a hit than any individual or small label could hope to do" (Jenner, 2010).

In the United States the reliance upon these so-called "quasi-monopolies" to get your merchandise to scale in a national or international fashion was a longstanding given. The ways that publishers and record companies negotiated this system were fundamental to conducting their business throughout the 20th century. Publishers' and labels' long-term investments in infrastructures of production, sales, and distribution were made to grow and maintain their significant claims on the most profitable sections of the music marketplace for almost over a century and a half. Had listeners not become users who moved their listening habits away from CD players to desktops, laptops, and MP3 players, the practices that ensured their dominance may have remained. The creation of the MP3 and other digital music file formats are part of longstanding efforts of capitalist demands to create ever-more efficient modes of information storage and exchange. Like any technology, as Jonathan Sterne reminds us, "The MP3 is a crystallized set of social and material relations. It is an item that 'works for' and is 'worked on' by a host of people, ideologies, technologies and other social and material elements" (Sterne, 2006, p. 826). Like other consumer audio technologies before it such as the long-play album, the cassette tape, and the compact disc, the MP3 has followed a long tradition of recordings that emphasize spatial compression and fidelity to store and reproduce the time-dependent labors of performers. However, because the MP3 is comprised of easily reproducible code, the limitations that ensured the continual purchase of recordings fell to the side as the marginal cost of reproduction practically reached a null point. By effectively moving the industry toward a system of files and ubiquitous networks, those practices and spaces that were both supported and demanded by an object-oriented industry of relative scarcity quickly lost their importance. As the law of supply and demand points out, if supply exceeds demand, then prices must drop. Accordingly, now that supply was no longer limited and users existed in an economy of seemingly unlimited abundance, musical recordings began to flirt with free.

For many, the problem of "free music" may appear obvious and have no clear solution. The development of ubiquitous broadband networks, mass storage devices, and compressed audio formats set the conditions for the widespread evolution and adoption of various peer-to-peer file-sharing practices. As a result, this new infrastructure of continually-networked end users quickly eliminated the need for a number of the physical dimensions of the record industry such as the need to go to record stores and purchase compact discs. However, free music has come in more varieties than file-sharing. As Eamonn Forde noted for the British trade *Music Week*, the first decade of the 21st century "has been the story of 'free'; from illegal and unlimited free (Napster 1.0) to legal and unlimited 'as free'" (Forde, 2009a). Between the arrival of Napster in 1999 to the development of cloud-based services in the late-2000s, the industry has struggled to determine whether or not "free music" could generate a set of profitable services. Forde notes that navigating between the extremes of both legal and illegal forms of "free" "has been the music industry's greatest challenge but it has also triggered its greatest period of innovation" (Forde, 2009a). A significant part of the difficulty has involved convincing the many players of the industry to recognize one significant fact: there will be no return to an industry that is primarily organized to move scarce or limited physical recordings. Although armed with a system of punishments, the industry has never been able to fully stamp out file-sharing. No matter how notorious the Record Industry Association of America (RIAA), no matter how often they won, and no matter how often students, parents, parishioners, and citizens have lost their cases, paid their fines, and promised not to do it again, file-sharing continues. Worse yet for the RIAA, consumers won something far more valuable: the many sympathies of the press and the eventual resignation of the RIAA from the practice of directly suing file-sharers (Moya, 2008). As one Warner Music Group executive put it, "we used to fool ourselves. We used to think our content was perfect just exactly as it was. We expected our business would remain blissfully unaffected even as the world of interactivity, constant connection, and filesharing was exploding." Because these labels stood still and did not adapt quick enough, the labels "inadvertently went to war with consumers by denying them what they wanted and could otherwise find. And as a result, of course, consumers won" (Quoted in Kot, 2009, p. 56).

By the latter half of the 2000s it was clear that music companies would take a two-pronged approach. First, instead of going directly after illegal downloaders they would begin to work with Internet service providers to develop a means of punishing these users. Second, labels would begin to steadily embrace and develop services that they once feared would cannibalize disc sales. In March 2008 the *Los Angeles Times* reported Sony was in discussions with other labels and partners to develop an Internet music subscription service. Furthermore, Warner Music Group began to discuss how to form a subscription service. Under the Warner plan, an income stream would come from a few dollars a month charge that could be added to an Internet bill that would allow consumers to "download, copy and share music." The revenues collected would then be divided among participating labels (Quinn, 2008). Although none of these efforts came to fruition, the days of denial, anger, bargaining, and depression about a paradigm lost were behind these labels. Instead, labels accepted that there were processes beyond their control and the question was how to do business in this environment. In the words of Peter Jenner, "Attempts to stop people copying are clearly a waste of time, and not only are they a waste of time, they make the law offensive. It's very similar to prohibition in America in the 1930s" (Anon., 2010b). Because the fight against filesharing was always unwinnable, the price of recorded music was quickly bottoming to null. As Jenner noted, "in the online world, the marginal cost of a digital file is essentially zero" (Anon., 2010b).

By the end of the decade more members of the industry began to acknowledge that they no longer could fight free unless they could provide a marketable alternative. To compete with free the industry would have to, to quote a former president of the National Association of Recording Merchandise, "make something better than free" (Quoted in Kot, 2009, p. 48). To make a product better that can beat free is something of a mantra for a new age of the music industry. However, that "something better" was not immediately clear. For a record industry led by major labels with executives who had spent their careers planning around how to make records, many of which were filled with posters, designer sleeves, liner notes, stickers, and sundry other items, there was a significant generation gap. Worse still, while 30-year-olds had abandoned compact discs in favor of digital downloads, the "digital millennials" had never become habitualized CD consumers. The UK magazine *Marketing* noted that in 2009 a generation of consumers existed that have "grown up expecting to get their music, newspapers, mobile phone handsets and broadband access without paying a penny. Over the past decade a tide of 'free' goods and services has washed over consumer markets, thanks to the spread of the internet and the deflation caused by technological advances and low-cost overseas labour" (Anon., 2009c). It is, as London's *Sunday Times* explained, a very real generation gap:

> If you're over 30, you think there's no such thing as a free lunch; if you're under 30, you assume all lunches are free. Look at your children: they know ways of getting movies, music and television free. They make phone calls free. They set up social networks or blogs using expensive software systems handed out free. They have free word processors, free web browsers, they can search every web page in the world for free. Over-thirties ask: "What's the catch?"; under-thirties shrug and say: "Nobody pays for this stuff, do they? Duh!" Why is all this stuff free? Because it has to be. The cost of the internet—band width, processing speed and storage—halves every year or so (Appleyard, 2009).

Copyright activist, lawyer, and scholar Lawrence Lessig argues that this generation may have shifted an entire culture's "expectations surrounding access" (Lessig, 2008, p. 46). This shift has also created, "a growing copyright abolitionism, a generation that rejects the very notion of what copyright is supposed to do, rejects copyright and believes that the law is nothing more than an ass to be ignored and to be fought at every opportunity possible" (Lessig, 2007). Lessig's assertion is borne out in the numbers. The online media measurement company BigChampagneMedia Measurement reported that in early 2010, "The volume of unauthorized downloads continues to represent about 90% of the market" (Goldman, 2010). As Luke O'Donnell writing for *The Australian* put it, for Gen Y, aka, 'Generation Free,' "Paid content is no answer" (O'Donnell, 2010).

Free not only means "free of charge," in this context free also means to be "free from contextual limits" both cultural and physical. When it comes to a new user-based economy there is more than a gap between our cultural practices of copying and the law. Furthermore, serving this new economy with music means reconsidering what this new generation of consumers value. Writing for the tech blog *Mashable*, Mark Mulligan argues that the needs of digital natives "differ so much from those of previous generations" because they have always had a completely different kind of consumer experience:

> Digital Natives don't have that analog era baggage. All they've known is digital. Online video and mobile are their killer apps. These Digital Natives see music as the pervasive soundtrack to their interactive, immersive, social environments. Ownership matters less. Place of origin matters less. Context and experience is everything. In a world beyond content scarcity, experience is now everything. With "free" infecting everything, the content itself is no longer king. Experience now has the throne. (Mulligan, 2011)

Communication and media scholars such as Nancy Baym (2011), Yochai Benkler (2006), Henry Jenkins (2006), Mark Deuze (2007), and Patrik Wikström (2009) each position this shift as the result of an across-the-board popularization of participatory media cultures. Baym points out that this shift to an emergent experiential media culture is being created in a space where "media are increasingly created, distributed, and reworked by loose networks of interconnected peers" (p. 24). Quoting Joshua Friedlander, the vice president of research at the Recording Industry Association of America, Baym notes that "the industry is adapting to consumer's demands of how they listen to music, when and where, and we've had some growing pains in terms of monetizing those changes." However, Baym warns:

> Friedlander's use of the term 'monetize', so common in music business parlance, may be indicative of the industry's troubles. For reasons that are deeply entrenched and not easily escaped, major media companies generally approach their audiences as markets. This leads to viewing audiences as people who either pay or steal. In contrast, participatory culture operates more like a gift economy. (pp. 24–25)

Baym's work on Swedish independent pop and rock music emphasizes what she terms "The Swedish Model," a model that encourages, "an alternative participatory, gift-oriented view of label's and audiences' practices and responsibilities" (p. 25). In this perspective, independent Swedish labels and audiences recast filesharing as a practice that adds value to those bands and musicians who search for international audiences. This is done most graphically by sharing files with the aim of building fan communities with whom they may directly interact through social media (pp. 26–26).

Baym claims that "The Swedish Model is just one manifestation of the broader phenomenon of media producers finding ways to come to the terms with participatory culture of the internet and the networked powers of their audiences" (p. 36). Indeed, this and other codeveloping variations of a "gift model" discussed in this chapter have always aimed toward fan engagement and future economic success. However, gift economies are nothing new and have long existed in the record industry. Gifts, both legal and illicit, have always been bestowed upon disc jockeys and promoters to feature their label's wares.[1] Simon Frith opens up his 1988 essay "Picking up the Pieces" by noting that the gifts he received in the 1970s as a record critic were numerous and that "being a rock critic was like being the object of a demented charity." Records that he reviewed not only came with posters and t-shirts, but in some cases "jars of marmalade, a road map of the British Isles, a clock, playing cards, [and] an in-car vacuum cleaner" (Frith, 1988b, p. 88). Although Frith states that it was "as if record companies could only guarantee the value of their own fleeting products by associating them with something really useful," the gifts were clearly given to generate a sense of obligation in the critic. Another variation of a gift exchange in the age of physical goods is the practice of the "loss leader." Long understood by distributors and manufacturers as a necessary means of lubricating exchange, retailers would often require goods that they offer at a steep discount or even in some variant of "free." These goods ranged from t-shirts, posters, "bonus discs," "demonstration discs," career samplers, etc., and were offered by retailers so that consumers would be drawn in, make purchases, produce profits, and grow their market share. Indeed, often forgotten is just how dependent the physical record industry was on loss leader practices. Major and independent retailers have and continue to offer freebies and discounts at the consent of their distributors. This includes "hot sales" of records and compact discs that distributors wanted to push. In other cases, distributors would offer records at a large discount as a way of clearing out old catalogue and other forms of overstock, as well as more standard fare such as concert tickets and chances to enter raffles for trips and other as a way to get consumers to buy their records.[2]

The music industry's emphasis on gifts should not be too surprising given the fact that all music rests upon listening, a social exchange between musician and audience. Researching these economies has deep roots in anthropology wherein the process of gifting is examined for the social aspects it engenders. Marcel Mauss argues that what gifts create are "feeling bonds" that cannot be ignored by recipients and, as I will discuss later regarding the importance of digital social networking for fans and musicians, they are viewed as key to creating a substantial economy based on cultural goods (Mauss, 1967). The key difference is that the population receiving gifts in this economy is not only comprised of professional critics, but fans, decentralized sets of users for whom gifts are essential to their experience of the art and the artists. From sample downloads, digital "mixtapes," and entire albums, the practice is widespread and in line with more wide scale, post-industrialist economic phenomena that have embraced flexible and decentralized labor pools as part of the systematic abandonment of central-ized industrial forms of production by North American and Western Euro-pean economies. Specifically, as investments in developed sectors of the world were made in communication and information technologies, these nations began to generate industries based on the creation of intellectual properties and "experiential goods" such as media, performances, litera-ture, software, etc. (Castells, 1996; Florida, 2004; Hartley, 2005; Harvey, 1991; Hesmondhalgh, 2008; Howkins, 2002; Jenkins, 2006). This trans-formation has affected every aspect of once-industrialized societies, partic-ularly those cultural industries resting on the production and distribution of physical goods. The development of a decentralized and somewhat "uncon-trollable" copy culture has been so shocking and profound that authors like Lawrence Lessig have focused on the need to fundamentally rethink the legal and cultural institutions. In Lessig's proposals sharing would play a significant role toward developing a "hybrid economy" where intellectual property is treated as something akin to a "raw material resource" that can be transformed and remixed by its users (2008, p. 77).

Despite advocates like Lessig and experiments by a few portions of the industry, the resistance toward the possibility of a "freer" hybrid economy built around the practices of gifting and sharing continued. This should not come as a surprise as this resistance is longstanding. Patrik Wikström reminds us that in the 1980s, "when the compact cassette technology was developed, it also incited a creative and social music listening culture with phenomena." A "home-taping" culture quickly rose that not only included the dubbing of albums, but the creation of "mixtapes" that were cassettes produced and shared between peers. Instead of embracing this blank cas-sette as a kind of supplement to a person's record collection, the industry decided to respond to this new form of audio culture by launching a set of campaigns designed to counter these practices. Such was the case with the International Federation of the Phonographic Industry's legendary "Home taping is killing music" and "it's illegal" campaigns. At the same time, "the industry also successfully lobbied against governments in order to introduce a levy on cassette recorders and on blank, recordable cassettes" (Wikström, 2009, p. 152). It is in this tradition of both shame and legal engagement of users that multiple elements of the music industry attempted to corral the widespread problem of illegal filesharing. One such response came in a much publicized reply to a blog post on National Public Radio's website. In the post, Emily White, an intern for the network's much-heralded *All Songs Considered* program, confessed to not missing physical forms of recordings (i.e., compact discs, LPs, etc.) and that she had purchased only 15 compact discs in her life despite having more than 11,000 songs in her iTunes file

(White, 2012). Lead singer of Cracker and Camper Van Beethoven, David Lowery, took it upon himself to respond in the blog *Trichordist: Artists For An Ethical Internet* in a post titled "Letter to Emily White at NPR All Songs Considered." Claiming that he had no intent to embarrass her, Lowery points out that he had spent the last two years teaching about the music industry at the University of Georgia where, "unfortunately for artists, most of [my students] share your attitude about purchasing music." For Lowery the problem of White and her peers is an ethical problem:

> You have grown up in a time when technological and commercial interests are attempting to change our principles and morality. Rather than using our morality and principles to guide us through technological change, there are those asking us to change our morality and principles to fit the technological change—if a machine can do something, it ought to be done. (Lowery, 2012b)

Lowery is hardly alone in his thoughts. Rick Carnes, a prominent songwriter based in Nashville and president of the Songwriters Guild of America (SGA) stated in 2010 that "The biggest challenge right now is changing the behavior of a generation of internet users to get them to pay for music" (Carnes, 2010b). Furthermore, "In a world of perfect justice," the CEO of the popular filesharing service Limewire "would have to personally pay back every cent that [it] stole from thousands of songwriters and artists" and "a life sentence of community service finding jobs for the songwriters and artists he helped put out of business" (Carnes, 2010e).

As tempting as it is to celebrate a new model and dismiss Lowery and Carnes as technophobes, it is not that simple. While some of this resistance, maybe of the knee-jerk variety, is based on what many of us resist in our daily lives, i.e. that those daily practices that so many have cultivated over years of negotiating cultural and economic struggles could simply be tossed aside by forces beyond our control. In this sense, Carnes is justifiably rankled by the devastating effects that free filesharing has wreaked on the industry. For example, Carnes points out that the Songwriters Guild has spent over 80 years educating songwriters about how to best negotiate the industry and has lobbied on their behalf. It's this kind of institutional legacy in education and advocacy that is especially important to many longtime music industry players. However, both institutions and players are engaging actors who are often unaware of the effects that their technologies have on financial, legal, and labor practices that took years to develop. This is one of the reasons Lowery holds the "Copyleft movement" in contempt. Led by Lawrence Lessig and others, the movement has worked to find ways of freeing art and culture from what they often perceive are the problematic restrictions of copyright. At the same time, the movement has become an occasional target for Lowery's posts where he argues for the significant virtues of a more conservative vision of copyright. Unlike most of those in the "tech blogosphere" who Lowery asserts "are knowing pawns in a cynical short term strategy to protect the profits of web and technology companies," he holds thinkers like Lessig in particular contempt for he is among "the most highly regarded voices on the web about the web" (Lowery, 2012a). Carnes also lays blame at some of those thinkers and groups that have advocated for reforming of copyright legislation and defended filesharers as a significant problem. For Carnes groups such as Public Knowledge have taken a dubious path by championing "ways to avoid detection of the crime of illegal downloading" under the banner of "free speech" (Carnes, 2010d). A nonprofit Washington, DC-based public interest group, Public Knowledge claims Lawrence Lessig as one of its board directors and is dedicated to rethinking intellectual property law. Indeed, Carnes has directed substantial amounts of public ire toward the group's president and cofounder, Gigi Sohn. In one post, Carnes noted that,

> as SGA vice president I fought alongside the Writers Guild of America, the Directors Guild, Screen Actors Guild, American Federation of Television and Radio Artists and the American Federation of Musicians to get the Bono Copyright extension passed. Public Knowledge opposed us. [Furthermore], where was Public knowledge during the 25 years I fought against the record labels on controlled composition clauses that insure that recording artists receive only 3/4's of their royalties on their own songs? Where was Public Knowledge when I was the lead witness to boost royalty rates for artists at the hearings before the Copyright rate board?

And finally,

> It is not surprising that Ms. Sohn doesn't get it. She has not spent her life as a creator or as an advocate for songwriters as I have. She has not watched as her friends and co-writers lost their jobs, their homes, and even their families, due to Internet piracy. She claims I ignore independent filmmakers. I guess she doesn't know that my daughter is a student Oscar winning independent filmmaker (*A Leg Up*) or that my wife is a recording artist? (*Hoagy N' Me*). Believe me, I'm intimately aware of what artists and filmmakers think. (Carnes, 2010c)

To be sure, Carnes' and Lowery's objections are neither examples of Ludditism or conservative reactions designed to affirm the dominance of major labels and big name publishers. Beginning his music career as an independent musician, Lowery has run an independent label, Pitch-a-Tent Records, for well over 20 years. Carnes on the other hand is openly progressive in his politics and has bemoaned that resistance he finds in left-wing brothers and sisters to work more "constructively with labor, with the creative classes (artists, musicians, songwriters, film makers) to build a digital economy that creates jobs and economic well-being" (Carnes, 2010a). Carnes' criticisms rest on the fact that he and his fellow practitioners have spent their lives invested in a set of rules and practices that are undergoing a paradigm change that they seem to have no control over. Both Lowery and Carnes relay anecdotes about how the changes in networking and distribution have had traumatic results for many of their peers who have spent their lives honing skills for a marketplace that has quickly dissolved. The trauma that accompanies any collapsing economy should be acknowledged as the legitimate and painful claim it is. Indeed, both Sohn and Carnes agree that business models centered on the sale of objects are preferable for musicians. However, Sohn and her colleagues have ditched the idea that the problems ubiquitous networks pose can ever be countered without a new model that somehow takes free into account and works with it. In Sohn's words, there must be "new business models that allow consumers access to a full catalogue of reasonably priced music" despite the pains that musicians and songwriters have suffered. While Public Knowledge is exploring new models, Sohn and her "allies are not in favor of stealing content. We don't devalue copyright and we don't think enforcing copyright law is 'trivial.'" Furthermore, "We don't believe that everything should be 'free,' as in 'free coffee.'" Instead, Sohn and her colleagues prefer "'free' as in 'free speech'" (Sohn, 2010).

Free is arguably *the* dominant concern for new music business models in the 21st century. The question of how to legitimately negotiate free to generate new income streams has been the source of numerous experiments. The counterintuitive aspect of an industry generating income from free is a significant problem as many are unable (and sometimes unwilling) to think of free as a set of practices. While we tend to think of free as a given pricepoint, free has its own history. In *Free: The Future of a Radical Price*, Chris Anderson points out that one of the reasons null points are hard to conceive of is that "we tend to think in terms of the concrete and tangible, yet free is a concept, not something you can count on your fingers" (Anderson, 2009, p. 34).[3] As a set of practices, free includes more than prices but the custom of tactical losses. Of course, no amount of digitization will ever get rid of the loss leader. Free downloads and bonus content remain effective practices for online retailers to draw consumers to spaces such as Amazon and iTunes. Another practice of free involves the freeing up of musical selections that were once seen as bound to albums. The importance of this rests in the industry's embrace of the compact disc and the its systematic abandonment of the "single."[4] Historically, the single was the entry-level product for the new consumer. With the lowest price point, the single was the product that most young record buyers acquired in the history of recorded pop. Abandoning the hit single in favor of forcing consumers into purchasing an entire disc worth of songs posed a significant problem, one that former president of the Record Industry Association of America, Hilary Rosen, acknowledged. For Rosen, without the single the consumer no longer had multiple price points for multiple means of market entry (Kot, 2009, p. 45). Furthermore, without the ability to purchase only the hit single many consumers felt "forced" or "tricked" into an-almost $20 purchase of twelve songs, only one of which was of quality. For some, this arrangement sowed a decade's worth of resentment, out of which Napster and others would find purchase and blossom.[5]

However, for every online Robin Hood who has advocated the righteousness of online piracy in the face of corporate greed, we should remember, as Chris Anderson points out, that piracy is also "a form of imposed Free" (Anderson, 2009, p. 71). Anderson's thoughts and opinions should not be dismissed. Unlike other pundits, Anderson's work has had a distinct impact in English reading communities that few authors can claim. "A guru of the information age," Anderson's position as an opinion leader for Internet culture in the English-speaking world cannot be discounted (Duncan, 2009). Editor-in-chief of *Wired*, the owner of The Sapling Foundation—a nonprofit 501(c)(3) that owns and hosts the TED conference—and author, Anderson's impact on new media practitioners cannot be underestimated. A tech evangelist who specializes in forums for new media ideas, Anderson is also a researcher and writer whose publication of two popular books, *The Long Tail: Why the Future of Business of Selling Less is More* (2006) and *Free: The Future of a Radical Price* (2009), have substantially influenced how new media businesses conceive of their practices. After finishing *The Long Tail*, Anderson noted that because "the new shape of consumer demand" was "enabled by the unlimited 'shelf space' of the Internet," a new understanding of "free" arose:

> There's only one way you can have unlimited shelf space: if that shelf space costs nothing. The near-zero 'marginal costs' of digital distribution (that is, the additional cost of sending out another copy beyond the 'fixed costs' of the required hardware with which to do it) allow us to be indiscriminate in what we use it for—no gatekeepers are required to decide if something deserves global reach or not. As I marveled over the consequences, I started thinking more about Free, and realized just how far it had spread. It didn't just explain the explosion of variety online, it defined the pricing there, too. What's more, this 'free' wasn't just a marketing gimmick like the free samples and prizes inside that we're used to in traditional retail. This free seemed to have no strings attached: It wasn't just a lure for a future sale, but genuine gratis. Most of us depend on one or more Google services every day, but they never show up on our credit card. No meter ticks as you use Facebook. Wikipedia costs you nothing. (Anderson, 2009, p. 3)

In short, "somewhere in the transition from atoms to bits, a phenomenon that we thought we understood was transformed. 'Free' became Free" (Anderson, 2009, p. 4).

Of course the Internet itself is hardly free. If anything, the Internet is composed of immense capital investments in hardware and coordinated practices.[6] It is much more precise to say that without the encumbrance of physical restrictions, users and businesses began to experiment with practices of free. More importantly, practicing free was an option only to those without large debts and other commitments. Major labels and publishers that are saddled with large-scale investments in the fixed costs of labor resources, infrastructure, complicated debt-finance structures, and the obligation of quarterly statements for their public investors would find it difficult to experiment with the wide-scale gifting of music. However, the practice of free has become such a hot topic for musicians of many stripes because of the relatively small-scale nature that many popular music investments demand. The problem that independent musicians and labels always ran into was not the production of music but its effective distribution that would allow it to go to scale. However, in a file-based economy, many of the logistical issues that accompanied the national distribution of discs were no longer necessary to bring product to market. Supply chains of warehouses and transportation and catalogue that connected with retailers have been replaced with third-party businesses that assist musicians and labels by placing music into digital retailers and services.[7] As the costs of distribution, both for promotion and moving products to retail, plummeted, so have the costs of create a reasonably quality recording. The problem for artists is to figure out exactly how to take advantage of these rapidly declining costs and create significant opportunities for profitability.

A significant part of this investigation by artists has involved documenting the many practical applications and failures of free to generate a viable and legitimate new music economy. Much of the discussion has occurred online through the maintenance of collective weblogs. One such site is *Music Think Tank* (*MTT*), a group blog that is hosted by Hypebot.com, a site dedicated to music, technology, and the new music business. Founded by educator and entrepreneur Andrew Dubber, *MTT* is open to and composed of musicians, music professionals, and industry observers as an information clearinghouse of practices and unsuccessful experiments. In early 2010, Mark Valente, the Director of Music Without Labels, posted on *MTT* the results of a less-than-scientific poll that his service posed on the social news site Reddit. In December 2009, Valente posted the query, "What needs to happen in order for music to become free and the artist still get paid?" Among the replies were to have musicians and acts focus on songwriting to help them generate and leverage performance rights as income streams; live performances would remain vital; find ways to increase the revenues from online advertising, instruction and other "nonmusic jobs." Finally, responses implored that the music industry consciously "break away" from a "MTV cribs' culture" of excess (Valente, 2010).

Music Without Labels' pursuit to find an answer to make music free yet make artists profitable was hardly altruistic. Other labels and entrepreneurs were in the long-term pursuit of properly revaluing musical properties, which meant understanding that simply because music was involved in practices of free it was not necessarily devalued. If selling massive amounts of iPods and the practices of illegal downloading, and remixing have taught us anything, it is that the appetite for recordings has not lessened. Although the numbers of recordings sold have plummeted, musicians continue to oversaturate the market with recordings. This is a key point: because neither production nor demand has abated, the music industry has been forced to reinvestigate how music is valued by networked users and consider that this may be significantly different from traditional music audiences. Value, not price, is the key term and it explicitly applies to a number of concerns far beyond those that guide monetary exchanges. Blaise Alleyne, musician and computer programmer, notes that artists are understandably wary of free because "zero" makes one "feel like their art is worthless." Alleyne explains further that "[Musicians] aren't hung up on scarcity. They're hung up on 'devaluation.'" This is a problem that the practice of free exposes: free demands that every actor in the music business rethinks how their wares are positioned in the marketplace and recognize that "value and price are not the same." Alleyne correctly explains that, "price gets driven down to marginal cost, but value factors into the demand side of the equation. Expensive things aren't necessarily valuable, and valuable things aren't necessarily expensive. I value oxygen a lot, but it seems silly to pay for the air I breathe" (Alleyne, 2009). Alleyne's point may feel like a stretch. However, it may have more purchase if we remind ourselves that in a user-based economy where value is accrued through the monitored and measured use and exchange of data, music, like air, is prized because it circulates within specific environments. The devaluation of recorded objects means investors have had to rethink their financial practices. Alleyne argues that musicians need to focus their resources on the production and distribution of ideas and experiences, and turns to songwriting to make his point:

> A recording is not the song, it's just an instance of it, and a digital audio file is just an instance of the recording. Equating these reduces music to recordings, to files. As important as recordings are, there's so much more to music! When you think of a song, do you think of the recording, or a memory you had connecting with the music? Do you think of the file and how much it cost [sic], or the emotions and relationships that the music conjures up? The recordings are just a means through which we experience the music. Songwriters (of all people!) should know that the value in music is so much more than the price of a recording. It's not devaluing music to give it away for free, but it can increase its value by allowing more people to connect with it, to know, love and understand it—to value it. It's through that experience that music is valued, not price!

Alleyne recognizes that the primary concern with free is economic with the key question being how will musicians and songwriters then make money. However, by understanding that because the price of digital audio files begins at zero Alleyne implores artists to "use as much of those abundant goods as possible." In this context, sharing for Alleyne would make "music more valuable and [lead] to more opportunities for monetization" by connecting with audiences and new fans. Once these connections are made, "the opportunity for monetization is in the associated scarcities—access, containers, community, merchandise, relationships, unique goods, the creation of new music, etc.—by giving people a reason to buy." For Alleyne, when a musician or label focuses on the "devaluation" of the file they are prevented from "seeing the opportunity—the necessity—to experiment with new business models" (Alleyne, 2009). Alleyne is not advocating free, but is responding to critics of free file-sharing. Alleyne's advocacy for a set of experiments in the search of new music business models comes from a feeling that the industry has no choice but to find innovative paths to monetization. As it turns out, many others agree in the industry and have begun to see results from rethinking how to monetize music. As Nick Clark reported in *The Independent*, after a "mixed year for Britain's entertainment and media industries" a Pricewaterhouse Coopers report emerged that recognized the value of these experiments. According to the report, media businesses have "reached a defining moment" and are poised for growth because they are "reevaluating and redefining [their] business models in ways that will ultimately redraw the value chain" (Clark, 2010).

The term "value chain" refers to every activity and intermediary through which a product passes as it seeks to accrue value. The chain includes logistics, assembly, distribution, and marketing, among others. Creating a deep understanding of the value chain that any product or service must negotiate allows businesses to plan strategically where they should allocate their capital resources. For over 100 years the value chain for the music industry made significant investments in the production, distribution, and retail of physical goods. Throughout history record labels and sheet music publishers developed and maintained similar value-chain logics and practices. For example, record label functionaries such as "artists and repertoire," aka "A&R," "rack jobbers," and record retailing practices of sample and display were all adapted from an economy focused on sheet music sales to one built around records. As products entered these value chains, the primary goal of selling objects remained the same, as did the fundamental issues of scale, gatekeeping, and the reduction of marginal cost. Indeed, the problems introduced by ubiquitously networked users for the record industry center on losing elements of the value chain such as retail, the placement of goods in the marketplace, and curation. The rise of digital retailers and business-to-business services has provided a number of solutions, although their presence are hardly curative. Indeed, what has remained problematic has been loss distribution techniques focused on promotion and marketing.

Because so many techniques were oriented around the purchase of musical goods, what the promoters and marketers have had to rethink is how to promote the utilization of music. It is in this vein that Chris Anderson complained in 2009 that "the traditional music business is a bunch of whiners" that want to retain the old model rather than develop a new model in light of this defining moment: "As you go through the process, trying to figure out what the new model is, often the voices of the losers are heard most loudly because they're feeling it so profoundly while the winners have not yet emerged" (Sydell, 2009).

In essence, what experiments in free focused on is a search for models that generate value through digital distribution. Two of the most noted and notorious examples of experimentations with free occurred in 2007. In spring 2007 Ozzy and Sharon Osbourne announced that admission to their touring heavy metal concert festival, Ozzfest, would be free. Later that fall, Radiohead announced that their latest album *In Rainbows* would be offered at a "pay as you wish" experiment, with the price of the entire DRM-less download beginning at zero. Finishing their contract with EMI in 2003, the band's lead singer, Thom Yorke, told *Time* magazine before recording the album: "I like the people at our record company, but the time is at hand when you have to ask why anyone needs one. And, yes, it probably would give us some perverse pleasure to say 'F___ you' to this decaying business model" (Tyrangiel, 2007). In actuality both were experiments in a search for value. In the case of Ozzfest, sponsorships would pay for the everyday expenses of staging the tour while bands ostensibly played for "nothing." Instead, bands were offered a chance to leverage the Ozzfest brand and promote themselves in front of the "tens of thousands of people" that would show up to the festival and to whom they could "sell CDs and merchandise to at our show" (Borden, 2007). The experiment did not become a permanent practice and in 2008 Sharon Osbourne declared that "We're going back to what we originally were. We've given the real good fans a free show for one time, and now, it's back to business as usual" (Harris, 2008). Although Radiohead's 2007 experiment was much more celebrated, its results are just as murky. Reports vary of how many units of *In Rainbows* sold and what the average price per unit was. In 2008 Thom Yorke noted that "We're the only people who know [how many people have downloaded 'In Rainbows']. It feels wrong to say exactly what happened. But it's been a really nice surprise and we've done really well out of it" (Anon., 2008). And like the Osbournes', Radiohead's venture into free would end and not be repeated. On December 31, 2007 *In Rainbows* was released through XL records as a physical CD with reportedly significant sales. Their next significant musical venture, the 2011 *The King of Limbs*, would be released in both physical and digital formats as for-purchasable entities with non-negotiable prices.

As important and ballyhooed as the Osbournes' and Radiohead's experiments in free and revaluation were, the most significant experiments in much less exalted terrain. These experiments occurred on an artist-by-artist basis as musicians explore the value chain through the development of gift economies or what Chris Anderson would call "nonmonetary markets." The gift economy is one of the four distinct practices of free that Chris Anderson identifies are employed by both commercial and noncommercial enterprises. These include the practices of: (1) direct cross-subsidization (p. 23); (2) the formation of "three-party markets" (p. 24); (3) the aforementioned "non-monetary markets" (pp. 27–29); and (4) freemium practices (p. 26). The first two of these, direct cross-subsidization and the formation of "three-party markets," have long been part of capitalist popular music practices.[8] However, it is the experiments with the nonmonetary and freemium markets where the majority of these new experiments have taken place. This is particularly true of nonmonetary markets where what is free is "anything people choose to give away." For Chris Anderson, "the incentives to share can range from reputation and attention to less measurable factors such as expression, fun, good karma, satisfaction, and simply self-interest" (Anderson, 2009, p. 27). The widespread embrace of nonmonetary markets in new media formations is the understanding that a good's or service's value is not limited to only "monetary markets." The abilities to gain attention and grow reputation are valued precisely because it is believed that they influence market choices and behaviors. Thus the question arises: what if we could treat attention and reputation as we do money? What if we could formalize them into proper markets so we could explain and predict them with many of the same equations that economists use in traditional monetary economics? To do so, we would need attention and reputation to exhibit the same characteristics of other traditional currencies, i.e. to be measurable, finite, and convertible. Indeed, the question of formalization will come back to haunt us in Chapter 6 in the discussion of the 1,000 true fans strategy.

For Anderson the ability of individual musicians to affect their overall standing in reputation has begun to emerge through the Internet's connector of choice, the hyperlink. Accompanying this digital binder are increasingly refined sets of user-based analytics and rankings that assess the "currency of [one's networked] reputation" (2009, pp. 182–183). Because they now participate in an ecosystem of cheap networks and abundancies, more and more musicians have begun to view their recordings as a kind of "calling card" that is exchanged to grow their reputation and ability to command audience attention. By cultivating value in these areas, musicians and bands seek to grow as a live act, pack venues, and sell merchandise. As a result, a number of musicians have begun to explore the practice of giving away their digital downloads as a means of advertising themselves. Writing for *Music Think Tank*, independent musician and specialist in micro-media branding Dexter Bryant, Jr. noted that the key is musicians re-imagining themselves as particularly social beings. As part of this process, musicians freely offer their recordings as a kind of greeting, a gesture designed to initiate relationships with audiences. The gift of music is a tactical offering, part of a strategy to forge affection-driven allegiances. The strategy demands much more than simply making "a few profiles on popular social networks, [throwing] your music up on your pages" (Bryant Jr., 2010). Recordings in this strategy are positioned as a low-risk, low barrier-of-entry "product sample." Ideally, after someone receives the download,

> they can easily dig deeper and sample some more of your music to get a better feel for your identity and what your brand represents. From there they can decide whether their values align with yours and if they would like to continue their relationship with you. If you and a potential fan are birds of a feather (so to speak) then chances are they will be ready to forge a deeper bond with you and take your relationship to the next level.

In this model "free music" downloads are posited as "the appetizers that will lure audiences to dine with you for a full meal" where your audience can gain a "clearer picture of your overall vision and your artistic identity." If the audience enjoys it then they can continue to enjoy your other, purchasable offerings such as tickets to a concert, merchandise, premium recordings (vinyl, signed compact discs, etc.), and other "unique experiences." Again, this practice begins with an important first step: musicians need to "stop complaining that the consumers you want to sell music to don't want to buy" (Bryant Jr., 2010).

Because recordings have been the primary income stream for the last half of the 20th century it has been difficult to alter the aspirations of many musicians raised wanting to go "gold" or "platinum" and persuade them to give away their music. This requires educating the musician and others that gift economies are economies rife with social commitments that force the gift giver to think about the needs and limits of his or her recipients, and vice versa. As Marcel Mauss argues, gifts are never truly "free." Instead, gifts entail significant obligations that recipients may not wish to engage (Mauss, 1967). In a gift economy of digital downloads the recipient's obligation is to share the musical gift with others. Without sharing, the potency of the gift wanes. The gift in this model isn't so much an offering for a relationship, but the agent that spurs a possible set of interrelated relationships. The gift is a critical social gesture to spark an economy based on sharing. Christopher Small notes that sharing plays a profound role in the creation of music cultures. This is true of small rural communities and metropolitan spaces where, as Small points out, "working-class social clubs; blues and jazz clubs; local repertory theaters; ethnic communities whose ceremonies of birth, death and especially marriage provide occasions; groups of friends who meet to make music together; sports and other activities clubs; and of course churches and other religious groups" (pp. 40–41). For Small, the "islands of community" that appeared as discos, popular theaters, and cabarets, etc., were something of an attempt to address a "great sea of impersonal relations" generated by modern urban spaces (Small, 1998, p. 41). Small's "sea of impersonal spaces" is one of the very problems that so many online spaces and social networks directly address. As part of this digital remedy that promises more personal, less anonymous connections, the musician's gift is an initial offering with hopes to engage and generate online communities that will include numerous exchanges and social obligations. Indeed, Billy Bones views free as a practice essential for new artists to cultivating the value of their brand position. For Bones, "new artists should utilize social media in order to build their following (their tribe), and rather than sell them music, [they should] acquire information from [their fans] such as e-mails and start to take notes of the different interests of your tribe" (Bones, 2010). A similar sentiment is held by Jonathan Ostrow, cofounder of Miccontrol, a music blog that is dedicated to connecting musicians with music bloggers. For Ostrow, artists with small fan bases should never give away their music as a gift unless it comes with explicit strings attached. The problem of a gift without strings is "unless you already possess quite a large fan-base along with the subsequent reach, giving your music away will be the last you hear from most of these new 'fans.'" What these artists need "is a way to turn this seemingly one-sided transaction, into one that is mutually beneficial." Ostrow advises artists that "you essentially want to continue charging for your product, but in a way that replaces value in terms of money with that of brand growth." In this practice, musicians should exchange music for anything that will "increase your reputation and reach, rather than increase your bank account" (Ostrow, 2010). For example, MP3s could be given to fans in exchange for their email addresses for future conversations, or musicians could demand that fans "tweet" or post a "Facebook share" on their personal pages to leverage their fans' social networks and widen their fan base. Whatever the case, there is no absolutely "free" exchange in this gift economy. Rather artists exchange their art in search of social capital. As we will discuss later, the search for a formalized model and sets of metrics that would allow musicians and management to ascertain when they have accrued this capital has become significantly important as part of employing a gift strategy.

It is important to understand that artists and entrepreneurs alike have engaged another version of the gift that Chris Anderson labels the "free-mium model." In this model, "free" involves giving a free service or version of a product and then offering "a premium paid version" that provides a noticeable improvement (Anderson, 2009, p. 26). Perhaps the most interesting example of this in popular music has been the consistent offering of the free, digital "mixtape" to hip-hop audiences. "Mixtape" refers to the practice of producing mixes of songs by DJs in a low cost manner for niche audiences. The practice began on cassettes, moved to compact discs, and has continued with the production and distribution of MP3 mixes as a way to promote future releases by artists and labels. Although giving away a portion of a song that is in a mix is a far cry from giving away an entire song, as Wesley Verhoeve of the independent label Family Records notes, the practice provides a significant lesson: "[if you expose] people to what's so special about your music, and if it's something they dig, they will be back and ready for you to close the sale and convert that into purchasing behavior, whether it's a shirt, more music, or a concert ticket." Offering a free mixtape is a strategic practice of free that artists and labels have embraced to promote their wares (Verhoeve, 2011). So widespread and important is the practice that at least one legal analyst has noted "[their] impact on the current hip-hop culture is undeniable" (Schantz, 2009). Although less widespread, a number of artists have experimented with the freemium model by offering a free tier of music that is somehow limited. These "freemiums" could come in the form of an older, less desirable portions of their catalogue, offer recordings that are significantly degraded in their sound quality, make their back catalogue streaming only, etc. And, of course, an artist may agree to offer a portion of an album (typically one or two songs). Key to this strategy is to keep these gifts incomplete and promise their completion and improvement upon the payment. In essence, the freemium gifts generate a possible moment for "upsell." Within this lies the basic value proposition of freemium: "Consumers demonstrably love music that is free or feels like free, but are still prepared to pay for it when they see the value" (Anon., 2010a, p. 18).

At the same time, the risk that the artist takes is relatively minimal. If an audience member only accepts the degraded or streamable version they at least have made a connection with the listener and the loss of a sale is offset by the potential of a future relationship where other sales and services can be monetized. Perhaps the most celebrated example of freemium offerings in the music industry has come in the streaming services of Pandora and Spotify. However, unlike an artist or an independent label, these services do not have the luxury of waiting for long-term relationships to develop. Because of their legal obligation to pay out royalties streaming services must immediately capitalize on the audience relationships they have developed. As a result, both of these services often engage in a form of freemium that is ad-supported and limits the amount of the service that users may access. Both Pandora and Spotify provide deep, entry level experiences that allow users to enjoy these services. Based out of the United States, Pandora's services emulate online radio in the sense that users may request an artist or a genre but they have no ability to demand specific selections. Spotify is also an online streaming service. However, unlike Pandora, Spotify is an on-demand streaming service that allows users to play whatever Spotify has licensed in their catalogue and as often as they like. Developed in Sweden, the service has headquarters in Stockholm and London, England, and, as of 2011, began to operate in the United States with headquarters in New York. The two demand more attention than I can offer here in this chapter. However, what is important for now is that both services offer successful freemium services that are ad-supported. Although there have been numerous attempts at ad-supported music streaming services, Pandora and Spotify are arguably the two most notable services as both have attracted large amounts of venture capital, media attention, and, what is more important, significant user bases who are willing to engage with freemium. For example, when Pandora first launched its radio service in 2005, the company provided an introductory offer of 10 free hours of streaming music. After this period, listeners were requested to pay a yearly fee of $36 a year. In an interview, Tom Conrad, Pandora's Chief Technology Officer, noted that, "In the first couple weeks we had 100,000 people come through and the vast majority listened to every last minute of their free ten hours. Then we asked them for their credit card and they would wander off into the wilderness." In November 2005 the company began to offer an ad-supported option, however the service did so without the aid of an ad staff or ad server. Further complicating the problem was that the user base quadrupled almost overnight and within three days Apple had called to buy out the ad inventory for the remainder of the month. Without professional ad staff, Conrad provided Apple with a $10,000 price tag and "literally hand-coded the ads on the page. We didn't want them to know, but every time they changed their creative we'd have to relaunch the entire site." In the past five years the company has become much more adept with ad services, with 20 million unique visitors and $50 million in ad revenue by 2010 (Gannes, 2010). In 2008 Pandora began to experience significant increases in its user base that was predicated on the release of multiple "smartphones" such as the iPhone and Android that allowed the service produce apps for portable streaming. That same year Pandora doubled-down on its freemium service and began to allow users to "get 40 free hours of music per month, supported by the usual ads, before they're cut off." Tim Westergren noted "[that] since only the top 10 percent of users log more than 40 hours per month on the site, Pandora is still free for the majority of users." And for those who are willing to pay the $36 a year fee, they would receive "Pandora One," a service that offers features such as "a desktop application, very high-quality audio and the ability to skip an unlimited number of songs" (Patterson, 2009).[9] Writing for the tech blog *GigaOm*, Liz Gannes notes that while subscription rates are well below 1% of the user bases, Pandora still claims 300,000 subscribers that account "for 1.6 or 1.7 percent of monthly uniques, and is expected to bring in 15 percent of 2010 revenue" (Gannes, 2010).

Spotify operates with a similar, ad-supported freemium model. Beginning in fall 2008 Spotify offered its users four distinct tiers of services, two of which involved the freemium approach. Those two services, "Spotify Open" and "Spotify Free," offer variants of freemium that were distinguished by invitation. While "Spotify Free" provided unlimited ad-supported music, it was offered only to select users. Far more common was the "Spotify Open" service that provided users free, ad-supported music for up to six hours a day, 20 hours a month maximum. While only initially available in the United Kingdom and a handful of European countries, the service was quickly celebrated by fans and journalists as "representative of the 'freemium' access movement" (Forde, 2009b, p. 16). Writing for *The Spectator*, Fraser Nelson celebrated the service for providing, "a seemingly limitless database of music all for £10 a month." The peculiar result for Fraser is that Spotify is a convenient service that generates demand:

> [Spotify] basically means I listen to music again. I had, stupidly, spent days digitally archiving my CD collection but it was so much hassle to play it that I'd given up. Wire up Spotify—from an iPhone or laptop— and you can instantly play a whole load of stuff that you thought you could never afford, or find. True to long tail economics, the greater supply of this free music leads to greater demand—in my case, spending ages discovering albums that I'd never buy on iTunes. But what is revolutionary about it is that its technology—instant streaming at perfect quality—will soon make the concept of music collections obsolete. (Nelson, 2010)

By providing a well-designed user interface, a robust database, applications for a multiple platforms, and an embrace of free, Spotify, in the words of Eamonn Forde writing for *Music Week*, "has done what Hoover and Google took years to achieve: it moved from being a noun to a verb" (Forde, 2009b).

Like Pandora, Spotify has made several changes to its freemium services. In May 2011 Spotify cut its users' free hours from 20 to 10 hours a week. However, it was its many new stipulations of Spotify's free service made it clear that Spotify's experiment with free was undergoing a radical shift. While the invitation-only "Spotify Free" continued to operate as it had in the past, the majority of new "Spotify Open" users would incur the new time limit and be limited to playing each individual track in the catalogue for free up to five times (Butcher, 2011). Writing for Spotify's blog, cofounder Daniel Ek noted that,

> Spotify's aim from the very beginning was to make music on-demand available to all. To give you the power to listen to, discover, share and manage your music the way you want to—simpler, faster, better— while making sure the artists whose music we all love continue to see the benefits as we grow. (Ek, 2011)

According to Ek, this means the company "can continue making Spotify available to all in the long-term" (Ek, 2011). However, commentary to Ek's blog post by readers such as "so long Spotify. It was nice nowing [sic] you. Guess I'll go back to pirating music again then" is the kind of user backlash every service hopes to avoid (Butcher, 2011). In 2011 Spotify opened in the United States with similar service options. But by 2012 the service had begun to offer an unlimited amount of the free ad-supported service. Like Pandora, Spotify's freemium practices exist in beta, ready to change as the service deems necessary.

Freemium may be a route for these services, however it, too, is not without its critics. The dominant concern for critics are royalty rates, particularly what some consider to be rather paltry and "unfair" when compared to other sources of residual income. The income from streaming will always be significantly less when compared to the amounts that come from music sales. However, the money that comes from licensing has always been significant to artists and investors alike because intellectual properties like songs and masters can be exclusively licensed for long periods of time.[10] The problem for most labels and the reason that so many resisted working with freemium services for as long as they could were the less-than-paltry receipts they gained from the likes of Spotify and others.[11] Further complicating this scenario was that while major labels were resisting freemium's entry into the U.S., they may have negotiated better rates than their independent competitors. For example, in 2011 it was revealed that Universal and Sony received more "revenue from Spotify than any other Swedish music service or digital and physical record store" (Lindvall, 2011). Spotify has never entirely denied this rumor. However, the company has defended itself stating that "We're working extremely hard with all labels, both indie and major, to provide sustainable revenues for the industry as a whole at a time when the vast majority of music continues to be downloaded illegally and not providing a single penny for artists" (McGivern, 2011).

The issue of equitable royalty distribution has been a consistent source of complaint made against the service. In 2009 a number of red flags were raised when reports surfaced that Spotify had disbursed a royalty check to a Swedish performing rights society for playing Lady Gaga recordings, at the time arguably the most popular recording artist in the English-speaking world, for the equivalent of $167. According to one blog, "this has led to much chattering that either Spotify are screwing the artists or, perhaps, the major record companies, who are shareholders in the streaming music company, are taking the lion's share of any royalty revenues" (Anon., 2009b). While this meager amount tells us next to nothing about the actual royalties paid out (Lady Gaga's specific payment arrangements with other coauthors and her label may be less than fair), the report began a narrative of suspicion that the service has yet to adequately quell.[12] The Spanish independent label Blancomusic Records noted in 2011 that "the rates offered to us as an indie label were so insulting that we'd prefer to forgo the 'privilege' [of being on the Spotify platform]" (Lindvall, 2011). To underscore the seemingly negligible per-play royalties that Spotify offered, in 2010 the blog *Information is Beautiful* culled data from various sources to generate a visual comparison of the service with other streaming services and sources of income. Employing the baseline of what it would take for a solo musician to earn the U.S. monthly minimum wage of $1,160, the blog noted that a musician selling self-pressed CDs sold at $9.99 would need to move 143 units per month. Using the CD Baby service the same musician would only have to sell 12 more physical copies to achieve the same goal. The numbers accelerate once the musician sells the same physical CD through a label with a "high end royalty deal." In this case the musicians needs to move 1,161 units per month, 1,229 if the same album is downloaded as a digital download on iTunes. By comparison, if a musician were to make his or her minimum wage from royalties earned by on-demand streaming, the numbers go up exponentially. For Rhapsody's paid subscription service an artist would have to be streamed 849,817 times per month to earn $1,160 a month. On Last.FM's free on-demand stream service the same artist would have to gain 1,546,667 plays. On Spotify that number more than doubles as the artist must receive 4,053,110 plays per month with the label receiving $0.0016 and the artist $0.00029 per play (McCandless, Flyn, Slater, & Key, 2010). The combination of Spotify's lowered rates and the fact that Sony Music had invested in the service raised many eyebrows. As Swedish noble, artist, and composer Magnus Uggla notes, Sony and other majors have continually sued illegal downloading sites and services for ostensibly not paying royalties to artists. Thus, Uggla concluded, "I would rather be raped by Pirate Bay than by Sony Music and will remove all of my songs from Spotify pending an honest service" (Gerard, 2010).

The dilemma of these practices is that it looks like Spotify is being cheap with artists; their counter has been that the service is streaming billions of songs per month, with billions scaling to millions of dollars, pounds, euros, and krona paid out in royalties. These are payments that must be made before any other expenditure can be spent to improve the service for listeners, most of whom are using a free version of the service. In 2009, Glenn Peoples noted in *Billboard* that companies invested in interactive streaming like Spotify are,

> able to offer a better user experience and probably generate interest from more avid (and thus more valuable) music fans. The hitch is the extra value offered must be converted into extra revenue in the form of subscriptions (or through selling downloads, tickets or other items). It's a brutal numbers game that requires innovative products and massive scale to succeed. Maybe somebody will make it work one of these days. (Peoples, 2009)

Running services like Spotify and Pandora may be particularly exciting as they embrace new models that work to both free-up musical experiences and create profits. Yet, these services are subject to costs of doing business that make the development of any free-oriented music service an extremely difficult task, one that requires deep pockets and investors with significant amounts of patience to bring it to maturity.

In every case, the success of freemium rests upon generating a more favorable balance between pay and free. Writing about freemium for South Africa's *Sunday Times*, Ian Mann underscored the common rule of 5%: "every user who pays supports 19 who don't" (Mann, 2009). The disproportionate nature of the premium versus free user base combined with the abovementioned issues of music licensing has led numerous leaders in digital music distribution to strongly question whether freemium can work at all. "The free model cannot work" stated Denis Ladegaillerie, CEO of the French digital distributor Believe. In 2009, Ladegaillerie declared that "on-demand streaming services will all come to a paid model." Still, the proliferation of on-demand services that offer freemium services such as Deezer, Jiwa, and Spotify in the French marketplace forced the streaming service MusicMe to adopt a similar strategy despite the fact that the service's own cofounder is more than suspicious of the practice. "We had to go free, considering the model had been legitimized by the music industry," MusicMe cofounder Ludovic Leu said in 2009, "but we don't believe in free" (Pichevin, 2009). Steve Purdham, the CEO of the UK-based freemium streaming service We7, underscored that the model had at least one significant advantage: "The good news is, the audience loves this type of stuff. They are prepared to accept the ad-funded model, because they get something they like—they get the music." The disadvantage is that the model now has to prove that it can work: "Now it's about getting real revenue and, more importantly, real, sustainable revenue" (Anon., 2009a, p. 26). Such concerns and pessimism led at least one music executive in 2009 to predict that "Spotify will be bankrupt in a year" (Ahmed, 2009). Still, as of 2013 Spotify is not bankrupt. However, it isn't clear whether Spotify is profitable and what its value is in the marketplace since it isn't publicly traded. The value of Spotify, Pandora, and other experiments in free rests in the solutions they offer a world where piracy continues unabated. Of course, free may not offer *the* solution but may be one of many. Even Peter Jenner, with his close to 50 years' worth of experience, feels that what lies ahead is at best brackish with one exception: "the more we drive the music into the grey or even dark zone the harder it will be to collect money and allocate that revenue fairly. The more we try and enforce our old-fashioned 20th century ways of looking at things, the worse shape we will be in. Devices can be bought that make copying easy, files can be exchanged for virtually nothing, the sweat shop is open-plan and the security guy is deaf, blind, and infirm" (Jenner, 2010).

BIBLIOGRAPHY

Ahmed, M. (2009, April 3). Spotify's Brave New Idea Could Pay Off For the Music Industry. *The Times*.

Alleyne, B. (2009, December 21). Free Music Doesn't Mean Devalued Music. Retrieved from http://www.musicthinktank.com/mtt-open/free-music-doesnt-mean-devalued-music.html

Anderson, C. (2006). *The Long Tail: Why the Future of Business of Selling Less Is More*. New York: Hyperion.

Anderson, C. (2009). *Free: The Future of a Radical Price*. New York: Hyperion.

Anon. Why Am I Limited to 40 Free Listening Hours Per Month? Retrieved from http://blog.pandora.com/faq/contents/1555.html

Anon. (2008, January 2). Radiohead: 'We've Done Really Well Out of 'In Rainbows.' *NME*.

Anon. (2009a, May 1). Is Time Running Out For Digital Music? *Revolution*, 26.

Anon. (2009b, November 24). Lots of Chatter About Spotify Royalties. Retrieved from http://www.thecmuwebsite.com/article/lots-of-chatter-about-spotify-royalties/

Anon. (2009c, May 20). Welcome to the Free World. *Marketing*.

Anon. (2010a, February 13). Musically: What Price Free Music? *Music Week*, 18.

Anon. (2010b, July 14). Westminster eForum: Peter Jenner on Digital Content Consumers.

Appleyard, B. (2009, June 28). What is the hidden price of our freebie culture?. The Sunday *Times*. Retrieved from http://www.thesundaytimes.co.uk/sto/ingear/tech_and_net/article175346.ece

Baym, N. (2011). The Swedish Model: Balancing Markets and Gifts in the Music Industry. *Popular Communication*, 9(1), 22–38.

Benkler, Y. (2006). *The Wealth of Networks: How Social Production Transforms Markets and Freedom*. New Haven, CT: Yale University Press.

Bodget, H. (2009). Malcolm Gladwell: Chris Anderson Is Wrong About "Free." *Business Insider, SAI*. Retrieved from http://www.businessinsider.com/henry-blodget-malcolm-gladwell-chris-anderson-is-wrong-about-free-2009–6

Bones, B. (2010, April 15). Build Your Tribe Before Selling. Retrieved from http://www.musicthinktank.com/mtt-open/build-your-tribe-before-selling.html

Borden, M. (2007, April 16). Headbanging Headliners Snub Free Ozzfest: Ozzy and Sharon Osbourne Are Taking Their Metalfest Free—Great News For Fans, But Will the Bands Play If They Don't Get Paid? *Fortune Magazine*.

Bryant Jr., D. (2010, January 27). Free Music = Free Advertising = Smart Business. Retrieved from http://www.musicthinktank.com/mtt-open/free-music-free-advertising-smart-business.html

Butcher, M. (2011, April 14). Spotify Takes the Axe to Its Free Service—Can It Now Claim to Slash Music Piracy? Retrieved from http://eu.techcrunch.com/2011/04/14/spotify-takes-the-axe-to-its-free-service-can-it-now-claim-to-slash-music-piracy/

Carnes, R. (2010a, September 29). Free Press: How (Not) to Win Friends and Influence People. Retrieved from http://www.huffingtonpost.com/rick-carnes/free-press-how-not-to-win_b_744405.html

Carnes, R. (2010b, June 9). Has Stealing Music Stolen Your Mind? Retrieved from http://www.huffingtonpost.com/rick-carnes/has-stealing-music-stolen_b_605441.html

Carnes, R. (2010c, March 24). Public Knowledge at Odds With Songwriters. Retrieved from http://www.huffingtonpost.com/rick-carnes/public-knowledge-at-odds_b_511678.html

Carnes, R. (2010d, May 4). "THE FIX" Is in. . . . Retrieved from http://www.huffingtonpost.com/rick-carnes/the-fix-is-in_b_563634.html

Carnes, R. (2010e, June 2). The LimeWire Decision and an Old Joke. Retrieved from http://www.huffingtonpost.com/rick-carnes/the-limewire-decision-and_b_598613.html

Castells, M. (1996). *The Rise of the Network Society*. Cambridge, MA: Wiley-Blackwell.

Clark, N. (2010, June 15). Get Creative to Beat Age of Austerity; The Media and Entertainment Sector in the UK Is Set to Increase Revenues Despite the Recent Slowdown, Nick Clark Reports. *The Independent*, 38.

Dannen, F. (1991). *Hit Men: Power Brokers and Fast Money Inside the Music Business*. New York: Vintage Books.

Deuze, M. (2007). *Media Work*. Malden, MA: Polity.

Duncan, E. (2009, June 28). Who Pays the Price of a Free-For-All? Chris Anderson Zeroes in on Our Giveaway Culture But Offers Few Answers As to What Happens Next, Writes Emma Duncan. *The Observer*, 21. Retrieved from http://www.guardian.co.uk/books/2009/jun/28/review-free-chris-anderson

Ek, D. (2011, April 14). Upcoming Changes to Spotify Free/Open. Retrieved from http://www.spotify.com/se/blog/archives/2011/04/14/upcoming-changes-to-spotify-free-open/

Florida, R. (2004). *The Rise of the Creative Class: And How It's Transforming Work, Leisure, Community and Everyday Life*. New York: Basic Books.

Forde, E. (2009a, December 12). DIGITAL: The Digital Decade. *Music Week*, 18.

Forde, E. (2009b, December 19). Review of the Decade: Fantastic Voyage. *Music Week*, 16.

Frith, S. (1988a). *Music For Pleasure: Essays in the Sociology of Pop*. New York: Pantheon.

Frith, S. (1988b). Picking Up The Pieces. In S. Frith (Ed.), *Facing the Music* (pp. 88–130). New York: Pantheon.

Gannes, L. (2010, March 26). Case Studies in Freemium: Pandora, Dropbox, Evernote, Automattic and MailChimp. Retrieved from http://gigaom.com/2010/03/26/case-studies-in-freemium-pandora-dropbox-evernote-automattic-and-mailchimp/

Gerard. (2010, March 19). Swedish Composer Has Some Interesting Words on Spotify. . . . Retrieved from http://www.playfairnow.org/?q=node/67

Gladwell, M. (2009, July 6). Books: Priced to Sell. *The New Yorker*.

Goldman, D. (2010). Music's Lost Decade: Sales Cut in Half. *CNNMoney.com*. Retrieved from http://money.cnn.com/2010/02/02/news/companies/napster_music_industry/index.htm?hpt=Sbin

Harris, C. (2008). Ozzfest Will Return In 2009, But It Won't Be Free, Says Sharon Osbourne: Tour's Mastermind Says Next Year Will Be 'Back to Business As Usual,' Most Likely With Ozzy Headlining. *MTV News*. Retrieved from http://www.mtv.com/news/articles/1597444/ozzfest-will-return-2009-sharon-osbourne.jhtml

Hartley, J. (Ed.). (2005). *Creative Industries*. Cambridge, MA: Wiley-Blackwell.

Harvey, D. (1991). *The Condition of Postmodernity: An Enquiry into the Origins of Cultural Change*. Cambridge, MA: Wiley-Blackwell.

Hesmondhalgh, D. (2008). *The Cultural Industries* (2nd ed.). Thousand Oaks, CA: Sage Publications.

Howkins, J. (2002). *The Creative Economy: How People Make Money From Ideas*. New York: Penguin Global.

Jenkins, H. (2006). *Convergence Culture: Where Old and New Media Collide*. New York: New York University Press.

Jenner, P. (2010, January 14). The Challenges of Digital Music: An Ex-Economist's View. Retrieved from http://collectiverights.org/192/peter-jenner-international-music-managers-forum-sincere-management-and-david-mazur-masurlaw/

Kirk, M. (Writer). (2004). The Way the Music Died. In M. Kirk (Producer). *Frontline*: PBS.

Kot, G. (2009). *Ripped: How the Wired Generation Revolutionized Music*. New York: Scribner.

Lessig, L. (2007). *Larry Lessig on Laws That Choke Creativity*. Paper presented at the TED2007. http://www.ted.com/talks/larry_lessig_says_the_law_is_strangling_creativity.html

Lessig, L. (2008). *Remix: Making Art and Commerce Thrive in the Hybrid Economy*. New York: The Penguin Press HC.

Lindvall, H. (2011, February 1). Spotify Should Give Indies a Fair Deal on Royalties: Independent Labels Have Threatened to Leave the Music Streaming Service, Claiming it Treats Them Unfairly. Retrieved from http://www.guardian.co.uk/media/pda/2011/feb/01/spotify-royalties-independents

Lowery, D. (2012a). Full Post: You Can't Have A Have A Healthy Market Economy Without Property Rights. Why Do So Many In Tech Blogosphere Want to Abolish Cyber Property Rights and Cripple The Cyber-Economy? Retrieved from http://thetrichordist.wordpress.com/2012/05/05/full-post-you-cant-have-a-have-a-healthy-market-economy-without-property-rights-why-do-so-many-in-tech-blogosphere-want-to-abolish-cyber-property-rights-and-cripple-the-cyber-economy/

Lowery, D. (2012b). Letter to Emily White at NPR All Songs Considered. Retrieved from http://thetrichordist.wordpress.com/2012/06/18/letter-to-emily-white-at-npr-all-songs-considered/

Mann, I. (2009, August 23). Today's Free Means Megabucks. *Sunday Times*.

Mauss, M. (1967). *The Gift: Forms and Functions of Exchange in Archaic Societies*. New York: W. W. Norton & Company.

McCandless, D., Flyn, C., Slater, T., & Key, J. (2010, April 13). How Much Do Music Artists Earn Online? Retrieved from http://www.informationisbeautiful.net/2010/how-much-do-music-artists-earn-online/

Mcelhinney, P. (2011). Revolution No. 9: What Does the Future Hold For Richmond's Home of Sonic Cool? *Style Weekly*. Retrieved from http://www.styleweekly.com/richmond/revolution-no-9/Content?oid=1486371

McGivern, C. (2011, January 1). Spotify Royalty Rates: Do Majors Earn More Than Indies? Retrieved from http://www.reviewexplorer.com/news/7184_spotify-royalty-rates-do-majors-earn-more-than-indies/

Meehan, E. (1990). Why We Don't Count: The Commodity Audience. In P. Mellencamp (Ed.), *Logics of Television: Essays in Cultural Criticism (Theories of Contemporary Culture)* (pp. 117–137). Bloomington, IN: Indiana University Press.

Moya, J. (2008, December 20). RIAA to Quit Suing File-Sharers, Wants ISPs to Disconnect Instead. Retrieved from http://www.zeropaid.com/news/9907/riaa_to_quit_suing_filesharers_wants_isps_to_disconnect_instead/

Mulligan, M. (2011, February 4). Why the Music Industry Must Change Its Strategy to Reach Digital Natives. Retrieved from http://mashable.com/2011/02/04/music-industry-digital-natives/

Nelson, F. (2010, July 1). In Praise of Spotify. Retrieved from http://www.spectator.co.uk/arts-and-culture/night-and-day/6115668/in-praise-of-spotify.thtml

O'Donnell, L. (2010, December 13). Compelling Content Is the Key to Gen Y. *The Australian*, 27.

Ostrow, J. (2010). Why Music Should Never Be Given Away For "Free." Retrieved from http://www.musicthinktank.com/blog/why-music-should-never-be-given-away-for-free.html

Patterson, M. (2009, September 1). Pandora Radio Ends Free Ride, But Appears to Leave Glaring Loophole. Retrieved from http://blogs.palmbeachpost.com/techtonic/mobile/pandora-radio-ends-free-ride-but-appears-to-leave-glaring-loophole/

Peoples, G. (2009, October 7). Analysis: The Cost of Streaming Billions of Songs. Retrieved from http://www.billboard.biz/bbbiz/content_display/industry/news/e3iecb83415cefdd2b0a43399437dff3e5f

Pichevin, A. (2009, March 28). Making 'Free' Pay. *Billboard.*

Quinn, M. (2008, March 28). Subscription Services Gain Interest Among Music Labels. *Los Angeles Times.* Retrieved from http://articles.latimes.com/2008/mar/28/business/fi-music28

Rose, L. (2012). David Geffen: 'I'd Kill Myself' Rather Than Get Into Music Business Today. *Billboard Biz.* Retrieved from http://www.billboard.biz/bbbiz/industry/tv-film/david-geffen-i-d-kill-myself-rather-than-1007644152.story

Schantz, M. L. (2009). Mixed Signals: How Mixtapes Have Blurred the Changing Legal Landscape in the Music Industry. *University of Miami Business Law Review, 17,* 293–324.

Small, C. (1998). *Musicking: The Meanings of Performing and Listening.* Hanover, NH: Wesleyan University Press.

Smith, E. (2011). A No. 1 Album But a Small Slice: This Week's Top Seller Marks Low Point, Underscoring Waning Sales of Music. *The Wall Street Journal.* Retrieved from http://online.wsj.com/article/SB10001424052748703951704576092213330550884.html

Sohn, G. (2010, March 18). Net Neutrality Not in Conflict With Copyright Enforcement. *The Hill.* Retrieved from http://thehill.com/opinion/op-ed/87657-qnet-neutrality-not-in-conflict-with-copyright-enforcement

Sterne, J. (2006). The MP3 As Cultural Artifact. *New Media & Society, 8*(5), 825–842. doi: 10.1177/1461444806067737

Sydell, L. (2009). Musicians Look For Pay In An MP3 World. *Morning Edition.* Retrieved from http://www.npr.org/templates/story/story.php?storyId=112065448

Tyrangiel, J. (2007, Oct 1). Radiohead Says: Pay What You Want. *Time.*

Valente, M. (2010, January 14). Free Music: Response to Reddit. Retrieved from http://www.musicthinktank.com/mtt-open/free-music-response-to-reddit.html

Verhoeve, W. (2011, March 2). The Importance of Free Music (or Give 'Em a Taste First). Retrieved from http://www.wesleyverhoeve.com/freedownloads

Webster, J. G., Lichty, L. W., & Phalen, P. F. (2008). *Ratings Analysis: The Theory and Practice of Audience Research* (3rd ed.). Mahwah, NJ: Lawrence Erlbaum Associates.

White, E. (2012). I Never Owned Any Music to Begin With. Retrieved from http://www.npr.org/blogs/allsongs/2012/06/16/154863819/i-never-owned-any-music-to-begin-with

Wikström, P. (2009). *The Music Industry: Music in The Cloud.* Cambridge, MA: Polity Press.

Willis, B. (2002). CD Price-Fixing Case Settled. *Stereophile.* Retrieved from http://www.stereophile.com/news/11461/index.html

Zeife, C. (2000). *Zero: The Biography of a Dangerous Idea.* New York: Penguin.

3 Retail Climate Change
From Selling Music to Selling a Service

The idea for Spotify struck [Daniel] Ek in 2002 when Napster stopped working and solving the piracy problem Kazaa was taking over. "I realised that you can never legislate away from piracy," he says. "Laws can definitely help, but it doesn't take away the problem. The only way to solve the problem was to create a service that was better than piracy and at the same time compensates the music industry—that gave us Spotify." (Neate, 2010)

By the end of the first decade of the 21st century if you were to ask the average music industry worker what the largest problem for the industry was they would most likely point to the pervasive practice of "illegal downloading" and with good reason. According to Forrester Research, in 1999 the total revenue from sales and licensing was $14.6 billion. By 2009, that number had been more than halved, plunging to $6.3 billion (Goldman, 2010). Worse, illegal downloading was a problem with no simple solution. As mentioned in the previous chapter, some musicians and services decided that the technological climate had shifted so significantly that experimenting with free was a better option than fighting piracy. However, while much of the legacy industry has balked at free, the same actors also initially resisted the creation of legal and convenient spaces to purchase downloads. Indeed, it would take close to four years between the closing of Napster until the advent Apple's iTunes Music Store in 2003. Still, by the end of the 2000s a number of legal, pay solutions had appeared in the North American marketplace. From iTunes to Amazon, Rhapsody to Spotify, a number of stores, services and gadgets such as iPhones, iPods, Zunes, Zens, PCs, and Macs were being used throughout a number of North Atlantic markets seeking ways to build better, legal digital music platforms that paid musicians and labels that could generate profitable returns.

Although some of these services and devices have found their way to the trash heap of disruptive innovations past, each of these is a part of a larger set of experiments in search of a viable retail model for the 21st century. While some of these services provide albums and songs for purchase, others have embraced some form of "cloud-based" subscription model where the user pays to access material that is kept on the service's database, ready to be streamed. In some cases services allow users to store their purchased files both on their computers and the service's database. In other cases, users pay a service subscription fees to access music that they do not nor will ever own. In each case the subscriber is allowed to stream a significantly large library of already-licensed music to any number of net-worked devices. The variety of these cloud-based services may feel incoherent, however we must remember that the sale of music-related products has always come in many forms. Even when the practices of record retail had been somewhat standardized, records could be purchased at a variety of spaces ranging from cinemas to gas stations and a number of spaces in between.[1] Indeed, as varied as they are the most successful services from iTunes to Spotify have one very important thing in common: they originated from third parties whose thoughts and practices have substantial roots in designing for users. From interfaces to backends, these services have continually pushed for ease of use, accessibility, individual choice, and portability. Their practices are significantly different than those of physical retailers who worked for years to sell physical goods to audiences. The common sense obsession over "units sold" and "charts" involves an assumption that physical and digital retail services hold goals of sales and downloads. However, many digital services value involve analyses on the backend where recommendation engines and social network integration. Indeed, while these aspects are often ignored as ancillary, they are in fact key to their long-term propositions. This chapter places the growth of digital retail into a context of change and adaptation where shifting circumstances and experiments have created a new landscape of online retailers and services whose primary aims are incommensurable with a previous system invested in the exchange of physical goods. Instead, these services are invested in significant amounts of end user data analysis that automatically match and promote music, musicians, and fans across the "social graph" as their key to value generation in a 21st century media economy. This change in valuation is difficult to grasp. Indeed, for musicians and labels alike, sales will remain important. However, the sale of musical recordings may no longer be the most important aim for the industry.

It is within this context of mutating retail that the very successful, veteran act AC/DC initiated the worldwide release of their 16th long-play album, *Black Ice*, in October 2008. As one of those rare acts that can state that every one of their long-play records released in the U.S. has moved over 1 million paid units (i.e., "platinum"), AC/DC has long benefited from loyal audiences who are willing to purchase their albums. Peaking at No. 1 in the United States, *Black Ice* went on to be certified as double platinum (over 2 million units sold) and, in defiance of all trends, became their best-selling new release since 1995. But most interesting was the band's reluctance to license *Black Ice* along with the rest of their catalogue to any digital service or online retailer, including the massively popular iTunes. Such defiance to popular innovations often spurs claims that moments of paradigmatic disruption and new practices rarely come from the elder statesmen of the field. "Almost always the men who achieve these fundamental inventions of a new paradigm have been young or very new to the field whose paradigm they change," stresses Thomas Kuhn (1996, p. 90). As true as this may be, even the least gracious observer could never accuse AC/DC of an inability to navigate change. Although the band's blues-based, hard rock music and reprobate schoolboy image has changed very little in five decades, the band has survived alterations that would cripple if not devastate most acts. The Australian act has lived through multiple recording formats, the loss of numerous musical personnel (up to 13 players can count themselves as former members of AC/DC), more than several generations of rock fans, and the death of an iconic lead singer and frontman, Bon Scott, in 1980. Still, AC/DC was particularly adamant about not placing their wares on the most iconic retail space of the digital age, iTunes. Explaining why the band had decided to not license their work to iTunes (and for advertisers), Steve Barnett, the chairman of Columbia Records (a division of Sony Music Entertainment), said, "They have a purist approach. Their instinct was always to do the right thing for fans, think long term and not be influenced by financial rewards" (Levine, 2008, p. AR1). For AC/DC this has meant an insistence on selling albums as physical entities in retailers throughout the world. Although, many believed that without a proper online retail presence consumers would simply pirate those files that they could not conveniently purchase (Ibid.). Even in 2010 when The Beatles had formalized a legal relationship with Apple's service to sell their albums and singles as digital downloads, Angus Young, lead guitarist of AC/DC, responded to questions about whether his band would reconsider their stance now that rock's most famous act had signed off on Steve Jobs' online service with a firm but respectful no. Young noted, "I know the Beatles have changed but we're going to carry on like that. For us it's the best way. We are a band who started off with albums and that's how we've always been. We always were a band that if you heard something (by AC/DC) on the radio, well, that's only three minutes. Usually the best tracks were on the albums" (Bennett, 2011).

AC/DC were not alone. Along with other big names like Garth Brooks and Kid Rock, the Australian act has asserted a resistance to iTunes and other digital services. Furthermore, each of these acts see itself as an "album oriented artist." Focused on the production of a group of songs that have a theme, one that forces the listener to listen for so-called "deep cuts," has long been the goal of many acts. Allowing users to download only the songs that the consumer wants may be a technological possibility, but it also violates a longstanding practice where the label or the musician decides on what should be released. The control that artists relinquish to the user is substantial and something that many have often cited as a reason not to legitimate these practices. Ken Levitan defended Kid Rock, his client, who refused to place his 2007 album *Rock'n'Roll Jesus* on iTunes and other online services by pointing out that "we get so caught up in technology and ease [of downloading a single] . . . there's nothing wrong with listening to a whole record from start to finish." Kid Rock was much more direct: "I tell people in my organization, 'Do not ever come up to me and say, 'This is what everyone's doing and how they're doing it.' Don't ever give me that lame-ass bullsh*t. As soon as someone says, 'You have to be on iTunes . . . they're the No. 1 retailer' . . . I don't have to" (Waddell, 2008). Country superstar Garth Brooks' criticisized iTunes as the proverbial road to hell paved with good intentions: "They truly think that they're saving music. I looked at them right across the table with all the love in the world and told them they were killing it. Until we get variable pricing, until we get album-only (downloads), then they are not a true retailer for my stuff, and you won't see my stuff on there" (Paulson, 2009).

Garth Brooks, AC/DC, and Kid Rock have acted as rare but instructive digital holdouts. Each are successful enough to effectively dictate a number of the circumstances surrounding how they should do their business. They harken back to a pre-user-oriented economy of discs and record shops, nostalgic for variable pricing practices and gatefold sleeves gone by. They are sweetened memories that, like all moments of nostalgia, remind us of what we valued but conveniently omit what we despised. Although these acts have dragged their collective feet, their reluctance pales in comparison to that of music industry's overall reluctance to embrace legal digital solutions as illegal downloading practices spread exponentially once Napster was eliminated. So widespread were illegal downloads that at least one network management software company, Packateer, announced that after demonstrating its products at 500 UK companies, as many of 80% of them had illegal music and video placed on their servers by employees (Adshead, 2002). With no quality legal alternative for almost four years after the shuttering of Napster, users had learned how to refine the procedures of piracy.

It would not be until 2003 when the almost-always-open online iTunes Music Store debuted as a major label-approved solution. The then-five major labels working with Apple would finally provide a convenient and legal way to download music onto computers and, more importantly, Apple's popular portable music device, the iPod. While the service has changed, its initial offerings were the result of substantial compromises between the demands of labels and Apple. To get the labels to sign on Apple presented labels with a digital rights management (DRM) technology that would limit how many machines and users could play these downloads. Titled "Fairplay," the technology was offered as way to get major labels to sign on to the file service that they had feared since the introduction of Napster. To gain the rights for the majority of the catalogue of recordings from Warner Music, BMG, EMI, Sony Music, and Universal, Apple glossed their wares with a DRM technology that would substantially limit a user's ability to share with others. Once the labels accepted the Fairplay technology, Apple was able to produce an accessible, legal, and easy-to-understand revenue generator. The final element of "easy-to-understand" rested on persuading labels to accept an initial $0.99 per-song and $9.99 per-album price points. The iTunes Music Store would be nothing less than a game changer for Apple. In 2008, five years after its opening, Apple reported its store now had over 50 million customers and 4 billion songs had been downloaded, thereby making it the second largest retailer of music in the U.S. (Neumayr & Roth, 2008a).

The story of iTunes is well documented in Walter Jacobson's biography of Steve Jobs. In the book, Jacobson notes that music retail was on Jobs' mind as early as 2000. As illegal file-sharing services proliferated so did the number of playlists burned onto blank CDs in the U.S. Estimated to be around 320 million, the number of user-burned CDs was only increasing. Jobs felt Apple had missed an opportunity and was now in catch-up mode. While Apple had added a CD burner to the iMac, Jobs wanted to "make it simple to transfer music from a CD, manage it on your computer, and then burn playlists" (Jacobson, 2011, p. 382), Jacobson points out that,

> Other companies were already making music-management applications, but they were clunky and complex. One of Jobs' talents was spotting markets that were filled with second-rate products. He looked at the music apps that were available and came to a conclusion: 'They were so complicated that only a genius could figure out half of their features.' (Jacobson, 2011, pp. 382–383)

In 2000 Jobs acquired SoundJam, a music management system, along with its founders and brought them into Apple. One year later Jobs debuted the iTunes music management system. Free to Apple users, the software was central to Jobs' "digital hub" strategy that would coincide with the release of the company's iPod (Jacobson, 2011, pp. 383–384). Working in tandem with Apple's most tangible music-oriented product, the iPod, iTunes was not just a hub but a digital "Trojan Horse." Because iTunes was initially a program for Mac OSX systems only, the popularity of the iPod began to lead consumers to Apple's Mac computer series. Yet the greatest achievement of iTunes software was the direct line it would provide consumers to Apple's iTunes store. In 2002 CD sales were just beginning their steep dive and the major labels' response was to offer very poor subscription services. So bad were the services that both Pressplay (Sony and Universal) and MusicNet (AOL, TimeWarner, Bertelsmann, EMI, and RealNetworks) would be listed in *PC World* as among the "25 worst tech products of all time" (Jacobson, 2011, p. 395). Jobs was able to persuade the five major labels to trust him to sell their digital wares through his Macintosh-only retailer, a platform that in 2002 reached only 5% of the personal computer market. However, Jobs had demands that emphasized the priorities of the user such as selling individual songs off of the records, not only entire albums. This was an initial problem for labels who wanted to continue the practice of bundling and have consumers pay the larger list prices that albums commanded. This single-song purchase condition would be central to Jobs' new store, one that emphasized ownership and embraced users' desires to poach individual songs. In 2003 Jobs debuted his company's new store with 200,000 tracks and the promise that it would grow on a daily basis. Within six days the store would move over a million downloads, prompting Jobs to claim another well-earned moment of hyperbole by stating that this would "go down in history as a turning point in the industry" (Jacobson, 2011, pp. 395–403).

On the face of it some of the solutions that iTunes offered seemed like an extension of what the music industry had engaged throughout the 20th century. The emphasis on selling goods that provided a sense of ownership was an aspect Jobs believed would remain essential to the music experience. People have an "emotional attachment" to their favorite music that he felt made ownership superior to subscription services, services where users paid a fee but did not own the music. In the subscription model music rests in a "walled garden" and can only be accessed with permissions that are granted in exchange for time, money, attention, data, etc. Jobs believed that the subscription model was such a loser that he told *Rolling Stone* "I think you could make available the Second Coming in a subscription model and it might not be successful" (quoted in Jacobson, 2011, p. 397). Jobs' prioritization of ownership provided a model that also matched 100 years of consumer and retail experience where purchases were, for the most part, designed with an emphasis on portability. Although the music was licensed to the consumer for private playback only, the "feeling of ownership" echoed the same feeling that followed the purchase and playback of sheet music and physical recordings. The ability to mobilize downloads as the consumer demanded was also one of the reasons that Jobs would eventually lobby for the elimination of DRM. Indeed, Jobs' comfort with the "FairPlay" arrangement quickly waned. By 2007 Jobs published an open letter criticizing the practice of music with DRM, even Apple's own Fairplay system, as nothing more than a "cat-and-mouse game" between labels and those with the time and wits to break these systems. There was no way for labels to win. According to Jobs, the argument that "once a consumer purchases a body of music from one of the proprietary music stores, they are forever locked into only using music players from that one company" had no basis in fact. Apple's own data from the end of 2006 highlighted this illusion by pointing out that although the company had sold 90 million iPods it had only sold 2 billion songs from the iTunes store: an average of 22 songs purchased from the iTunes store for each iPod ever sold. As Jobs explained in 2007, basic math made it clear that if DRM was doing its job then it was doing it poorly. With the most popular iPod holding close to 1,000 songs and its research telling Apple that the average iPod was "nearly full," Jobs reckoned that DRM never worked. Indeed, Jobs' research indicated "that only 22 out of [these] 1000 songs, or under 3% of the music on the average iPod, is purchased from the iTunes store and protected with a DRM. The remaining 97% of the music is unprotected and playable on any player that can play the open formats." Jobs opined that it was "hard to believe that just 3% of the music on the average iPod is enough to lock users into buying only iPods in the future." Furthermore, because this other 97% of music was not purchased from the iTunes store, iPod users were "clearly not locked into the iTunes store to acquire their music." Jobs' determination was to advocate for the abolition of DRM. The technology was clearly not working and Jobs wanted iTunes to sell products in tune with a world where, just like compact discs and long-play records, they could be "playable on all players" (Jobs, 2007).[2] By 2009 the majors relented and had also given up on DRM.[3]

No doubt the openness of a DRM-less ecosystem would provide a level of datamobility to music purchased from the iTunes service that would make it an even more attractive commodity. In one aspect this stress on openness emphasized practices that longstanding music consumers expected these were practices that mass retailers offered for over a century where a disc or piece of sheet music purchased in any small town could be played on devices and instruments throughout the world. However, embracing the openness of a DRM-less system is also one of the retail demands that dovetails with discussions of free from the previous chapter. As mentioned earlier, an aspect of openness is fundamental for the marketplace success of all experiential goods. This includes making samples of the product available and easy to access. While it does not necessarily mean making the entire stock available for free, it does mean finding ways to make stock "previewable." iTunes has always made its stock previewable, first in 30-second portions and beginning in 2011 extending the previews to 90 seconds. Drawing from the longstanding retailer practice of the "free sample", iTunes has worked with labels to promote and provide a selection of free weekly downloads from a variety of genres and musicians, both new and known. Beginning in 2007 iTunes worked with Starbucks coffee shops to offer a free, download-of-the-week card that customers could grab and get a code to use at their convenience. The Starbucks program continues and the iTunes store extended its free offerings to other goods such as applications, television episodes, and even occasionally feature films.

As mentioned in the earlier discussions of free, free is rarely without conditions. These offerings are a kind of "cost-free exchange." In the case of iTunes, free downloads demand that the user establish an iTunes account where the patron would deposit, at minimum, an email address. Other options such as associating a credit card or a PayPal account for future purchasing convenience are offered, but not required. What is important is that once the account is created iTunes can begin to record a user's downloads and other behaviors vis a vis the program. This includes what is played, when it is played, what playlists are made, what is rated, what is not, and so on. The value of this kind of data would be self-evident to any retailer and is particularly important to executing Apple's digital hub strategy. In 2011, Gil Elbaz, CEO and cofounder of the data platform Factual, explained that iTunes provides a model of distinct value because, "It is a place where data can be programmatically searched, licensed, accessed, and integrated directly into a consumer application." However, "the deepest value" for Apple is how, with a single click, iTunes "allows a developer to license data and have it automatically integrated into their particular application development stack" (Watters, 2011). Indeed, the value of iTunes' datasets has been evident to many of the content providers who sell their digital wares through the service. This is particularly true of those magazines who began to sell through the store. Because magazines have a long history of leveraging the data about their subscribers for ad revenue, the attraction of iTunes' datasets was obvious (Formeski, 2010). However, these sets remain unavailable to content providers of all sorts, a problem for those who retail through the store and are left only with "opt-in" options and develop their own apps to gather demographic information.[4]

This discussion of magazine retail may seem like an oblique item to mention in relationship to music retail. Yet, the history of record retail has rarely if ever been solely concerned with the sale of records. While the typical record store devoted the majority of its stock to records, it often dedicated shelf space to other goods such as T-shirts, jewelry, posters, blank cassettes, books, magazines, DVDs, VHS cassettes, stickers, and buttons. From a simple financial perspective most record stores could not avoid stocking these ancillary goods simply because their profit margins were far greater than the typical 15–30% markup on new compact discs and long-play records. Yet there is a second reason that record stores could not simply rely on records: record stores, particularly independent record stores that focus on specific genres, have always traded in lifestyle goods. These goods include music but extend into other realms devoted to areas of identity formation such as clothing and literature. Although the iTunes store does not sell physical goods such as shirts and posters, over time the store began to rent and sell films, books, television shows; distribute podcasts; and allow users to link up to a variety of streaming radio stations and applications. Organizing iTunes' music, film, podcast, books, and television programming in terms of genre (radio in formats) is a holdover from a longstanding practice in record and book stores. The connection between genre and the marketing of lifestyle goods, as Frith (1996) and Negus (1999) have pointed out, is key. Both authors point out that the music industry, from radio format to record sections, is organized with genre in mind. From A&R to record producers and so on, the industry has and continues to view genre as the route to reach consumers. However, the difference for iTunes and other digital services such as Amazon and Google that have established digital music retailers is that as they funnel their goods through genre categories the services accumulate data on their users. Like iTunes, both Amazon and Google music retailers demand the creation of accounts to access their services and that users grant permissions to monitor their use.

It is in data acquisition and analysis where the greatest source of value exists for digital music services. Amazon, Google, and Apple each tout policies explaining how they do not share individual profiles, however each service retains the right to share client information "in aggregate." For a moment allow us to speculate about the data that these services are trying to accrue. With the issue of scale eliminated, the traditional assets that secured market share such as access to premium spaces, quality distribution, effective logistic channels, and well-trained sales staffs no longer retained the value that they once did. Instead, deep data profiles that are ready to be mined in one experiment after another to secure higher probabilities of the sale and the use of music and other goods is where the value resides. For example, some of Apple's experiments like iTunes' "Genius" feature have become successful aspects of the program. Introduced in iTunes 8, the application allows users to take the songs in their iTunes catalogue (purchased and not purchased from Apple) and create instant playlists of songs through an association and recommendation algorithm. According to Christopher Mims, the probabilities of Genius' association algorithm are generated through the acquisition of a packet of usage data— data about the songs that a user has in his or her library and how and when s/he uses them—that is then aggregated into a larger database of iTunes users' usage data. Apple engineer Erik Goldman notes that the probabilities that generated Genius' recommendations "are computed globally at regular intervals and stored in a cache" (Mims, 2010). While the feature gives users another convenient tool to discover the music that they have in their own library, Genius also provides purchase suggestions. As one blogger put it, with iTunes Apple "has made a mainline to my credit card" and "every single time I fire up iTunes [I am able] to continue making regular donations to my favorite for-profit Cupertino-based charity" (Gray, 2008). Clearly other consumers felt the same way about iTunes services. By 2008 Apple was no longer the most successful online retailer in the U.S., but had surpassed Walmart to become the United States' No. 1 music retailer (Neumayr & Roth, 2008b). Two years later iTunes had sold over 10 billion songs to become the "world's most popular online music, TV and movie store" (Neumayr & Roth, 2010).

Apple's iTunes' other innovations have also offered some less-than-successful outcomes and, in other cases, the results are too early to determine. The service's most prolific failure has been Ping, an attempt to build a social network in iTunes that would build in another layer of discovery. Introduced in 2010, Steve Jobs claimed it would be "a social network all about music." For Jobs, Ping was "Facebook meets Twitter meets iTunes" and with it you could "'follow your favorite artists and friends and join a worldwide conversation with music's most passionate fans" (Anon., 2010). Although Apple had such a large share of the digital music market the service was never able to properly grow. By the summer of 2012 Apple announced that iTunes 10.6.3 would be the last version to include the Ping service. Shortly before Jobs' death in 2011, Tim Cook took over as Apple's CEO and one year into his tenure he determined that "we tried Ping, and I think the customer voted and said 'This isn't something that I want to put a lot of energy into.'" As one writer put it, the problem for Ping was that it "was focused far too much on enabling commerce, and far too little on enabling social interaction. It wasn't easy to find and connect with people on Ping. And that didn't resonate with Apple's customers all" (Paczkowski, 2012).

The latest iTunes innovation is a variation on a longstanding and controversial digital music model: the digital music locker. Each locker service offers different approaches to streaming and licensing, but every digital music locker offers users the convenience of offsite storage and the ability to access and upload their wares any time they wish. Titled "iTunes Match," the Apple service has a history that begins in 2008 with a Silicon Valley startup named Lala. Unlike other streaming-locker services, Lala offered a new technical and legal innovation: users could listen to a song at no charge once and, afterwards, purchase the right to repeatedly stream the song *ad infinitum* for 10 cents from the service's web-based platform. If the user wanted to purchase the song as a download, that, too, would be available for around 99 cents. Key to Lala was the service's ability to exploit an emerging flexibility regarding licensing among a few label executives. Lala executives credited "the labels' cooperation in the unusual licensing arrangement" with the result being the sale of "hundreds of thousands of songs a month" (Stone, 2009b). By October 2009 Lala developed an iPhone app that, in the words of a *Wired.com* headline, turned the mobile phone into a "ten cent jukebox" (Buskirk, 2009a). However, Lala's application would never appear in the company's iTunes app store. Instead, one month after Lala submitted the app Apple purchased the company. Apple is notoriously silent about its business motives and refused to comment on the reason for the purchase. Although the timing of the purchase made it appear that the company was impressed by Lala's iPhone app, at least a few reports had leaked that Lala had initiated discussions with Apple's iTunes division when it realized that its "prospect for turning a profit in the short term were dim." In Lala Apple had found a corps of engineers that had built a very elegant, usable cloud-based music service that they could employ to do the same (Stone, 2009a, p. B2). Almost two years after Lala's acquisition Apple would debut iTunes Match. For a modest annual fee of $25 the service applies Lala's "scan and match" process to the contents in the user's library and matches them with items in the iTunes database. Those items that iTunes does not have are then uploaded into an offline database to become available as downloads or streams to a variety of Apple devices. As of mid-2013 the service limits the user to 25,000 songs plus any song purchased on iTunes as part of an online locker. Because the service does not discriminate between legally purchased and pirated downloads the annual fee acts as something of a "get-out-of-jail-free card" as users can effectively launder their illegal MP3s into legal iTunes downloads.

As *CNET*'s Josh Lowensohn states, "[iTunes Match is] a solution for [a] problem Apple helped create" (J. Peterson, 2011). Other services had offered a digital music locker in the so-called "cloud" years before Apple, however the legal status of these services were always in question. One cloud-based locker service case in particular, MP3tunes, allowed users to pay for limitless amounts of storage and was sued in a United States District Court for copyright violations by EMI and 14 other record labels. Though the court found that although the service qualified for "safe harbor" status under the terms of the Digital Millennium Copyright Act, it also noted that the service was liable for "contributory copyright infringement" after it ignored multiple takedown notices for songs that labels claimed should be removed (Sandoval, 2011). As a result of the ruling, iTunes and others were soon able to provide online lockers with an understanding of the limits and conditions needed to operate legally. However, one of the conditions meant getting the approval of the labels involved so their product could become "streamable." As per agreement, iTunes pays copyright holders every time a song is re-downloaded or streamed. In 2012, Jeff Price, the president of TuneCore, a third-party service that assists musicians in placing their music on e-retailer sites, posted that in the first two months of iTunes Match his service had received over $10,000 in royalty payments. Price dubbed these royalties "magic money that Apple made exist out of thin air for copyright holders" (Price, 2012).

Along with Apple both Google and Amazon developed streaming online-music locker services after the MP3tunes decision. Like Apple, these companies offer users a limited amount of online storage and the proposal that these uploads plus any purchases made from their respective stores can be streamed and downloaded. Their services integrate both their digital retail spaces and their respective devices, thereby encouraging their users to buy specific hardware and software combinations. In each case, Apple, Amazon, and Google see their music services as one prong among many designed to keep users in their specific ecosystems. As mentioned earlier, the ability to use Match is tied to iTunes. While iTunes is developed for Windows and Apple desktop operating systems, its mobile versions are available only for other Apple devices. Once users purchase the Match service every one of their Apple-oriented devices, from iPhone to AppleTV, can stream the music in their lockers. The same logic adheres to Amazon and Google, both of which have invested in mobile devices and software. As Amazon CEO Jeff Bezos admitted about one of his company's mobile devices, the Kindle Fire, "we don't think of [it] as a tablet. We think if it as an end-to-end service" (Schonfeld, 2011). Bezos explained that "some of the companies building tablets didn't build services, they just built tablets" and that is a problem:

> In the modern era of consumer electronics devices, if you are just building a device you are unlikely to succeed. Today it is about the software, the software on the device and the software in the cloud. It is a seamless service—this is Kindle greeting you by name when you pull it out of the box. (Schonfeld, 2011)

The combined emphasis on software and hardware goods within the music industry is nothing new. Simon Frith points out that recordings cannot be divorced in the 20th-century history of popular music. Furthermore, the "history of the record industry is an aspect of the history of the electrical goods industry, related to the development of radio, the cinema and television" (Frith, 1988, p. 13). Within this context it is clear that investments in digital retail where consumers purchase items to use on their digital devices make sense, i.e. iTunes as the software for the hardware of iPods, PCs, etc. What has changed in the 21st century has been the extensive developments in information storage, personal computing, and digital networks. As the recording industry matures into this ecosystem what isn't clear is if an ownership model must remain dominant. Instead, a number of bets have been placed on a model of retail that is at odds with Jobs' lack of confidence in subscription streaming models. Subscription services provide users cloud-based streaming onto their networked devices for a monthly exchange. Music services have experimented with variants of this model since the early 2000s. For example, Roxio purchased Napster's assets in 2002 after the service had been litigated into bankruptcy and in 2003 it presented a new Napster service where individual downloads could be purchased with an option to subscribe to a service that allowed users to stream a catalogue of 500,000 songs and 40 radio stations. Perhaps more interesting, Napster introduced the service as part of a partnership with Penn State University. The announcement of their relationship came at the annual Educause meeting of information technology specialists employed by universities across the U.S. Explaining that Penn State students would not have to pay to use the service, the university president and cochair of the Committee on Higher Education and the Entertainment Industry Graham Spanier declared that this would be the "first step in a new, legal approach designed to meet student interest in getting extensive digital access to music" (Anon., 2003). Napster's president and COO, Mike Bebel, established student focus groups for feedback in an attempt to provide a "premium service [that] is designed to meet the needs of students who have demonstrated a voracious appetite for online music." According to Bebel, Napster had "improved upon the typical file sharing experience by delivering guaranteed high-quality tracks, a well-organized presentation of music and community features that music fans love" and that this joint venture would lead the industry by "paving the way for universities around the country to ensure that a legitimate marketplace for online music thrives" (Anon., 2003).

Napster's experiment is one among many music-streaming services. Some of these services have succeeded, others failed, but all of them embrace an architecture that walls off a portion of the proverbial "garden." Only subscribers are able to access and stream these songs. As mentioned earlier, Steve Jobs' bias against these subscription services was somewhat rooted in the fact that they were unable to give consumers a sense of ownership, the "emotional attachment" Jobs believed was so key for successful music retail. However, it's important to remember that Jobs' own experience as part of the "baby boom" generation, the first generation of listeners to be fully deposited into a music economy dominated by the sale and personal ownership of recordings, may have affected his own distaste of these earlier services. Jobs also made these statements in 2003, a few years before the rise of a mature media ecosystem of smartphone platforms and the popularity of wi-fi and 3G data services that allowed for more ubiquitous networks. Without this ecosystem, subscription services simply were not mobile. Without an infrastructure of portability users were effectively shackled to their desktops.

Furthermore, most of these services suffered from providing offerings from only a few labels. Unlike U.S. streaming services that "act like radio," on-demand streaming services cannot employ the compulsory "blanket license" that covers the playback of just about any recording an online radio station wishes to employ. As I will discuss in later in the book, the licensing structure that allows radio-like streaming services to operate in the U.S. was established with the passage of the Digital Millennium Copyright Act in 1998. The act specifically requires that these services *not* provide a compulsory "blanket license" option for the very thing that subscription streaming services like Spotify and Rhapsody offer: the on-demand streaming of specific songs and artists. Instead, subscription services have to establish licensing agreements with each and every label. During these negotiations copyright holders can demand different prices to stream different portions of their catalogues. As a result, it is not uncommon to find subscription services with large, gaping holes where important artists are not accessible to be streamed. Worse, some of these early services negotiated deals that, as Tim Westergren of the online radio service Pandora emphasized, "didn't make [economic] sense," "turned out to be unsustainable," and have "set a precedent" that has been difficult to renegotiate (Stone, 2009b). Indeed, with these many limitations at hand, Jobs' conviction that subscription-based streaming services could never succeed held significant weight.

By the latter half of the 2000s several of these limits had been addressed. Wi-fi and data rich 3G services had proliferated throughout the U.S. Furthermore, the 2007 introduction of Jobs' own iPhone would play a major role for streaming service. The hardware/software combination provided a space of innovation that would help solve some of the infrastructural needs for mobile streaming. Alongside other so-called smartphones, the iPhone's entry into the U.S. marketplace made it easier to exploit 3G mobile data networks and quickly transformed the landscape for all mobile delivery services, including music. Soon after its introduction a variety of streaming subscription services began to develop to mobile. These included services that had long been in the marketplace such as Rhapsody, as well as a number of newcomers like Rdio, Mog, and, most important for this chapter, Spotify. Beginning in 2006, Spotify began its development in 2006 with a team of developers in Stockholm, Sweden and by October 2008 it was able to launch a version of its application for public subscription. Although initially available in only a few European countries, Spotify's success was quick. Within a year the service claimed that it had assembled a catalogue that would demand "more than 34 years to listen to, no sleep allowed," had "tens of thousands new users joining everyday," and that "more than one in nine Swedes" had become Spotify users (Anon., 2009b). The service's rapid growth and expansive catalogue drew international attention. It was clear from across the Atlantic to even the most seasoned digital music user that Spotify was substantially different from its U.S. competition. By February 2009 *Wired* magazine indicated that the service was making a huge impression with those in the tech music community even though it was unavailable in the U.S.:

> Spotify is currently the biggest thing on the web among music geeks. Music bloggers and the tech elite have been raving about the sleek service, which lets users legally stream millions of high-quality tracks—including whole albums—from a deep library of mainstream and independent artists. There are no playback limits, only a 20-second ad once every half hour. Searches are lightning quick, and thanks to a combination of streaming and peer-to-peer technologies, tracks begin playing with virtually no buffering wait times. On top of that, the sound quality is exemplary. (Calore, 2009)

Enamored by the service, many users began to explore and find ways around Spotify's restrictions that kept those from nations where it was not licensed to stream from accessing it. The most common method was to establish an account and find a way to access it through a UK-based proxy server. As convoluted as this method was, for a service that Eliot Van Buskirk labeled in a 2009 *Wired* column as "already the best music app on the planet" it was well worth the effort. Buskirk effusively proclaimed "those who have tried Spotify know it's like a magical version of iTunes in which you've already bought every song in the world" (Buskirk, 2009b).

Like Apple, Spotify has placed a large amount of its efforts in making its services easier to use than those of its competition, which is one of the reasons for its critical accolades. Arguably the most important difference between Spotify and its competitors is that Spotify is not only a browser-based service: Spotify provides its users stand-alone apps that run on Windows and Mac desktops and a number of mobile operating systems. Furthermore, the application interface is very similar to Apple's iTunes application, thereby offering an application that borrowed from almost seven years of familiarity. This difference is crucial. Comparing the Spotify app with its streaming, browser-based competition, the user finds the difference immediately palpable since the Spotify application "isn't at the mercy of such slow or unstable environments as Flash-based [browser] systems" (Lopez, 2011). Thus, the application provides a functionality that web-based subscription services do not. For example, the ability to share a song or playlist is something that subscription services often tout as a means of differentiating themselves from more traditional download-oriented retailers. What makes Spotify's service exceptional is the emphasis it has placed on convenient sharing. The Spotify app allows users to create a unique URL for any user-created playlist that they can simply send to another user via email. The recipient simply clicks on the link and the playlist appears in the app, ready to use. The unique flexibility of this method has resulted in an unexpected outcome, whereby third parties soon began to aggregate, display, and promote these playlists. In January 2009, Spotify posted that one new Facebook application, Mixifier, had been developed to share playlists across a user's social networks. Furthermore, a number of third-party websites began to appear where users could share and find creative playlists. This one feature opened the possibility for a limited but rapidly growing ecosystem of user-driven participation with names like Listiply, Specifspot, Spotyist, Spotyshare, and Topsify and so on (Anon., 2009c). Writing for the tech blog *LockerGnome*, in 2012 Ryan Matthew Pierson noted that this aspect was one of the reasons he switched from Rhapsody to Spotify. As Pierson put it, "it's not so much that Spotify does something here that Rhapsody doesn't, but the real advantage (for me) is in how it does it. Execution is everything in software, and Spotify nailed it with this one" (Pierson, 2012).

When Pierson switched from Rhapsody to Spotify, the service had only been available for six months in the U.S. market. During the close to three years Spotify could not access North America's and the world's most significant music market, the service strategized how it could acquire the licenses necessary to enter the U.S. market with content similar to its European services. Securing the rights to stream the majority of the 15 million songs in its European catalogue to U.S. subscribers meant acquiring licensing agreements with every major and a majority of independent labels. Initially aiming to enter the U.S. market in 2009, the debut was delayed for almost two years as the company negotiated the licensing agreements. Spotify's hopes must have been buoyed by a European music industry that exhibited a new flexibility when it came to licensing. In 2008 the British-based music trade *Music Week* reported that the recent influx of new online music retailers were "being green-lit that once would never have stood a chance of gaining approval [in the past]." Although doors were opening for a wide variety of models, it still didn't mean the market was optimistic. In the words of one research analyst, "I think it is a good time to come in. I don't necessarily think it is a good time to make money, though" (Woods, 2008). As enthusiastic as labels were to sign on for European licensing in 2008, there remained significant reticence to sign over the rights of their catalogue for streaming in the U.S. The problem was that a poor deal for labels would set a significant precedent in the most important music market in the world and saddle copyright holders with just another set of less-than-impressive payments. Tobias Slater, singer of the band Tough Love, told one magazine that although he had signed up for Last.fm's "artist remuneration package" he didn't "expect any money from it." Worse yet, the magazine noted that although while it was a "very low rate," it was "still probably too high for it to base its long-term business model on." Thus, a label's reluctance for low rates was matched on the other side by streaming services plagued by the fear that as their user base grew they would quickly burn through venture capital and collapse under the weight of unsustainable debt (Anon., 2009a). *Music Week* underlined the fundamental concern of the industry in an interview with a Warner Music executive who asked to remain anonymous and emphasized that "if we don't get this business model right, it's going to be a lot harder to fix down the road" (Woods, 2009).

The reasons for the executive's skepticism at the time may have been the rather contentious negotiations that Warner Music Group was having in 2009 with the largest free streaming service for music in the world, Google's YouTube service. The rates Google offered were so low that Warner pulled out of negotiations. Yet the larger problem for Warner was the user-oriented video streaming site's popularity as a music service. This popularity was confirmed three years later in 2012 when the American media research company Nielsen reported that nearly two-thirds of the American youth they surveyed used YouTube to listen to music. By comparison only 56% reported listening to radio, 53% purchased songs on iTunes, and 50% listened to music on compact discs. And three years later the free, ad-supported video service was still involved in legal struggles over per-play rates (Michaels, 2012). Thus, when Spotify insisted that its service offer a freemium tier to its U.S. users the hostility from labels was no surprise as unacceptable rates and another failed service were in no one's interest. As discussed in the previous chapter, the freemium strategy provides a fully functional version of a service with some limits that can be lifted by purchasing a "premium" version of the service. The embrace of freemium by Spotify came from the insistence of the service's CEO, Daniel Ek who was also a former CEO of uTorrent, one of the world's more popular BitTorrent clients. Ek fully believes that "music is already available for free—95 per cent of all music downloads are currently illegal, it is pointless to resist that." Ek's argument is that the only way to make purchasing music an attractive proposition in a climate of free is to provide a free but legal alternative that contains content that is better than what one may get from an everyday downloading experience. Low rates from a freemium service provided labels with the proposition that in a future where there is no tangible difference between legal and illegal options Spotify may pay little now, but little pay will be better than nothing (Beaumont, 2009). Spotify continually asserts its "better than free" mantra by offering exclusive streaming for some albums and songs to users before they have been released to the general public with premium users accessing the same content but at a higher, better- sounding bit rate (Clark, 2009). As Spotify's UK managing director Paul Brown asserted in 2010 "a lot of our users have come in from piracy [and] we're trying to monetize those people who aren't buying music today" (Peoples, 2010).

Still, labels continued to argue that what streaming services offered was less than impressive. In 2010 ad revenues in the European version of the Spotify service were relatively small and worse the conversion rate from free to premium remained low (Pham & Guynn, 2010). Rumors abounded that in Norway the percentage of Spotify users was somewhere between 2%–4% of the nation's population. This significant number was matched by the fact that the typical payout was 0.3 cents U.S. per stream. The problem was clear: to make the seven U.S. dollars that a label would make on the sale of a typical $10 album download on iTunes, a "Spotify user would have to listen to an album of 10, four-minute songs twice per day for about four months" (Peoples, 2010). With payouts this low it is no surprise that the royalties from Spotify's European agreements began to come under scrutiny by numerous parties. One 2011 report in *The Guardian* made it clear:

> Although Spotify reportedly paid out about euros 30m to rights hold-
> ers and labels in the first eight months of last year, and in several Euro-
> pean countries is now making more money for rights holders than
> Apple's iTunes Store, some artists and labels complain that their royalty
> cheques are paltry. The UK rights collecting society PRS for Music says
> only 4.9% of its revenue came from digital services in 2009, compared
> with 2.9% in 2008. (Topping, 2011, p. 3)

Put simply, growth of income streams for digital music appeared to be "stut-tering." The International Federation of the Phonographic Industry (IFPI) claimed "that the global growth in digital music halved in 2010, with only 'single digit' percentage growth in the more mature US digital music sec-tor" (Topping, 2011, p. 3). The fear that the digital streaming market could never grow in a manner that labels considered significant was substantial. Thus, the prospect of opening up the United States to a questionable model that could establish a poor precedent was more than a difficult proposition. Worse, for many labels it was a problem without a good answer.

At least one research analyst in 2011 claimed that there may never be a solution acceptable to both labels and digital services. As a result, services like Spotify would have to take the lead in every area of innovation and recognize what "other failed services have shown is that if you play to the record labels' rule book you get nowhere. These startups need to make their own rules, and not let the labels lead the conversation" (Topping, 2011, p. 3). "Leading the conversation" in this case does not only refer to technological innovation, but the wholesale process of revaluation. Just as the problem of pricing that the previous chapter addresses is a signifi-cant part of the revaluation process, so is iTunes' investment in the sale of individual downloads. To be sure, while labels may have seemed to be a less-than-vigorous digital music marketplace, significant members of the traditional music industry were bullish on the prospects of the future of the music industry. Richard Conlon, BMI's expert in new media, pointed out, "There's every reason to be optimistic people are going to use music. Maybe consumers won't be buying CDs, or buying downloads for that matter. But whatever happens, music is going to be used." Furthermore, from the perspective of a performance rights organization, Conlon was convinced that their organization was well-positioned for a "usage-based economy." Representing publishers, Conlon explained that BMI "[does not] care about selling products or manufacturing discs. We care about monetizing use, and use is what's gonna happen, whether it's subscription or ad-supported or bundled services with ISPs" (Scoppa, 2009). The reassertion of publishing and its related interests have had numerous consequences on the new music industry, a few of which I will address later in the discussion of music supervision. Because publishing has long been invested in licensing revenues it is primed to assert its position in an economy based around usage such as one consisting of streaming services. Services like Spotify that are centered on monitoring and leveraging usage are attempts to successfully establish a model that may be the logical outcome of a field taken over by an information industry focused on users.

The trick for all streaming services is they must convince an already skeptical set of industry players to rethink how to value their holdings and invest in ways where every party can see the possibility of reward for their risk. In 2009 one of the founders of the "radio streaming service" Last. FM addressed the criticism that its streaming agreement guaranteed only $0.0005 per stream. Last.FM's proposition was that unlike the purchase of a CD or MP3 where the investor effectively gets paid once by the listener, "with a service like ours, every time somebody listens, there is a share of advertising, which means continuous payment to the artists and the labels" (Anon., 2009a, p. 26).[5] One of the promises that Spotify makes is that the issuance of micro payments is an answer to the "what choice do you give us?" argument that has long been mobilized to justify copyright infringement by so many users. The promise is that this excuse would subside if these services could deliver cheap, convenient, legal, and sometimes "free" on-demand streaming (Woods, 2008). As *Newsweek* reported in 2009, the problem revolved around the fact that according to estimates offered by the music industry, "about 95 percent of music downloads are illegal." The advantage of a streaming service "from the record companies' point of view, is that the service provides a way around the piracy issue: since there are no downloads, there's nothing to steal." As Julian Hobbins of the Federation Against Software Theft explained, "We have no problems with Spotify at all. Why would anyone pirate content or steal if they can get it as they want it for free?" (Underhill, 2009). With labels hemorrhaging cash, it was only a matter of time before they would begin to sign with Spotify in search of another income stream. After almost two years of courting major labels, in 2009 EMI became the first major to capitulate. Daniel Ek admitted that the two years of negotiations it took to get EMI and later other majors onboard was not only unusual but "unheard of" at the time (Ashton, 2009). By 2010 Ek would claim that Spotify had quickly become a substantial partner to record labels and was "a substantial revenue source for the whole of the music industry" (Neate, 2010). Two years later, after even more negotiations, labels cut Spotify licensing deals to bring its service into the U.S. market. The process of revaluation had hit an important threshold and had done so on Spotify's watch.

Revaluation isn't a process limited to those who produce, distribute, and retail music, but it must also involve the listener. Key to every streaming service's proposal to solving the problem of piracy is that it offers a resource so compelling that users will rethink their need to own music. As mentioned earlier, Daniel Ek and his colleagues at Spotify begin with the conceit that for many users music is already free, an admission not based simply only on technological possibilities but a generation's worth of consumer habits.[6] With its service Spotify is searching for a way not to solve the problem of piracy but to address the problem of ownership. Enthused about Spotify, Eamonn Forde of *Music Week* declared that "everyone else is a long way behind." Forde then offered a contrast that positioned Spotify in Biblical terms. For Forde, the BBC's "iPlayer," a service that allows free online access to the corporation's television and radio programming, is John the Baptist to Spotify's Jesus. In other words, iPlayer was "a powerful idea that led people further along the path. The idea has now exploded in the public consciousness." Furthermore, "for true apostles of the digital revolution, the path leads towards a future in which nobody will want to own music, films or even computer hard drives, instead accessing whatever they need whenever they want from central databases held on the internet" (Watt, 2009, p. 14). However, as messianic as the vision is, "it has been given the rather sinister name 'the Cloud'" (Watt, 2009, p. 14).

Part of what Spotify and other cloud-based services are in the process of doing is restructuring the consumption of music around a "utility model" where service, not content, is the primary sale point. Part of the excitement surrounding Spotify rested on the quality of the user experience it offered through its application. Indeed, the Spotify streaming application had been developed to also act as a platform for other services. Beginning in late 2011 Spotify opened up its platform for third-party development. Like Apple, Spotify would keep the applications within an environment and approval process that they would control. Although the service would keep all of these apps in the Spotify application interface, the service admitted that they "couldn't foresee the variety of apps that developers would create." Spotify's reason for this was its focus on offering "a more beautiful and seamless experience" that would get the user "closer to the song as well." While Daniel Ek would not comment on whether Spotify would allow apps to link back to a band's profile and other vendors that offer merchandise and tickets, Ek did comment that Spotify wasn't excluding "any particular app." The only guarantee Ek offered was the proclamation that Spotify would only approve apps that provide a "great user experience." Debuting apps from a music magazine (*Rolling Stone*), a fellow music streamer (Last. FM), a lyrics service (TuneWiki), and a concert-finder (Songkick), Ek also noted that the platform had "no monetization strategy at the moment" with regards to these apps. and that Spotify's licensing structure would "remain the same even as its scale balloons" (Piper, 2011). By May 2012 Spotify would unveil a second round of apps, many of which were tied directly to labels and social media (Barker, 2012, p. 2).

As mentioned earlier, amplifying the user's ability to create and share has long been a key to Spotify's service. The creation and exportation of playlists is an attractive aspect of the Spotify service, however the ability of Spotify users to share accelerated in 2009. That year Spotify announced it would produce an application that would allow users to share playlists through the Facebook platform (Anon., 2009d). By 2010 the Facebook application was released as part of what the Swedish company called Spotify's "most significant upgrade" since its initial launch and "moved a step closer to making music more connected." Called, "Spotify Music Profile," the aim of the application would be to use Facebook Connect and allow the user to create, store, and share playlists as well as tag favorite albums and tracks from personal computers and mobile devices (Kimberley, 2010). Because Spotify plugged into Facebook's API, Spotify users could see their Facebook friends Spotify activity. At the same time, the update of Spotify's desktop player allowed it to link to and play those music files on the user's desktop, thereby enabling the user to play all of his or her music from the same platform. In essence, these developments, as Paul Brown, Spotify's senior vice president of strategic partnerships, explained, "[was to] make it a social and sharing platform" (Forde, 2010, p. 10). Ek was even more emphatic: "Our job is to try to get you to share as much music as possible and to get recommendations from your friends. The more we can do that for you, the better it is for us as a business" (Levy, 2011, p. 19).

One of those early users was the CEO of Facebook, Mark Zuckerberg. Introduced to the service by Napster cofounder Sean Parker, Zuckerberg quickly understood its potential as a music application with social potentials. The day after his introduction to the service, Zuckerberg updated his Facebook status to "Spotify is so good." In many ways Zuckerberg's admiration should not have been that surprising. Both Facebook and Spotify share similar aims. Indeed, the two platforms provide social tools that embrace free as a bet that it will catalyze greater use and growth through ease of "social discovery." Working with the most popular social network in the English-speaking world Spotify took advantage of Facebook's "Open Graph" strategy, "an initiative that allows developers to create services that let people share everything—not just photos, messages, and status updates but movies, books, news articles, and so on" (Levy, 2011, p. 19). This is no small issue. Because of the strong connection that music has to users' identities, the music industry has organized itself around the intensely social worlds of music genre. Understanding the social nature of music, how it is distributed through a set of industrial *and* social coordinates, has always been key to successfully bringing music to market. Historically, the music industry has addressed this through understanding music genres and exploiting the social scenes and actor networks that compose them. What this has meant for the music industry is a continual embrace of relatively independent third parties like disc jockeys, rack jobbers, and street teams to help them connect with audiences. Because Facebook's goal is to create a set of intensely social tools, the service has followed a similar path and has embraced third-party developers that allow them to achieve a more flexible sociability. By opening up the Facebook platform to Spotify and other streaming services, Facebook is able to leverage the intense social aspects of popular music while avoiding the many knotty problems of music licensing and focus on enhancing the processes of discovery. In the words of Zuckerberg, "We're not trying to make a music product. We're trying to make something so that people can learn stuff from their friends and can share with them and express themselves." As Sean Parker noted, what Spotify and Facebook aimed to do was create a "ubiquitous music distribution plumbing for the entire Internet" that could amplify the use of streaming in a way that creates huge gains through the multiplication of micro payments (Levy, 2011). It was this strategy that compelled Spotify to hire the ad agency, VCCP Share, "to create a campaign that leverages Spotify's new global relationship with Facebook" and "focus on targeting music influencers and aims to highlight Spotify's music-sharing and playlist facilities" (Williams, 2011, p. 1).

Making Spotify's relationship with Facebook global was an essential part of Spotify's 2011 entry into the United States, an entry that all but consecrated the relationship between the two services. *Forbes* reported two months before Spotify's U.S. debut that the integration between the two services would become deeper throughout the year. This included placing the songs streamed from Spotify users (and users from other streaming services) into Facebook news feeds so that one could see what friends were playing in real time (Olson, 2011). At least one report noted that Spotify had generated promotional materials to give to advertisers that explained how integration with Facebook would help connect the streaming service with American culture. The goal for the Facebook-integrated Spotify was to acquire 50 million U.S. users within the first 12 months of operation (Perna, 2011). To achieve this number, Spotify initially planned to spend six months offering users a free version of Spotify with no limits to, in the words of Sean Parker, get the "[baked] in the system." During that six-month period users would "build their library, build playlists, become addicted to the experience, to the point where they want that experience with them everywhere they go." After the initial six-month period, limits on how many times a song could be streamed were to be enforced and, ideally, a large portion of these users would convert from free to premium (Levy, 2011, p. 19). These rules would change. Very quickly Spotify decided to drop its initial "six-month rule" and continue to provide a freemium version to users with ad support without song limits for an indefinite time. Perhaps the most interesting change took place almost two months after Spotify's U.S. launch when it announced that every new user would need to have a Facebook account to join the service. After introducing the requirement on September 22, 2011 at the Facebook F8 conference, Spotify reported an explosion in its active U.S. user base. Within eight months, Spotify increased its user base from 3.4 million users to 5.3 million, approximately a 56% increase (Buskirk, 2011). Soon thereafter, the streaming service MOG announced it would enforce a similar stipulation to access its free service (Sloane, 2011). MOG noted that the month after implementing the Facebook requirement the service claimed a 246% jump in monthly average users and early data suggested a 3–5% conversion rate to premium paid use (Ludwig, 2011).

Compulsory Facebook integration may have been a hit for some services, however the policy raised a number of red flags. That a service could demand others join another service as a condition for its use is problematic enough. For others displaying what songs a user plays on Spotify on the Facebook service became a substantial source of anger. When it was announced that these conditions would be applied to Spotify's UK users, *The Independent* reported that responses ranged from "smugly dispensed advice—'Spotify, this is not cool'—to demands that [users] file the case with our 'national competition authority'" (Marsden, 2011). Privacy concerns were quickly addressed with the installation of a "privacy mode" by Spotify so that listeners in the U.S. and UK could play without the scrutiny of their Facebook friends.[7] Still, it was clear to most analysts that the connection between services was key for Facebook and Spotify, both of whom were not monetizing music. Rather, Facebook and Spotify are monetizing "music-oriented experiences." *The Guardian* explained that this is part of a larger trend where "startups and investors are beginning to focus on services around the edges of music" (Topping, 2011, p. 3). The combination of Spotify and Facebook provides a possible ecosystem where the edges of experience are clearer, more exposed. The purpose of the ecosystem is to produce an environment where third parties can access user data and build other unique value propositions in the form of applications and advertising. In this sense the Spotify/Facebook environment is more like a complimentary imperative where associative data is generated through the integration of the services. Furthermore, by opening up Spotify's revamped API the importance of third parties is directly related to the value that these developers can find and generate. Eliot Van Buskirk explains that value of this API meant that, "a kid coding away in a basement all night, anywhere in the world, can build apps within the most popular music subscription service in the world. Want to play your friends' Facebook preferences? Create a party playlist automatically based on the people attending? Tag songs to locations so that others can stumble across them? . . . With the ability to include the apps within Spotify itself, the sky is the limit" (Quoted in Staff, 2011). Writing for *The Independent* Rhodri Marsden surmised the essence of the Spotify/Facebook proposal: "Your personal data has a value, chaps. If you want, you can exchange that data for a service. If you don't want to, don't" (Marsden, 2011).

It isn't simply personal data that Spotify's developers are mining. Unlike two other prominent social networks, Twitter and Tumblr, Facebook is based on an architecture of relationships that provides data on a user's social structure. It is this "'social graph' that represents relationships between its 700 million users and the things they care about: movies, books, videos, events and music" that *Billboard* cited as the unique asset that Spotify/Facebook integration offers (Peoples, 2011). The value of the Facebook's Open Graph API is that relational structures become more salient. As a result, companies that access this graph can build "more meaningful products that take advantage of consumers' social nature." As Clear Channel executive VP of digital Brian Lakamp dubbed it, the graph is the "social connective tissue" where the "value of millions of personal relationships" can be tapped. Facebook has invited this collaboration by generating a reputation as a warm, quality partner within the business community.[8] Reporting for *Billboard*, Glenn Peoples stated that while speaking with Facebook's F8 attendees, "Not a single executive had anything but positive things to say about his business' relationship with the company. Its executives and engineers have a reputation for being smart, agile and forward-thinking" (Peoples, 2011). This willingness to work with other businesses extended to Spotify. Beginning a partnership with General Motors' Chevrolet in 2011, Spotify started to explore deals designed to deliver some of the "edges" of music and target desired demographics as part of its U.S. debut. As part of this partnership with Chevrolet, in July 2011 Spotify provided close to 150,000 consumers with a six-month free trial. In exchange for the free service, consumers would agree to receive marketing emails and other communications. The cross promotion of Spotify's introduction to the U.S. and the fall release of Chevrolet's new 2012 Sonic allowed the two to work together and find value in their similar consumer bases. Christi Vazquez, communications manager at Chevrolet, confirmed this strategy, noting that, "We're looking for young professionals; we're looking at the Millennial market for this car. People who have recently graduated from college are experiencing a lot of firsts in their lives, so that's really the target for this vehicle." Angela Watts, Spotify's VP of marketing and communications, explained that these kind of "brand-partnerships" are part of a larger strategy that also involved companies such as Coca Cola, Reebok, and Motorola (T. Peterson, 2011). In the case of Kia Motors America, the car company quickly saw the value of engaging with Facebook users to create a "one-of-a-kind" crowdsourced Spotify-hosted playlist. Titled "Kia Rio Windows Down," within a month more than 1,100 songs had been submitted to Spotify "with song selections totaling 15 hours of music and an average of 24 minutes of time spent per user listening to the playlist, which provides an environment for users to listen, discover, and share the unique playlist with their friends" (Anon., 2012a). The list also provided its subscribers and contributors an environment of relationships that is ripe for analysis.

It was this environment of relational data that attracted the United States' largest live-event ticket dealer, Ticketmaster. In 2012 Ticketmaster created a Facebook application that would recommend events based on fans' listening habits, habits that were now easier to highlight because of Spotify integration. What differentiated this from other applications was that Facebook users could finish their purchase in the Facebook platform. This was a first for the platform, one that had been used primarily as a marketing platform. However, the Facebook platform had become robust enough that a Ticketmaster purchase could be made on it and provide "a transactional value of roughly $6" for Facebook. Kip Levin, Ticketmaster's executive VP of e-commerce confirmed that,

> the thing that puts this [app] over the top is the Spotify integration. Now, for anybody using Spotify through Facebook, it opens up a ton of information about what people like in terms of artists, and now we can actually access all that data. So instead of them coming to the web page where we're just saying 'here are the top-selling shows,' we can show them a list of shows based on what they're listening to.

And because one of the best ways to promote a tour is through "word of mouth," making the purchase of a ticket appear in friends' feeds acts as a type of micro promotion. Ticketmaster's interest in Facebook is how it allows friends to "connect the dots" of discovery:

> People who are friends on Facebook generally have very similar interests, and Spotify connected through Facebook is a great way to learn what other people are listening to. Music starts out with discovering a band, then you start to listen to a song, then the whole album, and then you listen to everything [the artist has], and then the next step in the progression is you go to the live event. Then you either become a fan or you don't.

Ticketmaster's Levin summed up the Spotify integration with Facebook as a conjunction that "just ties it all together really neatly" (Waddell, 2012).

To say that Spotify and Facebook "ties it all together" is not close to saying that a new paradigm is imminent. Questions about freemium may have waned, but they still persist. Perhaps more importantly is the skepticism that a micro-payments model is sustainable for artists let alone labels. Still, the experiment will continue. Valued at up to $4 billion, *The New York Times* reported that by mid-2012 Spotify was well on its way to raising $220 million in investment capital, with Goldman Sachs leading the way with close to $100 million (De La Merced & Rusli, 2012). Perhaps this kind of finance will be enough for the service to create a profitable model, one that benefits a number of players in the ecosystem including musicians and labels. Or maybe iTunes and Spotify will continue to co-exist as two successful services, leading two different business models. What is clear is that as digital user environments grow and change, every element of the industry will have to negotiate how their productions and contributions are valued and whether or not they may wish to participate. Such is the case of AC/DC who in November 2012 relented and placed their entire catalogue in the hands of iTunes for sale. Within a week iTunes reported selling 48,000 copies of AC/DC albums and close to 700,000 songs (Caulfield, 2012). That same month Kid Rock placed his new album on iTunes as well. Lee Trink, Kid Rock's manager, explained that "there are fewer record stores available, and there are fans who don't necessarily want to get in the car and drive to the store. They've been accustomed to buying it digitally. He's proven his point that he was able to have an incredibly successful record without iTunes, [but] that doesn't mean you can't reassess the landscape and take a look at people's buying behaviors" (Anon., 2012a). Kid Rock has also placed his catalogue on Spotify for streaming. Yet, at the time of this writing AC/DC continues to hold out and refuses to license any of its catalogue to the service.

BIBLIOGRAPHY

Adshead, A. (2002). Illegal MP3 Files Found on 80% of Firms' Servers. *ComputerWeekly.com*. Retrieved from http://www.computerweekly.com/news/2240048079/Illegal-MP3-files-found-on-80-of-firms-servers
Anon. (2003). Penn State and Napster Team Up. *Penn State Live*. Retrieved from http://live.psu.edu/story/4586
Anon. (2005). Sony Sued Over Copy-Protected CDs. *BBC News*. Retrieved from http://news.bbc.co.uk/2/hi/technology/4424254.stm
Anon. (2009a, May 1). Is Time Running Out For Digital Music? *Revolution, 26*.
Anon. (2009b). One Year Ago Today. . . . Retrieved from http://www.spotify.com/se/blog/archives/2009/10/07/
Anon. (2009c). Sharing Is Good, Share Your Spotify Playlists. Retrieved from http://www.spotify.com/us/blog/archives/2009/01/16/sharing-is-good-share-your-spotify-playlists/
Anon. (2009d, May 19). Spotify to Launch Facebook, Music Sharing App. *DmEurope*.
Anon. (2010). Apple's Ping Rival to Facebook and Twitter Launches With 160m users. *Belfast Telegraph*. Retrieved from http://www.belfasttelegraph.co.uk/news/world-news/apples-ping-rival-to-facebook-and-twitter-launches-with-160m-users-14931727.html#ixzz24QvwWS6I
Anon. (2012a). AC/DC Release Entire Catalog on iTunes After Long Holdout: Rockers Relent and Make Music Available Through Digital Store. *Rolling Stone*. Retrieved from http://www.rollingstone.com/music/news/ac-dc-put-albums-on-itunes-20121119

Anon. (2012b). Kia Motors' "Kia Rio Windows Down" Playlist on Spotify Gains Momentum As Facebook Users Submit Their Favorite Songs. *PR Newswire.*

Anon. (2012c). Spotify Launches For Germans Without Facebook. *DmEurope.*

Anon. (2012d). Spotify Tests German Law With Facebook obligation. *DmEurope.*

Ashton, J. (2009, March 8). EMI Has a New Spin on Record Market; New Chief Elio Leoni-Sceti Is Devising a Fresh Business Model, Writes James Ashton. *The Sunday Times, 7.*

Barker, A. (2012, March 23). New Spotify Apps Boost Labels' Grip. *Daily Variety, 2.*

Beaumont, C. (2009, April 25). Technology; Could the Success of Music-Streaming Services Such As Spotify Point to a Viable Long-Term Business Model For the Music Industry, Asks Claudine Beaumont. *The Daily Telegraph.*

Bennett, J. (2011). Rock Solid: AC/DC Stand Firm on Downloads. *Sky News HD.* Retrieved from http://news.sky.com/story/854279/rock-solid-ac-dc-stand-firm-on-downloads

Buskirk, E. V. (2009a). App Turns iPhone Into Dime Jukebox. *Wired.com.* Retrieved from http://www.wired.com/business/2009/10/lala-iphone-app/

Buskirk, E. V. (2009b). Spotify Becomes Platform, Makes U.S. Music Fans Even More Jealous. *Wired.com.* Retrieved from http://www.wired.com/business/2009/04/spotify-opens-a/

Buskirk, E. V. (2011). Spotify Usage Explodes After F8, Facebook Integration. *The Hollywood Reporter.* Retrieved from http://www.hollywoodreporter.com/news/spotify-usage-explodes-f8-facebook-242727

Calore, M. (2009). Spotify's Restrictions Can't Keep the Music Nerds Out. *Wired. com.* Retrieved from http://www.wired.com/business/2009/02/spotifys-restri/

Caulfield, K. (2012). AC/DC's iTunes Debut Sells 48,000 Digital Albums & 696,000 Songs. *Billboard.* Retrieved from http://www.billboard.com/articles/news/473957/acdcs-itunes-debut-sells-48000-digital-albums-696000-songs

Clark, N. (2009, August 29). Spotify Set For the Big Time As Regulators Scuttle the Pirates. *The Independent.*

De La Merced, M. J., & Rusli, E. M. (2012, May 18). Spotify's Financing Is Said to Lift Value to $4 Billion. *The New York Times, 7.*

Doggett, P. (2009). *You Never Give Me Your Money: The Beatles After the Breakup.* New York: It Books.

Forde, E. (2010, May 8). Overview: Taking Digital Up a Level. *Music Week, 10.*

Formeski, T. (2010). The Atlantic Publisher Wants Apple to Share Customer Data. Retrieved from http://www.zdnet.com/blog/foremski/the-atlantic-publisher-wants-apple-to-share-customer-data/1566

Frith, S. (1988). *Music For Pleasure: Essays in the Sociology of Pop.* New York: Pantheon.

Frith, S. (1996). *Performing Rites: On the Value of Popular Music.* Cambridge, MA: Harvard University Press.

Goldman, D. (2010). Music's Lost Decade: Sales Cut in Half. *CNNMoney.com.* Retrieved from http://money.cnn.com/2010/02/02/news/companies/napster_music_industry/index.htm?hpt=Sbin

Gray, L. (2008). The Real Genius in iTunes 8? Apple Will Make More Money. Retrieved from http://blog.louisgray.com/2008/09/real-genius-in-itunes-8-apple-will-make.html

Jacobson, W. (2011). *Steve Jobs.* New York: Simon & Schuster.

Jobs, S. (2007). Thoughts on Music. Retrieved from http://web.archive.org/web/20080517114107/http://www.apple.com/hotnews/thoughtsonmusic

Kehro, S. (2011). The iTunes Economy and Data Transparency. *Fast Company.* Retrieved from http://www.fastcompany.com/1752799/itunes-economy-and-data-transparency

Kimberley, S. (2010). Spotify Integrates Social Media in Major Upgrade. *Brand Republic*, 1. Retrieved from http://www.brandrepublic.com/News/999345/

Kuhn, T. (1996). *The Structure of Scientific Revolutions* (3rd ed.). Chicago: The University of Chicago.

Levine, R. (2008, October 12). Ageless and Defiant, AC/DC Stays on Top Without Going Digital. *The New York Times*, AR1.

Levy, S. (2011, November). The Second Coming. *Wired, 19*.

Lohmann, F. V. (2005). Are You Infected By Sony-BMG's Rootkit? *Electronic Frontier Foundation*. Retrieved from https://www.eff.org/deeplinks/2005/11/are-you-infected-sony-bmgs-rootkit

Lopez, J. (2011). First Look: Spotify. *InformationWeek*. Retrieved from http://www.informationweek.com/byte/reviews/personal-tech/digital-audio/231001850

Ludwig, S. (2011). MOG's Facebook users grow by 246% after its social integration Read. *VentureBeat. Retrieved from http://venturebeat.com/2011/11/01/mog-user-growth-facebook-integration/*

Marsden, R. (2011). Cyberclinic: The Songs Remain the Same . . . So Stop Whining. *The Independent*. Retrieved from http://www.independent.co.uk/life-style/gadgets-and-tech/features/cyberclinic-the-songs-remain-the-sameso-stop-whining-2362570.html

Michaels, S. (2012). YouTube Is Teens' First Choice For Music: Google's Video Streaming Site Is the Most Popular Way Young People Listen to Music, According to a New Survey. *The Guardian*. Retrieved from http://www.guardian.co.uk/music/2012/aug/16/youtube-teens-first-choice-music?newsfeed=true

Mims, C. (2010). How iTunes Genius Really Works: An Apple Engineer Discloses How the Company's Premier Recommendation Engine Parses Millions of iTunes Libraries. *Technology Review*. Retrieved from http://www.technologyreview.com/view/419198/how-itunes-genius-really-works/

Neate, R. (2010, February 18). Music Website Spot-On For Fans and Industry; Spotify's Founder Says His Company Will Be Worth 'Tens of Billions' After Solving the Piracy Problem. *The Daily Telegraph, 4*.

Negus, K. (1999). *Music Genres and Corporate Cultures*. New York: Routledge.

Neumayr, T., & Roth, J. (2008a). Apple Press Info: iTunes Now Number Two Music Retailer in the US. Retrieved from http://www.apple.com/pr/library/2008/02/26iTunes-Now-Number-Two-Music-Retailer-in-the-US.html

Neumayr, T., & Roth, J. (2008b). iTunes Store Top Music Retailer in the US. *Apple Press Info*. Retrieved from http://www.apple.com/pr/library/2008/04/03iTunes-Store-Top-Music-Retailer-in-the-US.html

Neumayr, T., & Roth, J. (2010). iTunes Store Tops 10 Billion Songs Sold. *Apple Press Info*. Retrieved from http://www.apple.com/pr/library/2010/02/25iTunes-Store-Tops-10-Billion-Songs-Sold.html

Olson, P. (2011). Facebook to Launch Music Service With Spotify. *Forbes.com*. Retrieved from http://www.forbes.com/sites/parmyolson/2011/05/25/facebook-to-launch-music-service-with-spotify/2/

Paczkowski, J. (2012). Apple's Ping to End With a Thud in Next Release of iTunes. *All Things D*. Retrieved from http://allthingsd.com/20120612/apples-ping-to-end-with-a-thud-in-next-release-of-itunes/

Paulson, D. (2009). Garth Brooks on Comebacks, Music Piracy, More. *USA Today*. Retrieved from http://www.usatoday.com/life/music/news/2009–10–15-garth-brooks-quote_N.htm

Peoples, G. (2010, July 24). Point of Low Return. *Billboard*.

Peoples, G. (2011). Facebook Music: The New Social Connectivity. *Billboard*. Retrieved from http://www.billboard.com/news/facebook-music-the-new-social-connectivity-1005368282.story

Perna, G. (2011). How Europe's Spotify Plans to Crash iTunes US Party. *International Business Times*. Retrieved from http://www.thefreelibrary.com/How+Europe's+Spotify+Plans+To+Crash+iTunes+US+Party.-a0262615901

Peterson, J. (2011). As Apple Debuts Cloud-Based Music Service, Effect on Online Piracy Uncertain. *The Daily Caller*. Retrieved from http://dailycaller.com/2011/11/14/as-apple-debuts-cloud-based-music-service-effect-on-online-piracy-uncertain/

Peterson, T. (2011). Chevrolet Trades Spotify Trials For Opt-Ins. *Direct Marketing News*. Retrieved from http://www.dmnews.com/chevrolet-trades-spotify-trials-for-opt-ins/article/207467/

Pham, A., & Guynn, J. (2010, September 3). Company Town; Music Labels Tuning In to Google; Firms Eager For a Digital Service That's Not iTunes Are in Talks With the Web Giant. *The Los Angeles Times*, B1.

Pierson, R. M. (2012). Why I Switched From Rhapsody to Spotify. *LockerGnome*. Retrieved from http://www.lockergnome.com/media/2012/03/27/why-i-switched-from-rhapsody-to-spotify/

Piper, G. (2011). Spotify Opens Platform to App Developers, But Retains Control. *Consumer Electronics Daily*.

Price, J. (2012). Apple's iTunes Match (aka iMatch): The First Royalties Are In. Retrieved from http://blog.tunecore.com/2012/02/apple-imatch-the-first-royalties-are-in.html

Sandoval, G. (2011). Court Says MP3tunes Protected By DMCA: U.S. District Court in New York Grants Summary Judgment Against MP3Tunes For Music That the Founder Uploaded Personally Without Permission But Grants Music Service Protection Under DMCA Safe Harbor. *CNET News*. Retrieved from http://news.cnet.com/8301-31001_3-20095599-261/court-says-mp3tunes-protected-by-dmca/

Schonfeld, E. (2011). Bezos: Kindle Fire Is an End-to-End Service. Retrieved from http://seekingalpha.com/article/296777-bezos-kindle-fire-is-an-end-to-end-service

Scoppa, B. (2009, May 1). Getting Paid. *Mix*. Retrieved from http://mixonline.com/studios/business/getting-paid//index1.html

Sloane, G. (2011, September 27). Spotify Caught in Cross Hairs. *The New York Post*, 28.

Staff, T. (2011). Spotify's New Apps: What the Critics Are Saying. *The Hollywood Reporter*. Retrieved from http://www.hollywoodreporter.com/news/spotify-launches-apps-applications-facebook-267806

Stone, B. (2009a). Apple Strikes Deal to Buy the Music Start-Up Lala. *The New York Times*, B2.

Stone, B. (2009b, May 28). Music Labels Ease Up to Assist Web Start-Ups. *The New York Times*, B1.

Topping, A. (2011, January 31). Media: Music's Leap of Faith: Major Labels Joined Forces Behind Streaming at Midem in Cannes Last Week, But Some Say They Must Change Their Attitude to Licensing or Face Losing the Battle For the Digital Future. *The Guardian*, 3.

Underhill, W. (2009, March 30). Music For Free, and It's Legal; The Music Service Has Caught On So Quickly in Britain That Some Analysts Are Hailing It As a Possible Rival to Apple's iTunes. *Newsweek, 153*.

Waddell, R. (2008). Kid Rock Living Large Without iTunes. *Billboard*. Retrieved from http://www.kidrock.com/news/kid-rock-living-large-without-itunes/

Waddell, R. (2012). Ticketmaster Launches New Facebook App. *Billboard*. Retrieved from http://www.billboard.com/news/ticketmaster-launches-new-facebook-app-1005921752.story#/news/ticketmaster-launches-new-facebook-app-1005921752.story

Watt, H. (2009, March 15). Why Spotify May Spell the End of Ownership; The New Music Website Shows Us How We Will Access Our Entertainment in Future. *The Sunday Times,* 14.

Watters, A. (2011). An iTunes Model For Data: Datasets As Albums? Entities As Singles? How an iTunes For Data Might Work. *O'Reilly Radar.* Retrieved from http://radar.oreilly.com/2011/04/itunes-for-data.html

Williams, M. (2011, December 1). Spotify Hands VCCP Global Digital Brief. *Campaign,* 1.

Woods, A. (2008, November 19). Digital: The Beat Is Online. *Music Week,* 19.

Woods, A. (2009). MIDEM 2009: Filling the Digital Space. *Music Week,* 24.

4 Opening Pandora's Box
The Problematic Promise of Radio on the Internet

Over a decade into the 21st century it is still the case that the best way to secure a hit song is to secure significant amounts of terrestrial, over-the-air radio airplay. While amateurs and experts continue to trumpet the many accomplishments of the Internet, over-the-air radio airplay is still the quickest, most desired way for popular music to reach audiences. With cars and kitchens tuned in, the easy-to-understand technology and trusted curatorial source is still unparalleled as a source of mass music discovery. The emphasis on curation and ease of use are the reasons that Pandora, the most successful U.S.-based webcaster, has designed its service the way it has. Tim Westergren, co-founder of Pandora, explained in early-2012, "Everything you hear on Pandora has gone through a very deliberate, methodical musical analysis" (Bordowitz, 2012). Pandora's musical reach is nothing less than a technological marvel. Its servers offer over 90,000 artists, 70% of them are independent allowing users to make all types of customizable music streams that feel like "radio." As part of a set of webcasting enterprises, like so many aspects of the new music industry, Pandora is continually experimenting to determine how best to deliver an online radio experience that is profitable. Unlike other areas of the new music industry that are dealt with in this book, webcasters like Pandora, more than any other practice in the ecosystem, have been governed by a number of pre-existing policies, institutions, and practices. Indeed, what has hindered webcasting are two significant structural issues: (1) The pre-existing model of radio broadcasting as it relates to ad revenue, and (2) the demands that the 1998 Federal Legislation known as the Digital Millennium Copyright Act (DMCA) places on webcasters. Successfully negotiating these two structuring agents is not only the key for long-term profit growth for this industry. It is also important to understanding how these structuring agents both enable and limit the very infrastructures that they engage. For U.S.-based webcasters this has meant performing a delicate and sometimes improvised dance around a variety of regulations, organizations, and investors as they have sought to produce a viable model.

Streaming audio was one of the first Internet-oriented investments to engage the music industry. Throughout the late-1990s the infrastructure necessary for streaming came into focus: as network bandwidth continued to grow, users began to access at-home Internet service providers, and a set of standard protocols began to be adopted, making the investment in this practice a viable option. In the United States companies such as Real-Networks created technologies devoted to streaming both audio and video events such as athletic contests and concerts. It wasn't too long before other companies, particularly major radio stations, began to create their own webcasting operations. Soon reports began to appear that a number of companies like Live365.com, Imagine Radio, and Spinner were offering everyday users the ability to easily produce their own "radio stations." Jeremy Berbach, a user who ran his own Brazilbient Lounge radio station from a computer in his living room, explained that, "This is really the evolution of music. It's like I made a mix tape to put in my Walkman, only I can listen to it anywhere and anybody else could listen too" (Goldberg, 1999). With these services just about anyone with a high-speed Internet connection and a relatively new PC with a soundcard could stream not-ready-for-drive-time programming (Kong, 1999, p. F01). Soon the webcasting industry exploded. In June 2000 Arbitron reported that 19% of the United States had tried Internet radio and that about 100 new webcasters were appearing each month offering a large and growing variety of programs aimed to fill the needs of even the most discriminating listener (Fridman, 2000). With consumers steadily adopting the technologies necessary to listen to streaming audio, words such as "critical mass" started to be used in discussions of Internet radio. By August 2000 the United States' largest radio group, Clear Channel, started to consider the new medium. Looking at its almost 900 radio stations, and television and outdoor venue holdings, the then-president of Clear Channel's Web Services, John Martin, told *Billboard* that his group was "just trying to figure out how to tie all these together and leverage them" (Saxe, 2000). As Clear Channel took notice, Live365's Chief Technology Officer, Peter Rothman, felt that too many radio broadcasters were ignoring this terrain and it "may come back to haunt them" (Saxe, 2000).

To be sure, one of the aspects embraced by webcasters small and large was, like the rest of the Internet, they would remain untouched by many of the content-specific restrictions that govern radio broadcasters. The proliferation of stations included material that rarely if ever would make it onto terrestrial or even satellite radio, as well as off-color, indecent programming. Still, webcasters have never been truly free from rules and regulations. Like all radio, Live365.com and its companion services were never released from their obligations to pay royalties to traditional performance rights organizations (PROs) such as the American Society of Composers, Authors and Publishers (ASCAP), and Broadcast Music, Inc. (BMI). However, these webcasters were also governed under the Digital Millennium Copyright Act (DMCA), federal legislation that many businesses viewed as the set of rules and regulations that make their enterprises possible. Passed in 1998, the DMCA established a legal framework that digital businesses could negotiate. Among other things, the DMCA established rules for what it identified as a "noninteractive sound service":

> An 'interactive service' is one that enables a member of the public to receive a transmission of a program specially created for the recipient, or on request, a transmission of a particular sound recording, whether or not as part of a program, which is selected by or on behalf of the recipient. The ability of individuals to request that particular sound recordings be performed for reception by the public at large, or in the case of a subscription service, by all subscribers of the service, does not make a service interactive, if the programming on each channel of the service does not substantially consist of sound recordings that are performed within 1 hour of the request or at a time designated by either the transmitting entity or the individual making such request. ("Digital Millennium Copyright Act," 1998)

This second clause about what "does not make a service interactive" is key, as it is the basis of defining the "noninteractive service" for webcasters who want to produce programming that "acts like radio." A number of other provisions such as "no more than four songs by an artist in a three hour period and no more than three in a row by the same artist" and "no more than three songs from the same album in a three hour period and not more than two in a row from the same album" define what constitutes a noninteractive service (Anon., *The DMCA Rules*). The importance of this definition rests in determining what kind of licenses the service may be able to purchase. In the case of webcasting, the ability to conveniently purchase licensed, legal programming material revolves around designing a noninteractive system that would make it eligible for a "compulsory license." The importance of the compulsory license cannot be overstated. As Richard Schulenberg explains in his work *Legal Aspects of the Music Industry,*

> The compulsory license is the grandaddy exception to the copyright owner's complete control over the use of the copyrightable material. The thinking behind the compulsory license is that music should be made available to the public. Without the compulsory license provisions, the copyright owner of a musical work could retain a monopoly on recordings of the musical work. With them, the copyright owner of a musical work only has that monopoly until the work has been recorded and distributed.

The compulsory license is borne out of the 1909 Copyright Act as part of a progressivist, trust-busting agenda (Schulenberg, 2005, p. 512). The design of the compulsory license provided a middle ground through which the public could access and use music for specific purposes without the consent of artists and copyright holders. In turn, copyright holders and artists would receive a just form of compensation. For the purposes of radio the most important application of the compulsory license has been in its acquisition of performance rights. The performance right is one of the rights generated when a song is written and needs to be acquired to play the song in public for nontheatrical purposes. Historically this is acquired through the purchase of a "blanket license," an annual purchase that allows venues to access an entire catalogue of music. In other words, like a blanket, the license "covers" the entirety of a catalogue. Venues and radio stations that are dependent on playing music in a nontheatrical manner purchase these licenses on an annual basis from PROs such as ASCAP and BMI. As mentioned earlier, webcasters are not immune to these payments and must send checks to these PROs to use the song catalogues they administer.

In the U.S., historically the performance right has only been offered to songwriters, often to be partially transferred to the publisher. Establishing a similar license in 1995 with the passage of Digital Performance Rights Act (DPRA), a performance right was also granted as an exclusive right "to perform the copyrighted work public by means of digital audio transmission" (Congress, 1995, 109 STAT. 336). However, the DPRA amended the Copyright Act of 1976 and established a performance right in the sound recording, thereby establishing, for the first time in U.S. history, a performance right to performers on the recordings. Modified by the DMCA in 1998 to establish a framework for a compulsory licensing schema for the application of the DPRA, webcasters had the federal licensing framework necessary for the industry to operate.[1] While clarity was one aspect that the law offered, it also demanded that webcasters purchase a compulsory license that would bring with it three significant issues. First, unlike terrestrial broadcasters, webcasters would be compelled by law to purchase two distinct performance rights: one for the song and the other for the recording. Second, unlike the compulsory licenses needed to acquire the performance rights for songs, those involving recordings would have their prices arbitrated by a government body rather than a negotiation between the programmer and the PRO for a blanket license rate. The difference between the webcaster and the broadcaster would extend further by the fact that the compulsory license for digital transmission is measured on a per-stream basis rather than on the basis of a market estimate. Finally, the compulsory license would only be effective if the funds could be adequately collected and delivered to those that had earned them, i.e., the recording performers. In the case of the performance right for songs, publishers developed the aforementioned PROs. The genius of the PRO is it acts as a clearinghouse for large numbers of publishers who want their wares' performance rights licensed. Instead of going to each and every publisher or songwriter to acquire a compulsory license for the performance right, the PRO acts as a one-stop shop for any vendor who wishes to purchase them. With the DMCA ratifying a compulsory license and assigning the responsibility for rates to the U.S. Copyright Office, the next question would be who would issue the bill?

The answer would come in the formation of another PRO. Initially formed in 2000 as an unincorporated division of the Recording Industry Association of America (RIAA), in 2003 SoundExchange became an independent entity. Exempt from taxation as a nonprofit corporation, SoundExchange incorporated in the State of Delaware as a 501(c)(6) "Collective Under Statutory License" with the Licensing Division of the United States Copyright Office (Anon., 2000b). Controlled by a board of artists, label executives, and other industry representatives, SoundExchange is unlike any other PRO in U.S. history. PROs devoted to the collection of song performance rights are member-driven, meaning that publishers are not compelled to join. Instead, publishers can choose a PRO or even decide to administer their own rights. On the other hand, SoundExchange's mission is mandate-driven. Because SoundExchange is the only PRO that exists to collect this new, Congressionally-mandated royalty payment, the organization receives payments for many performers who have no idea that they have earned these monies, let alone that they are entitled to a performance right (or even what a performance right is). This has been a sore subject for many musicians: because the U.S. Congress allows SoundExchange to absorb funds that have accrued but had gone unclaimed by performers after three years, a number of musicians and those that represent them have raised concerns about the organization. One attorney, Fred Wilhelms, called out to SoundExchange in a guest post in *Techdirt* where he complained about the organization's less-than-open communication practices about unpaid royalties and artists who were "missing" from their lists. Wilhelms' largest complaint was that the organization had done a consistently poor job of contacting artists and spreading the word about the thousands of artists that they could not contact. Particularly galling was that by using the list that SoundExchange provided on its website he had a fairly easy time contacting performers that the organization claimed that they couldn't find. Wilhelms explained that,

> people outside SoundExchange, like me and dozens of others, started contacting people on the list; cold calling them and telling them about SoundExchange. And an even funnier thing happened; the list began to shrink. All this time, SoundExchange was telling everyone how hard a job they were doing in finding people, with clearly limited success, and, lo and behold, an unfunded, uncompensated, grassroots effort was able to do what SoundExchange had failed. (Wilhelms, 2010)

Although the company had refused to absorb these escrowed funds, the complaints about SoundExchange continued. For example, in 2012 SoundExchange posted on its site that if performers had not registered with the organization by October 15, they could "risk losing any royalties collected three or more years" (Anon., 2012). The problem with this announcement was that a number of artists on the 2012 list of "unregistered artists" were anything but unfamiliar names. Indeed, as of early September 2012, recording artists and acts such as Skrillex, Bernie Taupin, Boston,

Billy Bob Thornton, Geto Boys, Rob Zombie, N.W.A., Steve Van Zandt, P. Funk, Fleetwood Mac, and President Bill Clinton were listed as unregistered (Resnikoff, 2012). As one blogger pointed out,

> there's one name on the list that is stunning: Gene Simmons. Simmons is famous for being focused almost entirely on getting money, even to the point of saying that artists should sue their fans. You'd think that somewhere along the line he'd notice that he should register with SoundExchange to get what's owed to him. (Masnick, 2012)

Despite these names, the same blogger noted that while these criticisms were legitimate, "having watched their efforts over the past few years, they really have done quite a lot to try to get artists to register" (Masnick, 2012).

While the criticisms remain, SoundExchange provides a clear, one-stop shop through which webcasters can purchase a compulsory license. As such, every webcaster, as long as they adhere to the DMCA and have purchased their compulsory licenses, could use practically any recording for their programming repertoire. Now the goal of a particular webcaster would be to find the most effective way to differentiate its services from the competition. For services dedicated to differentiating themselves from broadcasters through the production of niche services. How to best explore these niches through unique programming become the order of the day. In one case users decided to take advantage of the moment and in 2000 *The Philadelphia Inquirer* reported that fans of the defunct Philadelphia classical radio station WFLN-FM were forming the online service WFLN.com to stream classical music. In another example, students at The University of Pennsylvania would create and run WQHS.org for everyday streaming, thereby avoiding the many engineering and federal licensing issues necessary to acquire and maintain an over-the-air broadcast service (K.L. Carter, 2000). As a business model, Live365.Com's proposition that users could program these niches for each other was embraced by other services and by 2000 other webcasters such as OneSonicnet and netradio.com began to provide multiple, unique user-provided streams (Graham, 2000). In the case of Christmas programming, a December 2000 *Billboard* article reported that Live365.com offered more than 200 unique Christmas- and holiday-oriented streaming-audio shows with names such as "Women Out Loud Christmas" and "Gothic Christmas" (Saxe & Stark, 2000). Embracing his status as a user, a musician, and a label owner, Trent Reznor worked through his management to connect his label, Nothing Records, with Live365.com to deliver a "branded streaming music service" titled "radio nothing." Featured programming would highlight the label's catalogue and programming from the label's artists, staff, and fans with material such as "feature concert Webcasts and live broadcasts, Internet-only tracks, demos and works in progress, and sneak previews of upcoming major releases" (Anon., 2000a). By March 2001 Live365.com could sport 29,000 stations (Saxe, 2001).

Not every service decided to follow the user-generated path to programming. In 2000 RadioFreeVirgin.com established a service guided by the belief that "people want to be programmed to" and "In general, people aren't great programmers—if they were, they would do that for a living" (Saxe, 2000). Although RadioFreeVirgin.com closed in 2007, its disavowal of user-generated programming continues in the form of what is undisputedly the most popular and important webcaster in the United States, Pandora Radio. Founded in 2000 as Pandora Media, the service was an outgrowth of the Music Genome Project. While in August 2012 Pandora Radio could claim 6% of all United States radio listening, it has hardly had a primrose path to success(Atkinson, 2012). Running out of its first run of venture capital by 2001 and being "flat broke for about 2 1/2 years" much of the staff didn't take salaries. In 2004 the service hit two substantial turning points as it received new funding and hired Joe Kennedy as the company's CEO (Kessler, 2007). As a service, Pandora emerged as a service with a widespread 2005 launch that included a substantial experiment with freemium pricing. What distinguishes Pandora from its competition is the manner in which it explores niches and enables music discovery for its users. The distinct genius of the service is that it allows users to create a stream that is customized to their tastes with relative ease based on a combination of proprietary and user-generated data points. The process begins with a user entering a particular group or artist or song into the service. In return, the service offers a large, professionally-curated database of songs and artists. Since 2000 a team of volunteers (and eventually professionals) trained in music analysis have applied the Music Genome Project's proprietary method of categorization to a large and growing database of music. By 2005 the result was an "extraordinarily deep and detailed" database that, combined with the service's algorithms, provided an easy-to-explore service that allowed users to find "songs with similar melodic style, rhythms, and instrumentation" (Turnbull, 2005). Throughout the process, the interactions between the user and the Pandora database are the key to the process. If users hear an artist or a song that they like or do not like they are encouraged to "tag" the song with by clicking on a "thumbs up" or "thumbs down" icon that represents a positive or negative opinion, respectively. The combination of a sizable, curated database and a focus on the musical and sonic connections that tether one selection to another quickly made Pandora among the more popular mediums in the new media ecosystem to discover music. As such the system can provide the user a number of surprises. Writing for *The Oklahoman* in 2005, George Lang reported that when he initially tried the service he was impressed by Pandora's catalogue but found negotiating it something of an adventure:

> Early offerings were promising, including The Shins, Teenage Fanclub and Built to Spill, but then Pandora.com took some strange and unfortunate turns. Specifically, it tried to foist upon me Hootie and

the Blowfish and the poor man's Hootie, Sister Hazel, as well as a con-spicuously bland singer-songwriter named Geoff Byrd. I hit "thumbs down" as quickly as possible, prompting a sweeping qualitative uptick: Mercury Rev and Death Cab for Cutie showed up, along with lesser-known stylistic brethren such as Dios (Malos). (Lang, 2005, p. 8d)

A 2006 headline in *The Denver Post* perhaps explained how it programs best: "It knows what you like. Like a hip friend, the website Pandora.com wants to turn you on to sounds you might enjoy" (Wenzel, 2006, p. F01). One year after its widespread launch, 2006 became one of a number of "breakout years" for the service. In May 2006, Pandora reported that it had a base of 1.8 million registered users that skewed young (18–34) and male. Pandora was adding close to 300,000 to 400,000 listeners a month (Klaassen, 2006).

As part of Pandora's music experience, one of the advantages that the service touts is that it provides a way to minimize the influence of "other people's taste" in the design of a user's personal radio stations. Pandora is designed so that "music-liking becomes a matter decided by the listener and the intrinsic elements of what is heard" (Walker, 2009). According to a 2009 *New York Times* interview, so committed to listening before judg-ment, "early on, [Pandora's cofounder, Tim Westergren] actually pushed for the idea that Pandora would not even reveal who the artist was until the listener asked" (Walker, 2009). Westergren believed that this "struc-ture would give users a kind of permission to evaluate music without even the most minimal cultural baggage." This aversion to the social aspect of music discovery explains Westergren's dismissal of "hipster blogs" who often indict artists for committing the crime of popularity. For Westergren "that's just snobbery, based on social jockeying that has nothing to do with music" (Walker, 2009). To be sure, such a commitment to a "purer" discov-ery process is often celebrated by Westergren:

[Westergren] likes to tell a story about a Pandora user who wrote in to complain that he started a station based on the music of Sarah McLachlan, and the service served up a Celine Dion song. "I wrote back and said, 'Was the music just wrong?' Because we sometimes have data errors," he recounts. "He said, 'Well, no, it was the right sort of thing—but it was Celine Dion.' I said, 'Well, was it the set, did it not flow in the set?' He said, 'No, it kind of worked—but it's Celine Dion.' We had a couple more back-and-forths, and finally his last e-mail to me was: 'Oh, my God, I like Celine Dion.'" (Walker, 2009)

Westergren comments that while "his anecdote almost always gets a laugh," "Pandora doesn't understand why that's funny," which is an essential part of the service (Walker, 2009). These programming choices leave Pandora open for other associations and strange, often independent alliances. Because Pandora does not discriminate between major and minor label releases, independent musicians have found a platform upon which their releases have a competitive shot at airplay. The promise is that these "clairvoyant computers" could rescue independent artists by offering users a trusted technology that acts "like a good friend who knew your music tastes," "introduce[s] you to new bands and songs, but only those that you would most likely enjoy" (Leifer, 2006).

The trope that Pandora acts as a benevolent "techno-friend" that understands your personal needs is abundant in its early press releases. As mentioned earlier, in 2006 *The Denver Post* wrote that the customizable Internet radio stations that the service provided was "like a hip friend" (Wenzel, 2006). That same year *The International Herald Tribune* reported that one executive in the technology industry compared the experience Pandora created to "something like you're talking to the clerk at your favorite record shop" (Leeds, 2006, p. 11). Indeed, Pandora's ability to provide such close analysis and surprising recommendations provides what one user labeled a more "human approach," one that in the interface between the program and the user suggests that "we as human beings can intuit and understand something about music far beyond what computers can do" (Coddington, 2006, p. C1). This development of a customizable technology that provides an even more human sense of discovery positions the service firmly within the terrain of other user-generated musical guideposts and gatekeepers such as music blogs and review sites. As one media analysis company noted in a 2006 report, Pandora was part an emerging ecosystem that, by 2010, would drive around 25% of online music retail transactions. According to Mike McGuire, coauthor of the Gartner report, Pandora was part of a system of empowered fans that would lead to the "the slow death of programmed content" (Leeds, 2006, p. 11).

As important as the service's popularity was, Pandora also needed to evolve and has embraced a "Web 2.0" ethic that sees services and applications as never finished and existing in a state of "perpetual beta." Even as reporters and bloggers continually praised the early version of the service as a simple and reliable means to produce quality individualized stations, Westergren claimed that Pandora would find a way to become even more personable and user-friendly. In 2006 this meant three things: (1) continue to curate and tag new additions for Pandora's library; (2) work hard to make Pandora more than a laptop or desktop-only service by placing it on mobile devices; and (3) invest in an infrastructure that could disrupt terrestrial radio.

Although all three goals are discrete, each is deeply connected to and amplifies the other. For example, the importance of adding curation is fundamental to improving the experience Pandora provides its users, as well as adding to the infrastructure of choices needed to grow market share. Tim Westergren explained in 2011 that the collection was acquired through three processes: research of multiple sources (charts, reviews, historical research, etc.); the acceptance of submissions (from artists, labels, etc.);

and information gathered from listeners whose searches for artists and songs resulted in "misses." Throughout the curation process each song is analyzed with the question "Would this song enhance the listening experience for the audience who enjoys this kind of music?" applied to each piece (Westergren, 2011a). By 2011 the service claimed to have over 900,000 songs from over 90,000 different artists. And in October 2011, Tim Westergren claimed that "over 95% of those songs played on the service in July" (Westergren, 2011b). The acquisition and development of Pandora's catalogue has been part of a long-term strategy that not only emphasizes a quality experience for listeners to discover music but an ethical commitment to providing a space for undiscovered musicians in the marketplace. For Westergren, this kind of niche-oriented service may not help musicians "sell 50 million records, but they'll sell 50,000 and have a career" (Hutsul, 2006, p. C03). The combination of an expansive catalogue and a productive, niche-oriented discovery system would provide unknown artists a shot to find the exposure critical to make a living. In 2010 Westergren explained in an interview that "in the last year, 40 to 50 musicians have written to us and said, 'We are now making a living thanks to Pandora.' To me, that's just the most gratifying thing imaginable" (Harrington, 2010).

Just as Pandora consistently adds to its catalogue, the service has continued to add other features to make it more accessible. In 2009 Pandora worked with the music database service Gracenote to provide lyrics to a few songs in the Pandora catalogue for listeners to read as they played them (Linder, 2009). In the same year Pandora also integrated a "sharing toolbar" that allowed users to let other users know what they were listening to through their Twitter and Facebook accounts (Caceres, 2009). However, the service's most important changes would come in Pandora's search to tie its service to a growing field of mobile computing devices and services. Pandora's earliest search for mobility came when it struck collaborations with Sprint mobile telephone service and Sonos, a company that specializes in wireless home music systems (Rothman, 2007). Yet, by far the most important development for a more mobile Pandora was the 2007 introduction of the Apple iPhone. Soon after its introduction, third party developers found it easy to develop to the iOS platform and Apple soon after opened up its system to these third-party applications. Following this development Pandora began to develop to the iOS platform. The key for this platform was Apple's demand that iPhone users purchase significant mobile data plans and that the devices integrated with wireless Internet. The result was that Pandora could offer an app that could practically deliver program streams anytime and anywhere. It released its application on July 11, 2008, and by July 17, 2008 Pandora claimed it had streamed 3.3 million songs to iPhone users (Shields, 2008). Furthermore, the quality of Pandora's application was recognized when *Time* magazine named it as the iPhone app of 2008. By December 2009 Pandora would report that its iPhone app had 10 million registered users (Hendrick, 2009; Shar, 2009).

The rapid growth spurred on by the iPhone excited Pandora executives enough to believe that the company had finally found a path to profitability. For Westergren, "The iPhone single-handedly kicked off that phenomenon. It changed the way consumers think about what Internet radio is. You're no longer limited to thinking it's just a computer radio." In August 2009 Pandora confirmed that this shift was showing up in its research and it reported that 70% of those it considered to be "new members" were coming from those using mobile devices, particularly the iPhone (Evangelista, 2009). Eventually Pandora would develop to Apple's iPad, mobile devices running Google's Android operating system, Blackberry phones, and other domains that would permit the service such as televisions and DVD players. As Pandora developed it has consistently aimed to be a post-PC service. Westergren explained, "we are always looking at ways to expand our reach beyond the PC in order to make the service available to our users anytime and anywhere they want to listen to music" (Anon., 2009b). Such an approach could be ecumenical because Internet connectivity had continued to expand far beyond wired domains. The steady introduction of multiple modes of wireless connectivity combined with the increasing ubiquity of low-cost networked computers enabled what one reporter in 2010 referred to as a "device-agnostic" Internet (Van Grove, 2010). This meant Pandora would stream directly from multiple tablets, Roku television devices, and even a refrigerator developed by Samsung that included the service along with a number of other applications (Hampp, 2011).

Just as important as the quest for mobility was finding a place for Pandora in cars. Soon after the release of the Pandora iPhone application listeners began to plug their iPhones into auxiliary connection ports in the car stereos to use Pandora. By 2009, Pandora's Chief Technology Officer, Tom Conrad, noted that half of Pandora's mobile users listened to it in the car (Warren, 2009). Conrad's notes are particularly surprising given that in 2009 Pandora had yet to find its way on the dashboard of any American automobile sound system. Of course, this, too, was in Pandora's sights. In a 2010 interview Tim Westergren announced that his company was deep in the process of developing products both with car companies such as Ford and Mercedes, as well as "after-market stereo companies such as Pioneer and others" (Pham, 2010). Although Westergren acknowledged that the Pandora phone application was being used in the car, his company could not endorse this behavior due to the "safety concerns involved when you're driving and trying to control your phone at the same time" (Ibid.). Developing for the car was not simply an ethical move. Westergren explained that, "Simply put, half of radio listening happens in the car. People spend 20 hours a week listening to music; 17 hours of that is from radio. About half of that radio listening, or 8.5 hours, occurs while they're in a car. So that's the holy grail" (Ibid.). In short, a significant portion of the company's future would rest "in being able to control Pandora right from your steering wheel" (Ibid.). To go further into the market in March 2010 Pandora hired George Lynch, an employee of the leader of satellite radio, Sirius XM, for 11 years and its vice president of automotive partnerships beginning in 2004 (Peoples, 2010). By January 2011 Pandora had placed its application onto nine of Kenwood Corporation's new 2011 in-dash car stereo models (Palenchar, 2011). In July of the same year car manufacturers Buick, Chevrolet, Hyundai, GMC, and Toyota as well as other after-market stereo manufacturers like Alpine Electronics and JVC had established partnerships with Pandora (Merino, 2011). The importance of this investment cannot be underestimated and the effort behind establishing this foothold should not go ignored. Unlike a web or phone app where you can work with one platform at a time, developing for an auto manufacturer is a much more complex process. Pandora's executive vice president of business and corporate development, Jessica Steel, explained that working with even "a single car line for one automotive OEM (Original Equipment Manufacturer), there may be 3 or 4 suppliers that Pandora needs to work with to make the product work" (MacManus, 2011).

Pandora's investments in mobile phones and automobiles have been fundamental to challenging pre-existing radio infrastructures such as AM/FM and satellite broadcasting. A threat to Sirius' per-share values in the late-2000s and early-2010s, Pandora's ubiquity has often been cited as a problem for this fee-driven business (Anon., 2010). But by far the loudest concerns were voiced by established broadcasters who viewed Pandora and other "streamies" as a "threat to terrestrial radio" (Anon., 2010b). The biggest threat for terrestrial broadcasters was the fact that the behavior of young listeners was trending away from over-the-air radio stations to streaming radio. While terrestrial broadcasters began to make investments to stream their product, *Variety* reported that a 2010 study by Edison Research noted that "20% of respondents aged 12–24 had listened to Pandora in the past month, with all online streams of AM/FM radio reaching only 6%" (Barker, 2010, p. 15). Furthermore, those who did respond reported that they spent "nearly three hours a day on the Internet and a little over one hour listening to terrestrial radio," almost exactly the inverse amount of time that studies noted this demographic spent with Internet and radio 10 years earlier (Barker, 2010). Writing for *Huffington Post* in 2011, tech reporter Eliot Van Buskirk noted that the threat posed by smartphones had reached a critical point for FM'ers throughout the U.S. and that "the FM broadcasting trade magazine *Radio Ink* carried the following all-caps warning to FM stations: 'WARNING! WARNING! PANDORA TARGETING RADIO'S ADVERTISERS AND STATION CLUTTER.'" To make its case, Buskirk pointed out that the *Radio Ink* column included statistics about Pandora's growth and that "one out of every two American smartphones has the Pandora app installed on it" (Buskirk, 2011). So large was Pandora's growth and holdings that by 2011 its data problems demanded that it hire Gluster, a service that provides open source, scalable solutions to storage, to help manage its ability to deliver music to its more than 75 million register users in the U.S. (pyliana, 2011).

Pandora's sizable advantage in the online marketplace has not always established itself as the clear winner for every user. For some it was Pandora's lack of genre-specific channels, a popular feature that most American broadcasters provide. In 2010 Pandora addressed this and began to provide genre-oriented stations that curated relevant and fresh content for those who simply want to hear new country, jazz, hip-hop, etc. (Mickie, 2010). Other complaints were more difficult to remedy. For example, Pandora's automated discovery process left some listeners wondering what they had just heard: without a human or electronic DJ to back-announce songs, those using Pandora's mobile app in their cars would have to look at the screen and possibly compromise their driving safety (Pegoraro, 2009). Yet this was hardly Pandora's most significant problem. For all of Pandora's advantages, questions of marketplace success and the ability of radio streaming to deliver profits have plagued the industry from its beginning. As mentioned earlier, unlike over-the-air broadcasters, digital streamers have to purchase two compulsory licenses to the one compulsory license for the same piece of music that a broadcaster airs. Furthermore, broadcasters have at times offered artists (most of whom are independent) the opportunity to waive their performance rights in return for placing their records in over-the-air programs as a kind exchange for promotion. Critics of this exchange have pointed out that while this is not illegal, is technically questionable (Ulaby, 2007). Finally, as mentioned earlier, terrestrial broadcasters purchase "blanket licenses" from their PROs (in this case BMII, ASCAP, and SESAC) annually at prices determined through various criteria including market size. The key for the terrestrial broadcaster is that this once-a-year expense is a purchase around which budgets can be formed. However, this is not the case in the digital sphere. As mentioned earlier, unlike terrestrial broadcasters digital streamers are able to record every instance that a song is streamed and pay royalties on a per-stream basis. As a result, content acquisition can never occur in a way that creates an economy of scale for these services because unlike traditional broadcasters Pandora and other streamers see costs rise in direct proportion to audience usage.

What this means for Pandora and others in the webcasting industry is that any path to profitability is made more difficult by significant legal impediments. From its inception until summer 2011, Pandora ran on wave after of wave of venture capital. Although years of venture capital suggest that analysts believe in the long-term success of the service, Pandora's troubles with royalties have always been understood as a significant structural flaw that would have to be addressed. In many cases analysts saw this royalty issue as simply too insurmountable to guarantee its survival. For example, Pandora offers its service only to the U.S., New Zealand and Australia because multiple licensing issues have rendered most of its international efforts sterile (Evans, 2007). Nations where Pandora had been trying to establish legal beachheads such as Great Britain and Canada no longer seem viable. In the case, of Great Britain, after spending a significant amount of time and capital to enter the UK marketplace in 2007 Pandora had no choice but to walk away once the nation's Copyright Tribunal enforced a royalty rate of 6.5% for interactive webcasters and a compulsory minimum rate of .0085p per stream. Pandora's international managing director, Paul Brown, explained,

> Our business model works in terms of listener-hour revenue. So, every hour of music we stream to our listeners is an economic unit where we say, "how much can we earn per listener-hour from advertising revenues?" In a nutshell, 0.085p per track absolutely doesn't support the ad-supported web radio model, which is predominantly what webcasters are. (Benzine, 2007, p. 1)

Despite an attempt to work with the Copyright Tribunal, by the beginning of 2008 Pandora had closed its UK operations (N. Kelly, 2008).

While these international copyright issues halted Pandora's ability to grow internationally, the domestic threat of rising royalties was much greater. In March 2007, after 40 days of testimony, the Copyright Royalty Board (CRB) of the Library of Congress issued a ruling that would almost triple the amount of the per-stream statutory rate from less than a penny per user hour to $.03 per user hour. Tim Westergren called this decision "absurdly high" and explained that in 2006 Pandora paid $2 million in royalties, which would result in, at minimum, a $6 million bill for fiscal year 2007. In other words, 50% of Pandora's gross revenue would be lost thereby making its model "economically unsustainable" (Doyle, 2007). Westergren also noted that while his investors had no desire "to fund a business that has no long-term future," they were willing to fund a lengthy defense of their position and attempt to be heard on the need to rethink royalty rates (Bruno, 2008). Pandora immediately launched a public relations and lobbying campaign and reached out to the services' users to call their congressional representatives (Kessler, 2007). As webcasters across the U.S. began the process of filing with the U.S. Court of Appeals to delay the implementation of the rates, the public began to become more concerned about the loss of these services. The combination of the PR campaign and lobbying caught the attention of Senators Ron Wyden (D–Oregon) and Sam Brownback (R–Kansas), who cosponsored the Internet Radio Equality Act of 2007 to overturn the CRB decision and offer a new rate of 7.5% of a service's total revenues that would be mandated by Congress (N. Anderson, 2007). Although the legislation was ultimately abandoned, the demand that negotiations continue was heard loud and clear.

Perhaps the loudest complaint was not about the cost of the royalties, but the fact that terrestrial broadcasters did not have to pay any kind of performance royalty for musicians and performers. In interview after interview, Westergren decried the structural inequity as an injustice that determined who could win in the marketplace. When asked about this issue by *Billboard*, Westergren replied, "If I'm a legislator right now, there's no way I'd give power to [the CRB] to do to broadcast radio what they're doing to Internet radio. They've shown no level of responsibility with the existing rate that's wrecking Internet radio. I think they should show great pause before giving them that power in the context of broadcast radio" (Bruno, 2008). Indeed, a number of terrestrial broadcasters spent their time criticizing the CRB's decision. W. Russell Withers Jr., who oversaw 12 radio stations in Illinois, Kentucky, and Missouri as president of Withers Broadcasting Cos., explained to a U.S. Senate commerce committee in October 2007 that Internet radio was not a threat. Instead, the executive framed it as a complimentary medium that needed to be nurtured rather than punished by "unreasonable and debilitating" royalty rates (Doyle, 2007). At the same time Pandora reached out to the U.S. terrestrial broadcast giant Clear Channel, a company that, according to Westergren, is a service that did not "pay royalties on over 90% of what they broadcast." Pandora arranged for a simple trial with the company by adding a "Clear Channel station" to its offerings. In return, Clear Channel would act as a Pandora distribution partner and Clear Channel would "[pay] the licensing and [handle] the economics of it" (Bruno, 2008). As Westergren explained, "Companies like us are always wise to look at new distribution partners. If we can get Pandora in front of more people that's nothing but good" (Bruno, 2008). Perhaps more important was that this would get Clear Channel involved not only in webstreaming, but a larger discussion about the structural inequity of royalty payments between over-the-air and Internet radio.

By 2009, well over two years after the CRB offered its initial royalty rate decision, webcasters and the Royalty Board were able to negotiate a new rate that called for these services to either pay 25% of their revenue or a specific amount per song, starting at $.08 per stream, or whichever is higher. For webcasters with less than $1.25 million in sales the royalty rate would be between 12% and 14% of their revenues. While the structural inequity remained intact, Pandora believed that this reprieve offered the company the license to move forward and it accepted the terms.[2] At the same time, Pandora continued to grow at a rate of 50,000 to 60,000 new members a day and was expected to double its income to $40 million and had expectations of reporting its very first profit (Lewis, 2009). With Pandora's outlook appearing rosier, July 2009 brought the service another substantial influx of venture capital. Writing for *TechCrunch*, MG Siegler reported that "the Internet streaming radio service has raised a new $35 million round of funding." Although Pandora remained silent on the number, it did report that Greylock Partners, one of the oldest and most reputable venture capital firms in the United States, led the round and would join a prestigious set of already-existing firms investing in Pandora that included Crosslink

Capital, Walden Venture Capital, Labrador Ventures, King Street Capital, Hearst Corporation, DBL Investors, and Selby Ventures (Siegler, 2009).

As impressed as the investors were, there remained the substantial problem that Pandora's model was still not profitable. The service needed to find a way to grow profit margins and its options were limited to either lobbying for lower royalty payments, increasing revenue on a per-hour use basis, or both. With a royalty agreement achieved and an agreement that Pandora not lobby for a set period of time, Pandora would try capturing a larger share of advertising dollars, a task easier said than done. Writing for *Billboard*, Antony Bruno noted that webcasting's success would be a balancing act between "their pursuit of greater ad dollars with their need to manage user expectations." Furthermore, "the lack of advertising has long been one of the key attractions of Internet radio, along with the personalized listening experience that it offers. Whether the latter can trump the former will be crucial to retaining loyal users" (Bruno, 2009). Early in its history Pandora placed a focus on creating unique online advertising methods. In 2006, Pandora's VP of ad sales, Cheryl Lucanegro, explained the services' aim was to create and only charge for ads where the "listener is leaning forward and interacting with the site." Thus, as Lucanegro claimed, if a listener was "just leaning back and listening and not looking at the site, we're not refreshing the ads" (Klaassen, 2006). It is indicative of Pandora's devotion to a strategy of engaged contextualization where ads address and captivate listeners. Rather than creating ads that simply played in the background, Pandora was dedicated to bringing a user-centric focus to advertising. When asked about one standard ad metric for online impressions (cost per thousands or CPMs), Pandora CEO Joe Kennedy explained that advertisers would not find "a site where you see 15 ad banners and buttons simultaneously" but a different way of thinking about advertising:

> We built our ad model around any given moment. The advertiser gets a lot of advertisement to engage the consumer. We think that's really key because in the Internet world, a lot of people are focused on impressions but that's not really what an advertiser buys. Advertisers buy an opportunity to engage with a consumer. (Francisco, 2009)

The key to these ads rested in combining a highly customizable approach that would act as if Pandora gave the advertiser the "inside front cover of [a] magazine." The advertiser would "surround the [Pandora] experience with their ad," while Pandora would do all that it could to "preserve the user's experience" (Francisco, 2009). In some cases this preservation would come in the form of limiting the number of audio ads and, later, through campaigns that would do all they could to provide a specific context for the user. In 2010 Pandora reportedly targeted its then-60 million users with 500 simultaneous advertising campaigns involving 45 of the nation's top 50 advertisers. Westergren told *Billboard* that he felt like the company had finally "cracked the nut on how to effectively monetize a streaming radio service." The formula would involve building "a radio business that looks a lot like the traditional radio business," but with one significant and very important difference. Pandora would include,

> a scalable mechanism for selling national and local advertising so we can do everything from big, branded national campaigns to local pizza joint specials. They can be delivered as graphic ads, as audio ads, as video ads. We're pitching big ad agencies who have historically bought broadcast radio and pitching them to shift that money to the Web. (Bruno, 2010)

For example, among the station's offerings would be a "Blue Cross" station that streamed "workout music" sponsored by the health insurance company (Duck, 2010). 2010 also saw other first-time Pandora clients such as Walgreen's, Disneyland, Farmers Insurance, Allstate, Ford Trucks, Marie Callender's, and Verizon purchase "national audio, display and video buys." Perhaps most importantly, chains such as Whole Foods started to experiment with local ads that would take advantage of Pandora's "dynamic targeting capabilities" by streaming within a 30-mile radius of San Francisco and targeting women in their 30s. *Advertising Age* explained that, "This is where Pandora's promise of personalization really kicks in. Because Pandora knows all of its listeners' ages, demographics and ZIP codes when they register, the site was able to broadcast those ads only to the direct target" (Hampp, 2011, p. 82). Thus, when Pandora worked with the Simmons Jewelry team for a campaign, the service would provide a "lean-forward experience" that leveraged Pandora's "advertising platform and sizable user-base" to engage a "receptive audience" (Anon., 2010d). In the case of Whole Foods, its ad buy was so targeted Tim Westergren would claim that, "No man heard those ads, or if you were a 40-year-old woman, you wouldn't have heard it either, because you were outside the demo. We hear from 74-year-olds who say, 'I haven't heard an ad yet when I listen to you.' That's because we haven't targeted you yet" (Hampp, 2011, p. 82).

The aim of creating this kind of "intuitive audio" ad was to allay some of the fears that local advertisers have for digital and pry open a vast, untapped source of income (Hampp, 2011). One reason for the vast distance between webcast revenues and those of traditional over-the-air broadcasters is that webcasters had not yet found their way into most American's cars. Despite Pandora's alliances with car manufactures, this was a long-term strategy that had yet to take hold and left the webcaster still unable to take advantage of the drive time advertising hours that local advertisers value (A. Levy, 2010). However, more problematic was discovering how to connect to these local advertisers and explain to them that an ad purchased on a webcaster like Pandora can actually be a better use of their promotional budgets. This demanded tapping already-established reservoirs of trust to deliver the message and assembling a sales force who knew and connected with these buyers. In August 2009 *Billboard* reported that Pandora would again partner with Clear Channel Communications and engage its subsidiary for Internet ad sales, Katz Online Network. Along with handling terrestrial radio accounts, Katz also handles "advertising for such Internet radio services as AccuRadio.com, RadioIO and Digitally Imported" and would be able "take on a 'significant portion' of Pandora's digital audio advertising inventory" (Anon., 2009a). The director of audio sales at Pandora, Doug Sterne, stated that not only would Katz "represent us in our uncovered territories," but Pandora's then-small audio sales team of five people would "have access to Katz's 12 dedicated digital sales executives, plus the 200 Katz Radio account executives that also sell into the Katz Online Network." In return, Katz Radio would add 4 million more monthly visitors to its services through Pandora's huge user base, thereby growing its listener inventory almost 66% and making its experiments with geo-specific ad delivery even more successful. Brian Benedik, president of Katz 360, the digital sales arm of Katz Media Group, noted that the timing of the partnership was a driving force to come together as, "More advertisers understand the space and growth [of online radio] has been exponential. You're seeing four to five times the revenue going into the medium compared to last year [2008]" (Bachman, 2009).

Within a year reports emerged that Pandora was researching and targeting local advertisers with whom it wished to work. As Pandora's VP of sales, Brian Mikalis, explained, "We do research into who is advertising in the radio and local newspapers and will give those advertisers a call and let them know what opportunities are available on Pandora." Pandora would work with clients to develop Pandora-specific campaigns that could be highly targetable and offered at no additional cost to the ad buy (A. Ostrow, 2010). Mikalis explained that he was receiving so many inquiries from "small to mid-size businesses" that Pandora's premium sales staff was being overtaxed by the simple burden of fielding calls. The company soon responded with a new local sales staff that would be stationed in the company's Oakland, California headquarters. Mikalis committed to work with his local sales team to sell Pandora not so much as an online service but more like a "radio station" (Quenqua, 2010). By 2012 Pandora reported securing over 400 local marketing campaigns. One example included working with the Planet Honda dealerships of New Jersey who ran audio ads targeting adults 22 and older in specific New Jersey counties. Another campaign involved Wayne State University in Detroit, Michigan. The institution desired to provide information on admissions to a target audience without wasting its money on impressions it didn't want. Pandora provided an audience of teens from 13–17 and adults 18–24 in the metro regions of Detroit, Grand Rapids, and Toledo (Hess, 2012). Pandora's pitch to prospective clients is that its technology would target so effectively that every "dollar spent on Pandora [advertising] is better than a dollar spent on terrestrial radio" (Sisario & Vega, 2012 p. B4). Getting this message out has been the key to currying clients, some of whom discover other advantages to buying ads from the service. William Feinstein, the president of the previously-mentioned Planet Honda dealerships, started his relationship with Pandora with a $10,000 ad buy in January 2012. In less than four months Feinstein witnessed his web traffic quadruple and increased his buys to a total of $20,000. As important as the increase in web traffic, Feinstein pointed out that the buy was logistically much simpler than it would be working with terrestrial radio to get the same amount of geographic coverage: "we don't have to buy five radio stations. We can buy one" (Sisario & Vega, 2012 p. B4). With such geo-specific targeting capabilities in hand and a number of successful experiments behind his firm, Westergren began to hint that another Pandora service might come in the form of a geo- and taste-specific "tour promotion" and help address "the most important or second most important challenge for musicians—how to get people to come see you play live" (Shaw, 2011). In March 2012 Westergren provided specifics about how his company could provide such an innovation in his keynote address at "Re:Think," the Advertising Research Foundation's annual convention in New York City. Westergren explained that in at least one 2011 case, to target potential concertgoers Pandora had planned and promoted a successful concert featuring Aimee Mann at the Los Angeles venue Largo. To get the audience, Pandora listeners who had clicked a "thumbs up" for any of Mann's songs and lived within driving distance of the venue were sent messages about the event. Westergren's point was to show that this kind of targeting would allow promoters and marketers to put micro-targeted audiences and plan events in a way "that you really couldn't before" (Dostal, 2012).[3]

As important as these innovations may be, Pandora had still not reaped what it considered its "fair share" of advertising dollars. Speaking in November 2011, Pandora's CEO, Joe Kennedy, laid out the company's case onstage at *Billboard*'s "FutureSound Conference," explaining first that the current advertising market was between $13 and $14 billion dollars a year. As such, because Pandora had a 3.7% share of all U.S. radio listening, the service should be collecting close to $480 million a year in ad revenues. In stark contrast, its last fiscal quarter report of 2011 had ad sales at $66 million with a projected rate of $260 million a year. Finally, Kennedy argued, in the most bullish scenario, without any market growth Pandora should be able to double its sales numbers (Rosoff, 2011). Further aggravating Kennedy was the fact that research showed Pandora's substantially rapid growth in those demographics most desired by advertisers, adult listeners 18–34 and 18–29 in top local markets (Anon., 2011a, 2011b). So speedy was Pandora's growth that in early 2012 Kennedy proclaimed that Pandora would be "the largest radio station in each of the majority of U.S. markets" (Trager, 2012). Simultaneously, Arbitron, the United States' most prominent radio audience measurement service, continued to report that radio listening among younger audiences was declining with a majority of the decline would coming from FM broadcasters (Trager, 2012).

Still, Arbitron's good news was outweighed by the significant problem that as of 2012 Arbitron did not measure webstreaming radio. For buyers and sellers who purchased and sold audio ads Arbitron's measurements and reports remain the industry standard and act as the "neutral" ground floor for transactions. This was so problematic for Pandora that in May 2012 *Advertising Age* reported the company hired the measurement firm Triton Digital to report such measurement metrics needed to communicate the effectiveness of its service such as cumes and average-quarter-hour audiences using the service. The resulting numbers were impressive. Triton's reported that when comparing its numbers to Arbitron's, on a national level Pandora was the largest radio network for listeners age 18–49 (Del Rey, 2012).

The need to quickly grow ad income was no doubt spurred on by Pandora's preparation to become a publicly-traded company. As Pandora prepared its IPO filing, the service was forced to open up about its future plans and its vulnerabilities. *Variety* reported that although Pandora was clearly the leading webcasting service, nearly half of its revenues went toward paying royalties needed for content acquisition. Worse yet, Pandora "had losses of $328,000 in the nine months ending Oct. 31 [2010]" and their music licensing fees were "set to escalate over the next four years" (Lowry & Barker, 2011, p 5). Still, the considerable buzz that accompanies significant public filings such as Pandora's allowed the service to claim an initial valuation somewhere between $7 to $8 per share, i.e., $1.3 billion, in June 2011 (Lynley, 2011). When Pandora's stock went public the valuation rocketed and stock began to sell at $16 per share, resulting in an initial Wall Street valuation of $3.75 billion. This valuation came despite the fact that 2011 revenue estimates were $250 million for 2011 and there were no profits in sight (Brand, 2011).

These numerous structural problems have remained significant for the service and while Pandora's stock rose close to $20 per share in July 2011, by March 2012 the service treaded below the $10 range. As an analyst writing for the online business forum *VentureBeat* put it, the reason for the rapid devaluation was simple. The company's IPO opened with strong results that dwindled as many questioned its ability to turn a profit (Cheredar, 2011). Although investors pinned their hopes on the growth of ad revenues, this would take some time and its speed would be dependent on the long process of sales outreach to educate local advertisers about Pandora's ability to connect with audiences.

Even this outreach would not necessarily ensure profits as long as Pandora and webcasters could not solve those issues surrounding royalty payments that placed them at a significant disadvantage when compared to its broadcast brethren. Without this, doubts about Pandora's profitability simply would not go away. As *The New York Times* published a mixed analysis of Pandora's June 2011 IPO, that the company had severe structural problems that would hinder its ability to be profitable. Pandora's primary competition, AM/FM radio, still retained a significant amount of America's listening time. Furthermore, Pandora still did not have "the financial scalability of a Facebook" as "the more people who listen, the more royalties the company pays for music" (Goldfarb & Arnold, 2011). Without somehow addressing the issues behind these fixed costs, Pandora would remain a "good service but poor investment" (Sandoval, 2011). Perhaps *Variety*'s analysts put it best when they noted that the "IPO opens Pandora's box of questions." The near-term threat of royalty increases may have scared off investors, but as Chief Strategy Officer Tim Westergren explained, "We're thinking about years down the road. We're still only 3% of a huge category (total radio listening), so we don't really think about that in the near term."

While Pandora is so significant that it remains the only U.S. webcaster of note, even this position is hardly secure. Reports that Apple wanted to exploit its deep infrastructure purchase in music services with the intro-duction of a service called iRadio surfaced in 2012. In June 2013, Apple announced that the service would debut later that year. *Billboard* reported that the company had decided to avoid the purchase of compulsory licenses and establish a direct licensing agreement with both Warner Music and Universal Music Groups. In the case of the Warner Music Group, Apple simultaneously negotiated licensing deals with its recording labels and pub-lishers. In fact, reports indicated that both the agreements with labels and publishers alike included rates that were substantially larger than the com-pulsory licenses as well as percentages of any ad revenue that Apple was able to generate. Furthermore, these "multi-year contracts give Warner a guaranteed minimum amount of money rather than an advance" (Pham, 2013). The advantage of this type of direct agreement is that it would allow the service to become instantly global. Unlike Pandora, which had finally negotiated license rates with Australia and New Zealand, iRadio would have a potentially greater reach the minute it debuted (Peoples, 2013). Whether or not this would result in a profitable business, it had the ability of crowding an already confusing marketplace. As deep-pocketed services whose mobile devices and operating systems that can leverage pre-estab-lished contacts and agreements in the music industry, we may indeed soon see a Google or Amazon radio service soon. What this means for Pandora is uncertain. Indeed, the only thing certain for Pandora is that there will be anything but certainty for its near future.

BIBLIOGRAPHY

Anderson, N. (2007). Senate Hears the Internet Radio Blues, Takes Action. *Ars Technica*. Retrieved from http://arstechnica.com/tech-policy/2007/05/senate-hears-the-internet-radio-blues-takes-action/

Anon. The DMCA Rules. Retrieved November 3, 2012, from http://www.gomu-sic1.com/Upgrade/WebCasting/The_DMCA_Rules/the_dmca_rules.html

Anon. Why Am I Limited to 40 Free Listening Hours Per Month? Retrieved from http://blog.pandora.com/faq/contents/1555.html

Anon. (2000a, December 16). Merchants & Marketing Newsline. *Billboard*, 63.

Anon. (2000b). *Notice of Designation As Collective Under Statutory License.* Retrieved from http://www.copyright.gov/carp/notice-designation-collective.pdf

Anon. (2009a, August 22). Bits & Briefs. *Billboard*, 8.

Anon. (2009b, July 8). Prodea Systems Partners With Pandora Internet Radio, Bringing Their Personalized Music Service to the Prodea Systems Digital Life Command Center™ Service Delivery Platform. Retrieved from http://www.prodeasystems.com/events-press/2009–2/prodea-pandora/

Anon. (2010a). Jacobs Media: Pandora Presents Emerging Problem For Broadcast Radio. *Radio: The Radio Technology Leader.* Retrieved from http://radiomagonline.com/IT_technology/streaming/jacobs-pandora-problem-radio-0429/

Anon. (2010b). Pandora and Simmons Jewelry Co. Team in New Lifestyle Campaign. Retrieved from http://www.highbeam.com/doc/1G1–245558217.html

Anon. (2010). SIRIUS Financial Take: Howard Stern/Pandora Risks (SIRI, AAPL). Retrieved from http://247wallst.com/2010/01/22/sirius-financial-take-howardsternpandora-risks-siri-aapl/

Anon. (2011a). Pandora Posts November Listenership Results. Retrieved from http://www.highbeam.com/doc/1G1–274992659.html

Anon. (2011b). Pandora Publishes Latest Local Market Radio Ratings. Retrieved from http://www.highbeam.com/doc/1P1–198184803.html

Anon. (2012). Unregistered Artists. SoundExchange. Retrieved November 8, 2012, from http://www.soundexchange.com/performer-owner/does-sx-have-money-for-you/unregistered-artists/?search=Artanker#results

Atkinson, C. (2012, August 30). Facing the Music: Artists Protest Pandora's Proposed Royalty Fee Cuts. *The New York Post.* Retrieved from http://www.nypost.com/p/news/business/facing_the_music_1Gj3Do2NM1BSGOj92lQ6NJ

Bachman, K. (2009). Katz to Rep Pandora. *AdWeek.* Retrieved from http://www.adweek.com/news/television/katz-rep-pandora-113083

Barker, A. (2010, November 29). B'cast Radio Faces the Music; AM/FM Feeling the Squeeze As Internet Jukeboxes Branch Out. *Variety*, 15.

Barker, A. (2012, March 23). New Spotify Apps Boost Labels' Grip. *Daily Variety.*

Benzine, A. (2007, July 28). Pandora grabs UK lifeline. *Music Week*, 1.

Bordowitz, H. (2012). The Lost Audience: Pandora Founder on Music Discovery. *The Huffington Post.* Retrieved from http://www.huffingtonpost.com/hank-bordowitz/pandora-founder-on-music-discovery_b_1201820.html

Brand, C. (2011). Pandora IPO Reminds Us What 1999 Felt Like. Retrieved from http://www.peridotcapitalist.com/2011/06/pandora-ipo-reminds-us-what-1999-felt-like.html

Bruno, A. (2008). 6 Questions With Tim Westergren. *Billboard.biz.* Retrieved from http://www.billboard.biz/bbbiz/content_display/industry/news/e3i92f29f82847baa415a5ad5f2e12fd164

Bruno, A. (2009, July 25). Shake Your Moneymaker. *Billboard*, 121, 18.

Bruno, A. (2010, July 17). Pandora: Thinking Outside the Box. *Billboard*, 14–17.

Buskirk, E. V. (2011). FM Broadcasters Are Freaking Out About Pandora. Retrieved from http://www.huffingtonpost.com/eliot-van-buskirk/terrestrial-broadcasters-_b_897063.html

Caceres, C. (2009). Pandora Joins Social Media Bandwagon. Retrieved from http://vator.tv/news/2009–10–28-pandora-joins-social-media-bandwagon

Carter, K. L. (2000, March 26). Now the Net Is Becoming Radio Active. *The Philadelphia Inquirer*, I01.

Cheredar, T. (2011). Pandora Beats Analyst Estimates, Reports $67M Record Revenue. Retrieved from http://venturebeat.com/2011/08/25/pandora-reports-record-revenue/

Coddington, M. (2006, August 14). Pandora's Box of Musical Treats; Music Fans Are Turning to This Web Site to Get Turned on to New Rock Groups. *Buffalo News,* C1.

Del Rey, J. (2012, May 28). Pandora's New Data Not Turning Heads; Tired of Waiting on Arbitron, Streaming-Radio Firm Goes Elsewhere, But Buyers Say That's Not Key Issue. *Advertising Age, 83,* 3.

Digital Millennium Copyright Act. (1998).

Dostal, E. (2012). Pandora Founder Talks Targeting, Advertising in Keynote Address. Retrieved from http://www.dmnews.com/pandora-founder-talks-targeting-advertising-in-keynote-address/article/233915/

Doyle, T. (2007, October 26). Radio Execs Complain of New Royalty Rates. *SNL Kagan Media & Communications Report.*

Duck, B. (2010). BlueCross Feels The Need to Launch A Pandora Internet Radio Station? Marketing . . . Marketing . . . and More Marketing. . . . Retrieved from http://ducknetweb.blogspot.com/2010/10/bluecross-feels-need-to-launch-pandora.html

Evangelista, B. (2009, August 8). Pandora Bounces Back From Near Bankruptcy. *The San Francisco Chronicle,* DC1.

Evans, M. (2007). Sad Day For Internet Radio. Retrieved from http://www.markevanstech.com/2007/05/03/sad-day-for-internet-radio/

Francisco, B. (2009). Pandora Sees Revenue Up 80% This Quarter. Retrieved from http://vator.tv/news/2009–05–26-pandora-sees-revenue-up-80-this-quarter

Fridman, S. (2000, June 22). MP3 Summit: Innovation Is Key For New Devices. *Newsbytes.*

Goldberg, A. (1999, October 14). Internet Discovers the Allure of Sound. (News Agency Article). *Deutsche Presse-Agentur.*

Goldfarb, J., & Arnold, W. (2011, June 6). Listen Carefully For the Sour Notes. *The New York Times,* 2.

Graham, J. (2000). You Turn it On: It's a Web Radio Tailored to Your Tastes. *USA Today,* 3D.

Ha, A. (2011). Pandora Looks Beyond Music to Sports and Talk Shows. Retrieved from http://venturebeat.com/2011/02/11/pandora-ipo-future/

Hampp, A. (2011, January 17). Fridges, Fords and Phones: How Did Pandora End Up in Everyone's Box?; On the Brink of Bankruptcy As Recently As Four Years Ago, It's Become the De Facto Radio App For Virtually Every New App-Enabled Device. *Advertising Age, 82.*

Haring, B. (2000, February 29). Protected or Locked Put? Foes of Copyright Act Say It Hampers Net's Growth. *USA Today,* 3D.

Harrington, J. (2010). Thinking Inside the Box: Pandora Reinvents Internet Radio. *Contra Costa Times.* Retrieved from http://www.highbeam.com/doc/1P2–21223060.html

Hendrick, D. (2009). Pandora Passes 40 Million Users. *SNL Kagan Media & Communications Report.* Retrieved from SNL Kagan Media & Communications Report website.

Hess, S. (2012). Pandora Local Radio Ads and Larger Audience: Interactive Music Service Is Tracking Usage and Releasing Numbers on a Monthly Basis. Retrieved from http://www.webpronews.com/pandora-local-radio-ads-and-larger-audience-2012–04

Hutsul, C. (2006, February 13). An Awesome Way to Hear New Music. *The Toronto Star,* C03.

Kelly, N. (2008). The Day The Online Music Died. . . . *Computing,* 6. Retrieved from http://www.computing.co.uk/ctg/analysis/1845169/the-day-online-music-died

Kessler, M. (2007, May 23). Net Radio Faces Swan Song If Fees Increase; Rising Royalties Could Kill Stations Like Pandora. *USA Today,* 5B.

Klaassen, A. (2006, May 3). Advertising Age. *Find Music That's Just Your Style*, 76.

Kong, D. (1999, November 4). The Internet Can Turn Music Lovers Into DJs. *The Philadelphia Inquirer*, F01.

Lang, G. (2005, October 28). Web-Based Radio Station Personalizes Playlists. *The Oklahoman*, 8D.

Leeds, J. (2006, September 6). Music Fans Become Their Own Gatekeepers. *The International Herald Tribune*, 11.

Leifer, A. (2006, January 20). Clairvoyant Computers Come to the Rescue. *The Stanford Daily*.

Levy, A. (2010, October 20). Pandora Pursues Drive-Time Radio After Capturing Mobile Market. *The Pittsburgh Post-Gazette*, E2.

Lewis, H. (2009). Pandora No Longer on Verge of Collapse, Set to Be Profitable Next Year. *The Business Insider*. Retrieved from http://articles.businessinsider. com/2009–05–19/entertainment/30094802_1_pandora-tim-westergren-ads

Linder, B. (2009). Pandora Internet Radio Adds Lyrics . . . For Some Songs. Retrieved from http://downloadsquad.switched.com/2009/04/02/pandora-internet-radio-adds-lyrics-for-some-songs/

Lowry, T., & Barker, A. (2011, February 14). Pandora Opens Up on Risks. *Variety*, 5.

Lynley, M. (2011). Online Radio Pandora Claims Valuation of $1.3B. Retrieved from http://venturebeat.com/2011/06/02/pandora-ipo-valuation/

MacManus, R. (2011). UX Evolutions: Pandora Inside Cars. Retrieved from http://www.readwriteweb.com/archives/ux_evolutions_pandora_inside_cars.php

Mann, I. (2009, August 23). Today's Free Means Megabucks. *Sunday Times*.

Masnick, M. (2012). SoundExchange, Once Again, Warns Artists That If They Don't Register, It Might Keep Their Royalties. Retrieved from http://www.techdirt.com/articles/20121012/12292520690/soundexchange-once-again-warns-artists-that-if-they-dont-register-it-might-keep-their-royalties.shtml

Merino, F. (2011). Pandora Teams With Scion, Breaks 100M User Mark. Retrieved from http://vator.tv/news/2011–07–12-pandora-teams-with-scion-breaks-100m-user-mark

Mickie. (2010). Pandora Launches Genre Specific Radio Stations. Retrieved from http://mickieszoo.blogspot.com/2010/08/pandora-launches-genre-specific-radio.html

Ostrow, A. (2009). Internet Radio Gets a New Deal; Pandora Adjusts Accordingly. Retrieved from http://mashable.com/2009/07/07/internet-radio-deal/

Ostrow, A. (2010). Pandora Brings Mobile Advertising to Small Businesses. Retrieved from http://mashable.com/2010/10/18/pandora-mobile-small-business/

Palenchar, J. (2011, January 6). Kenwood Adds Pandora Control to 9 Heads. *Twice, XXVI*, 1.

Parr, B. (2011). Pandora Adds 10,000 Comedy Clips to Its Archives. Retrieved from http://mashable.com/2011/05/04/pandora-comedy/

Pegoraro, R. (2009, May 31). Web Radio Hits the Road. *The Washington Post*, G02.

Peoples, G. (2010, November 6). Car Market Merges Ahead. *Billboard*.

Peoples, G. (2013). Business Matters: Apple iRadio's Licensing vs. Pandora's Licensing. *Billboard*. Retrieved from http://www.billboard.com/biz/articles/news/digital-and-mobile/1565657/business-matters-apple-iradios-licensing-vs-pandoras

Pham, A. (2010). Pandora's Tim Westergren Goes After Radio Where It Matters Most: The Car. Retrieved from http://latimesblogs.latimes.com/music_blog/2010/10/pandora-goes-after-radio-where-it-matters-most-the-car.html

Pham, A. (2013). Warner Music Group Inks iRadio Deal For Publishing, Recorded-Music Licensing. *Billboard*. Retrieved from http://edit.billboard.com/biz/

articles/news/digital-and-mobile/1565596/warner-music-group-inks-iradio-deal-for-publishing

Pham, A., & Guynn, J. (2010, September 3). Company Town; Music Labels Tuning in to Google; Firms Eager For a Digital Service That's Not iTunes Are in Talks With the Web Giant. *The Los Angeles Times,* B1.

pyliana. (2011). Gluster to Help Manage Data Growth for Pandora. Retrieved from http://jobincapriga.blogspot.com/2012/02/gluster-to-help-manage-rapid-data.html

Quenqua, D. (2010). Pandora Goes After Local Advertisers. Retrieved from http://www.clickz.com/clickz/news/1713828/pandora-goes-after-local-advertisers

Resnikoff, P. (2012). Unbelievable: The Following Artists Are Not Getting Paid by SoundExchange. . . . Retrieved from http://www.digitalmusicnews.com/permal ink/2012/120904soundexchange

Rosoff, M. (2011). Pandora Wants Its "Fair Share" of Ad Dollars. Retrieved from http://articles.businessinsider.com/2011-11-17/tech/30409310_1_mobile-ads-advertisers-ad-sales

Rothman, W. (2007). Pandora Hits Sprint Phones and Sonos Remotes. Retrieved from http://gizmodo.com/262741/pandora-hits-sprint-phones-and-sonos-remotes

Sandoval, G. (2011). Pandora, a Good Service But Poor Investment. *CNET News.* Retrieved from http://news.cnet.com/8301-31001_3-20071325-261/pandora-a-good-service-but-poor-investment/

Saxe, F. (2000, August 5). Streaming Sites Promise Evolution—Some Warn Traditional Stations Must Expect Competition. *Billboard, 93,* 96.

Saxe, F. (2001, March 24). Programming Newsline. *Billboard,* 65.

Saxe, F., & Stark, P. (2000, December 23). Programming Newsline. *Billboard,* 65.

Schulenberg, R. (2005). *Legal Aspects of the Music Industry: And Insider's View of the Legal and Practical Aspects of the Music Business.* New York: Billboard Books.

Shar, G. (2009). Dockers Pockets BlackBerry Pandora Marketing With Discount Code. Retrieved from Wireless and Mobile (WiMo) News website.

Shaw, L. (2011). Pandora's Westergren at The Grill: Is Tour Promotion Next? Retrieved from http://www.thewrap.com/media/column-post/pandora-co-founder-westergren-thegrill-tour-promotion-next-31154

Shields, M. (2008, July 17). Pandora's Success With iPhone Bodes Well For Internet Radio. *Adweek.*

Siegler, M. (2009). Confirmed: Pandora Raises a Huge Round, Post Streaming Rate Agreement. Retrieved from http://techcrunch.com/2009/07/10/confirmed-pandora-raises-a-huge-round-post-streaming-rate-agreement/

Sisario, B., & Vega, T. (2012, April 16). Pandora Courts Local Advertisers, by Offering Well-Defined Listeners. *The New York Times,* B4.

Trager, L. (2012). Pandora Eyes Beating All Stations in Most U.S. Markets, CEO Says. Retrieved from http://consumerelectronicsdaily.com/Content/Pandora-eyes-beating-all-stations-in-most-US-markets.aspx

Turnbull, G. (2005). E-Business : Pandora Has a Box of Tricks That Might Just Interest Everyone. *Birmingham Post,* 22. Retrieved from http://birmingham-post.vlex.co.uk/vid/pandora-box-tricks-interest-everyone-69889678

Ulaby, N. (2007). Clear Channel: Swap Exposure For Royalties. Retrieved from: http://www.npr.org/templates/story/story.php?storyId=11250011

U.S. Congress. (1995). *Digital Performance Right in Sound Recordings Act of 1995.* Washington, DC.

Van Grove, J. (2010). 6 Tips on Starting a Digital Business from the Founder of Pandora. Retrieved from http://mashable.com/2010/10/14/digital-business-tips/

Walker, R. (2009, October 18). The Song Decoders. *The New York Times Magazine*. Retrieved from http://www.nytimes.com/2009/10/18/magazine/18Pandora-t.html?pagewanted=all&_r=0.

Warren, C. (2009). Your Next Car Radio Might Be Pandora. Retrieved from http://mashable.com/2009/12/08/pandora-car/

Wenzel, J. (2006, May 16). It Knows What You Like: Like a Hip Friend, the Website Pandora.com Wants to Turn You On To Sounds You Might Enjoy. The Marriage of Music and Technology Doesn't Always Succeed in Predicting Users' Tastes, But It's Got a Lot Going For It. *The Denver Post*, F01.

Westergren, T. (2011a). How Does Pandora Determine Which Songs to Include in Its Database? In Other Words, What Is Their Curation Process? Retrieved from http://www.quora.com/Pandora-Radio/How-does-Pandora-determine-which-songs-to-include-in-its-database

Westergren, T. (2011b). How Many Songs Are in Pandora's Database? Retrieved from http://www.quora.com/How-many-songs-are-in-Pandoras-database

Wilhelms, F. (2010). Responding to SoundExchange ... By Their Numbers. Retrieved from http://www.techdirt.com/articles/20100107/1632237663.shtml

5 Radio on the TV
Music Supervision Taken Seriously

Everyone in my dorm watched that show, and each episode had a really different range of music. As soon as the episode was over they had all the songs listed in the website, and a few minutes later you could be listening to it on your hard drive. You couldn't buy it or download it from their website, but you could obviously find it somewhere else. They played Death Cab. They played Spoon. They played Rooney, Phantom Planet. They played Modest Mouse before Modest Mouse was getting played on the radio. They had the Killers on before the Killers even started getting out there. It was stuff that really wasn't getting played a lot or at all on the radio. That's how I know a lot of people got into Death Cab. It's kind of silly, but the way they used music was totally cool. Sometimes you'd watch and you'd tune out the scene. You were just listening to this song and it'd be like, 'Oh, God, What's that? I need this.' (Maggie, a sophomore at Marquette University in Milwaukee when *The O.C.* debuted[1])

Debuting in 2003 on the Fox Network, the United States began what would be a brief but intense four-season love affair with the American teen drama, *The O.C.* As with other teen dramas, issues such as insider/outsider status, emerging sexuality, and class distinctions found their place in a narrative where adolescents and their attendant spaces of bedrooms, high schools, and parties explore their audience's collective pathos. Unlike other teen dramas of the time, Josh Schwartz, the program's producer, would hire Alexandra Patsavas as his music supervisor to look at his music budget not as a means of acquiring background sounds, but as an essential element of his storytelling process. According to Patsavas in a 2006 interview, "Josh Schwartz always intended for music to be a character." Patsavas said "it's up to me to help him find the artists, both on camera and for source and theme music, to support the drama" (Trakin, 2006, p. S9). With Schwartz and Patsavas as both "self-described music nerds," the relatively small licensing budgets of the new program "made it imperative to seek out music that wasn't on the mainstream radar—Patsavas's specialty." For *The O.C.*, "the music that [best fit the program had] an indie sensibility: stuff that's innovative, different, that hasn't been overplayed and overhyped." Patsavas explained, "I didn't need to find twelve good songs. I needed a great song to fit a scene, and it doesn't matter where it came from. There's a lot of freedom in that" (Kot, 2009, p. 76). Patsavas' freedom to discover new music from various sources was also complimented by *The O.C.*'s corporate connection to Warner Bros. Records. As a Warner Brothers television show,

The O.C. mined a connection that allowed the program to introduce five new songs from Beck's then-forthcoming *Guero* record in a 2005 episode. The program also worked with Warner Bros. Records to release a series of *The OC Mix* soundtracks and a website listing the songs appearing in each episode "linking to the individual bands' music, as well as its own iTunes space." Put simply by Patsavas, "The audience discovers new artists on *The OC*" (Trakin, 2006, p. S9).

While this type of synergy may seem obvious, it could not be accomplished without the specific skills of Patsavas and others like her. In his work on media convergence and transmedia storytelling, Henry Jenkins points out that, "Political economists and business gurus make convergence sound so easy. But from the ground, many of the big media giants look like great big dysfunctional families, whose members aren't speaking with each other and pursue their own short term agendas even at the expense of other divisions of the same companies" (Jenkins, 2006, pp. 7–8). This is why Patsavas' skillset has become so vital. As Patsavas states, "Music supervision, at its core, is really about helping the producers define a sound for their show." As Jon Burlingame noted in a *Daily Variety* article, "that [music supervision] means not only supplying from three to nine songs an episode for each series she handles, but negotiating the prices and red tape to clear them with artists, labels and publishers" (Burlingame, 2006, p. A18). Patsavas' skillset emerged from a past as a fan of independent and alternative rock and continued to grow as she booked rock shows while at the University of Illinois at Champaign–Urbana in the 1980s. After leaving college Patsavas began working for a BMI music agency, and later provided music supervision for over 50 Roger Corman productions and numerous made-for-television movies. In 1999 Patsavas opened her own business, Chop Shop Music Supervision, ready to act as a licensing liaison for Hollywood (Kot, 2009, p. 76). Since founding Chop Shop, Patsavas' standing has slowly grown from learned negotiator to something of an aesthetic impresario in her own right. Working on series such as *Roswell*, *Boston Public*, and *Criminal Minds*, Patsavas grew her business throughout the early 2000s until she began her more celebrated work on *The O.C.*, *Grey's Anatomy*, and *Mad Men*. By December 2010, *Billboard* would list Patsavas as the fifth most important woman in the music business (Anon., 2010b).

As Patsavas' Chop Shop has grown in stature, so has its reach. In 2007, Patsavas announced that she would be launching her own label, also named Chop Shop. Working with the Warner Music Group, the idea was "first broached in a meeting with Atlantic president Julie Greenwald at the Coachella music festival." According to Patsavas, "a label seems like a natural extension of what a music supervisor does. . . . You can come across things very early, and there have been bands along the way I would have loved to have worked with more closely." In essence, what Patsavas describes when she notes how she "can come across things very early" is an

A&R function that has been a longstanding element for the music industry. As Atlantic Records GM/executive VP of new media Livia Tortella put it, "We realized really quickly that how she picks music for shows is very unique and very different. She really gets into the psyche of her characters—she has an innate A&R ability. She has ears" (Donahue, 2008b). Focusing on indie rock, Chop Shop looked to "be an extension of the kinds of artists that have been featured on 'The OC' and 'Gray' soundtracks. Many of those artists have been unsigned or signed to small labels" (Garrity, 2007a, p. 3). While how much "synergy" would occur from this arrangement of label and music supervision shop was unclear at the beginning, it was clear that Patsavas would most likely "gravitate to acts she views as 'syncable'" (Garrity, 2007b, p. 9). For example, one year after scoring a sync placement on the Patsavas supervised program *Gossip Girl* in 2007 the band, Republic Tigers, signed to the Chop Shop label. As *Billboard* reported, the act was offered what the label offered all of its acts: "[they would] be top of the list for music placements in the TV shows and films she and her team supervise" (Donahue, 2008b). That same year *Billboard* also noted that Patsavas had signed The Little Ones with the promise that the band's records could find better promotion through television syncs such as the one they received on a 2007 episode of *Gossip Girl*. One of the band's cofounders, Ed Reyes, noted that Patsavas being a music supervisor made the label that much more attractive. For Reyes, "Music is discovered through different channels now. Kids might hear us in a TV show—that's the new way of the digital age" (Wood, 2008, p. 58).

It may seem counterintuitive that placing a song on television would be the "way of the digital age," however, as this chapter argues this is not the only odd aspect of the music supervisor in the 21st century. Once a below-the-line facet of the film and television community who dealt with the even less-glamorous, back-of-the house "special products" divisions where most record companies ran their licensing operations, the once lowly position of the music supervisor has blossomed into a sometimes above-the-line consideration in this age of digital convergence. Once considered a minor credit, the music supervisor has become ever-more important in this new media ecosystem because of the position's close association with taste, licensing, and clearance. In a multichannel universe with ever-increasing programming options, gaining the ear of a well-placed music supervisor has not simply become important, but a key to breaking new music. The rise of the music supervisor is also indicative of three specific changes in music industry systems as they have responded to a climate of crisis and change: the reassertion of the role of publishing in the music industry, the change of what it means to be a "record label," and the strategic need for media branding in a new media environment. This chapter examines the rise of the music supervisor from a once obscure credit to a position of significant power in this new media ecosystem. Throughout I focus on the trade discussions about the practices and practitioners that have changed the profession. Furthermore, these practices and practitioners are placed in a context of new actors, technologies, and industrial demands that have changed and affected music licensing and consumption.

Let's begin with Jeff Smith's 2001 article, *Taking Music Supervisors Seriously* (J. Smith, 2001), a paper which succinctly sums up how relatively disregarded the status of the trade was at the turn of the century. After conducting a number of interviews in the 1990s, Smith summed up the general disdain and antagonism held toward the profession at the time:

> Margot Core (*Big Night*, *Mickey Blue Eyes*) told me that several directors with whom she worked regarded her as little more than a clerk or administrative assistant, whose only task was to fulfill their will regarding the kind of music that appears in their film. If this is indeed true, then it would appear that in most productions, music supervisors are caught in the proverbial middle. Since supervisors are generally responsible for any music in the film that is not orchestral score, composers treat them either as corrupt agents of record companies or as despotic representatives of directors and producers. At the same time, however, directors typically treat music supervisors as a necessary evil, one of the many industrial constraints and encumbrances that potentially conflict with the director's own artistic agenda. Of course, what makes the music supervisor's position doubly interesting is that other industry craft persons are generally not treated with the same sense of contempt. Although it is always difficult to imagine one treating a cinematographer, production designer or even a composer as a mere clerk (J. Smith, 2001, pp. 125–126)

Even in an era of relative respect where music supervision has moved from below-the-line to above-the-line status, one of the more respected music supervisors in Hollywood, Randall Poster, admits that the supervisor's job is still sometimes devalued: "a lot of people think they can do music supervision just because they love music, and the job can be something of a dilettante's lair" (Crisafulli, 2007).

Still the importance of the supervisor rose drastically in the early portion of the 2000s, a fact observed in a 2003 issue of *Electronic Musician*, a monthly magazine aimed at musicians and producers:

> the change is due largely to a timely convergence of three major factors. Most important is the explosion of cable TV, which has created a huge demand for content to fill the programming hours. That in turn has created a huge boom in all types of content production, from shot-on-DV reality shows to traditional film-based productions—all of which need music. On your side of the fence, the low cost of high-quality recording equipment has created an unprecedented supply of master-quality recordings looking for a home. Finally, there is the limited

music budget that most of these productions now have. Producers of every show would love to have songs by big-name stars but simply can't afford them. (Adams, 2003, p. 8)

As a result of these changes producers turned to a number of agents such as publishers, licensing agents, music libraries, and, of course, music supervisors to use these properties (Adams, 2003). And as popular music has become increasingly prominent throughout television programming, the demand for it has grown. To quote Billy Gottlieb, music supervisor for the crime drama *Bones*, "It used to be the bastard stepchild—the last thing a studio wanted to do was put extra money into the music. But now there's an expectation that audiences want to hear new music and not some standard needle drop" (Whitmire, 2005, p. 33). This expectation has meant that the most significant elements of the music industry have looked at music supervisors as new positions that they need to acquire and develop. In 2010 the British trade magazine *Music Week* reported that Sony aimed to capitalize on the "valuable source of income" that sync licenses represent and hired veteran music supervisor Ian Neil for the corporation's newly created position, "director of music for film, TV, advertising and computer games." Noting that sync licensing had become much more important than it was in the past, Neil was quoted as stating that "the difference between now and 10 years ago is that now every managing director wants to know what you are doing and the international guys and marketing men too because sync generates a lot of money" (Ashton, 2010).

To be sure, sync income is part of the reason majors have looked to music supervisors. The other half of this story, as noted earlier, is the exposure a record receives when it is played in film and television programming, a factor which is the result of the manner in which broadcast radio was altered in the United States beginning in the 1990s. The changes that took place after the passage of *The Telecommunications Act of 1996* made it easier to acquire and consolidate radio stations, which made it even more difficult for more artists to find their way onto their playlists. Such consolidation was met with the growth of satellite and Internet radio, and developments in mobile electronics such as the iPod made broadcast radio an even less attractive option for a growing number of listeners, particularly younger ones. According to Joel C. High, music supervisor for *Little Britain USA* and *Madea Goes to Jail*, whereas radio used to be the way to best promote and break records into the marketplace, "Now if you put something to good use in a big motion picture, more people are going hear that song than if it's played on a few stations in some sort of rotation. And those people will then go to a Web site to find that music, thanks to the rise of the Internet." The result, according to High, is that "music supervisors have really come into their own in terms of being tastemakers" and "now music supervisors are one of the surest ways to help break records" (Mitchell, 2010, p. 35).

With the ability to generate sales came respect and media. Indeed, the role of the music supervisor has become something of a celebrity role with celebrities themselves sometimes taking the position. As labels searched for a way to replicate the multiplatinum success of the soundtrack to *The Bodyguard*, studios offered musicians such as Courtney Love, John Cale, and David Byrne an "opportunity to flirt with moviemaking" and entice them and other "frontline musicians to take an occasional walk below the line" (Arkoff, 1995). However, this "walk below the line" became an above-the-line opportunity when in 2006 MTV looked to Chris Carrabba, the frontman for Dashboard Confessional, to act as "guest music supervisor" for the reality program *Laguna Beach*:

> Carrabba, whose own music has been featured in several previous "Laguna Beach" installments, is overseeing scoring of the episode and handpicked four tracks that will be included in the show. The songs Carrabba selected are "Ageless Beauty" by Stars, "This Isn't Farmlife" by Essex Green, "Lloyd I'm Ready to be Heartbroken" by Camera Obscura and "Pin Your Wings" by Copeland. In addition, a Dashboard Confessional track "Currents" will also be featured in the episode. (Garrity, 2006, p. 8)

While MTV wouldn't "aggressively market" Carrabba's stint as a supervisor before the episode airs, the network flagged the end of the show to alert viewers to his role and that the tracks were available for online purchase. Still, not all of Carrabba's picks made the program. Carrabba chose 20 songs, "the majority of which were left out." As Carrabba joked, "I learned that they are not programming to what I like exclusively" (Garrity, 2006, p.8). Further respect began to appear in other forms of media such as radio programming. Writing for *The Hollywood Reporter*, Ada Guerin noted in 2006 that "the delicate art of music supervision finally is beginning to receive the recognition it has long deserved" as Indie 103.1, a popular Los Angeles alternative-rock station, recently began devoting "three minutes of its daily airtime to Amanda Scheer-Demme, a veteran music supervisor responsible for such groundbreaking soundtracks as 2004's *Garden State* and *Mean Girls*." As a set of three-minute spots, the segment titled "The Reel Minute" aimed to "educate" by illustrating how movies and music are mutually dependent (Guerin, 2006). The growing respect accorded to musicians and composers by filmmakers was a trend of mutual appreciation where filmmakers could work with music supervisors for greater aesthetic impact and musicians could find another position in the marketplace for both licensing and promotion. As Matt Shay, then VP of A&R and marketing at RCA Music Group pointed out in 2007, "a film placement can bring an artist attention it might otherwise take years to cultivate." Epic marketing VP Scott Carter made it even clearer: "*Garden State* was almost like an hour-and-a-half-long commercial for the soundtrack" (Paoletta, 2007c).

There really is no question that a band like The Shins benefited commercially from their inclusion in the *Garden State* soundtrack. While Natalie Portman's character tells Zach Braff that their song "New Slang" would "change your life," the film most definitely altered The Shins' career. According to Sub Pop licensing VP Jen Czeisler, "That was definitely a turning point. In this case, sales of *Oh, Inverted World*—a record that at that time was already 3 or 4 years old—went through the roof." Moving over 500,000 copies, *Oh, Inverted World*'s post-*Garden State* success at a time of across-the-board collapse in sales was promising, yet one with no guarantee. As Czeisler also noted, "Sometimes you license something to a soundtrack and you don't really see an effect on sales" (Paoletta, 2007c). Trying to discover what practices do and do not work, the role of the music supervisor was a one-day theme for the fall 2007 "Hollywood Reporter/ Billboard Film & TV Music Conference," a first for the annual affair (Anon., 2007a). Focusing on what was then a loose community of practitioners, discussions centered on the limits of representation by a guild. Starting at the previously mentioned conference's "town hall" luncheon in November 2007, talks of such an organization began. Reporting for the Hollywood reporter, Chuck Crisafulli noted,

> one worthy advocate for the cause is music supervisor Maureen Crowe, who, as a recent president of the Los Angeles chapter of NARAS, helped secure RIAA voting rights for music supervisors (a right they have yet to be granted within the film and television academies). "I think it's important for us to lay out some parameters of the job and let the industry know what the expectations of service should be," says Crowe. "It's nice if somebody knows their way around iTunes, but that's not music supervision. When you bring in a true music supervisor, a project moves to another level, and a supervisor who can help a project out creatively, financially, legally and in terms of efficiency—a music supervisor who can help you make your day because problems were taken care of before they became problems—that kind of supervisor can be a producer's or director's best friend."(Crisafulli, 2007)

In 2010 the invitation-only Guild of Music Supervisors was established. With Maureen Crowe as the guild's president, the guild claims committees dedicated to Membership, Events and Fundraising, Health Care, and the creation of a "Mission and Roles of a Music Supervisor Statement." That importance of the statement, as president Crowe notes, is it will provide a compulsory set of standards that lets all possible employers know that every guild member is respectable and trusted, "committed to the Guild's mission statement and definition of the role a Music Supervisors. Once a Music Supervisor is accepted into the Guild, the GMS stamp is a sign to producers, directors and executives that this is a qualified Music Supervisor" (Crowe, 2011).

In the annals of American music history respectability for pop on film and television has always been wanting. Furthemore, television has long held a reputation as a crass popularizer. Norma Coates points out that the reasons for this are many, including a longstanding dominance of rock as a dominant genre in popular music. Rock's attendant emphases on "authenticity" and "masculinity" combined with television's association with feminine domesticity has tended to make the marriage a difficult one and, as Coates points out, "for rock and roll to succeed as a counterculture, television was discursively constructed as representing the worst of mass culture" (Coates, 2002, p. 30). Nevertheless, as Murray Forman points out, "music, including symphonic and popular idioms" has long been "of central concern" since the growth of U.S. television in the late 1940s (Forman, 2002, p. 255). Simon Frith summarizes what he labels "The Uneasy Relationship of Music and Television" by noting the following:

> In the popular music literature there are two broad views of television. On the one hand, it is understood as a medium of great importance. It is the most effective tool of star-making and record promotion. Television programmes from American Bandstand to Top of the Pops to Yo, MTV Raps! have shaped the social meanings (and our memories) of artists and genres. On the other hand, television is thought not to be very important at all. Music has not been a central part of its programming. The television audience is rarely conceived as a music audience. TV-made pop stars almost always lack musical credibility. (Frith, 2002, p. 277)

Furthermore, Frith notes in his 2002 piece, "if it is arguable that television was the most significant medium of political and commercial communication in the twentieth century, it is not clear that it has been a very effective means of musical communication" (p. 279). The question then arises, why has the music industry, particularly those bands from "indie rockers" that Alexandra Patsavas' Chop Shop specializes in signing and placing, embraced music television and film? The short answer is the crisis that the music industry went through with the advent of broadband digital networks and peer-to-peer technologies quickly decimated a record industry based on the sale of physical goods. No doubt there is some truth to this position.

However, accepting this explanation as gospel essentially hides the numerous other crises and practices that informed the rise of the music supervisor from an afterthought to an important part of the music industry. The first of these crises occurred nearly four decades ago. Writing in 1988 about the then-recent popularization of rock, pop, and soul catalogues in television commercials, Simon Frith noted that "the starting point for any understanding of the music business today must be the 'crisis' that hit the industry in the 1970s." For Frith the crisis of the record industry at the time was that sales had reached that critical point of possible market exhaustion:

> After more than twenty years of steady growth (and a decade of spectacular growth—the value of worldwide record sales rose from $4.75 billion to $7 billion between 1973 and 1978), record companies found that sales had peaked and that their rock-oriented working practices (the signing of numerous acts, the huge investment in studio time, the optimistic expenditure on promotion) made increasingly less economic sense. The year of truth was 1978–79, when music sales fell by 11 percent in the United States (from $4.13 billion to $3.69 billion) and by 20 percent in Britain, but the decline continued until 1981–82. (Frith, 1988, p. 92)

The crisis affected every level of the industry and included significant revaluation of resources and practices. What that meant throughout the 1980s was that a significant amount of investment capital would be directed away from the sales of records and toward the acquisition and exploitation of pre-sold musical properties to satisfy the needs of emergent markets such as cable television and home video. This practice would eventually morph into the exploitation of these pre-sold properties, namely master tapes and music publishing, as remastered compact discs. As mentioned earlier, coupling the significantly greater margins that CDs afforded these companies with the relatively minimal investments in remastering most master tape sources, the focus on pre-produced and pre-marketed holdings allowed the record industry to grow again until its collapse in the 2000s.

What is significant are the numerous practices that these labels abandoned and adopted. What they quickly dropped are what Frith labels the "rock-oriented working practices" that focused on the long-term investment in artist development aimed at the sale of physical goods. Instead, many labels began to redefine themselves and embrace new practices in their search for synergy. Again, this was part of a long-term trend. As music, television, and film industries became conglomerates, Frith could confidently write that by the late-1980s "commercial popular music no longer depends on the sale of records; it can no longer be understood in terms of a fixed sound object; it is no longer made in terms of particular sort of audience, rebellious youth" (Frith, 1988, p. 129). Frith's point about this paradigm shift is that the industry's new investment in the acquisition and curation of intellectual properties was predicated on the ability that these industries control their legitimate utilization and reproduction. Indeed, in the same essay Frith notes that in the 1980s the International Federation of Phonogram and Videogram Producers had already envisioned a future without physical goods (vinyl, compact discs, cassettes, etc.) where networked home-computers and databanks would provide on-demand music. Of course, the rise of new transmission systems would only be acceptable if piracy could be controlled (pp. 114–115). Frith also argues that the effects of this search synergy in the 1980s can be seen in the success of soundtracks such as *Dirty Dancing* and the resurgence of Ben E. King's "Stand By Me" in a late-'80s commercial for Levi's jeans and as the key song for the hit film of the same name. These examples and others were part of a world of cross-media tie-ins that Frith termed "the rock version of the postmodern condition" (Frith, 1988, p. 91). Blockbuster successes such as the soundtracks to *The Big Chill* (Kasdan, 1983) and *Top Gun* (Scott, 1986) made it clear that the soundtrack could be a substantial investment for synergistic exploitation, a fact that would become clear in the 1990s and into the 2000s as more conglomerates acquired the skilled practitioners necessary for the proper exploitation of their rather complex assets.

The goal may have been synergy, but how it would be achieved by labels and media conglomerates was not always clear. For example, one of the initial aims of this move toward an economy built on intellectual properties was to become much more aggressive in placing popular music into commercial television programs and advertisements. The question was how to do this. In 1987, Lincoln Diamant, then-president of Spots Alive Consultants, noted that advertising agencies who wanted to move a number of those elements of the business that drive advertising placements up in costs into production houses as a money-saving measure may be taking on significant risks. Diamant asked if agencies understood the exigencies of the music industry well enough to predict whether or not if there would "be any shift in compensation for 'below-the-line' production services—casting, music supervision, typography, artwork, color correction, etc.—currently performed by the agency for the price of commissions? Under any new formulas, how will 'client savings' eventually be identified?" (Diamant, 1987). This is an interesting question and reminds us that some specific media systems and operations may never be completely internalized by conglomerates. Ad agencies and other content producers have to weigh the possibility of saving costs against that of taking on the roles of actors who possess skills that are often unclear and whose values are attached to the social networks they supply. The value of intermediaries is a question that has always plagued the music industry. In his sociological study of recorded music studio producers, Antoine Hennion notes that studio producers work to "represent the public" to musicians and singers. In short, a producer's ears provide a kind of intermediation that listens as if it were the public in search of the ever elusive hit. This kind of intermediary has always been key to the music industry where, "between production and consumption there is nothing like the abyss separating the technical and the social" (Hennion, 1989, p. 402). The result is that the music industry relies upon multiple actors who act as "interposed operatives" that bridge the gap between music production and social consumption to reduce risk, whether this means trying to retain on-staff A&R or hiring any number of free agents from rack jobbers and song pluggers of the past to the radio pluggers and music supervisors of today. It's not always clear whether these functionaries can be adequately centralized, which means the terrain of the music industry will most likely always have a number of professional liaisons, third parties needed to bridge the gaps for independent and major firms alike.

In the case of a new digital music economy the shift has demanded a new set of third-party actors like the music supervisor to build and maintain connections between producers and consumers. The amplification of the music supervisor as this once-ignored intermediary has come at a time when publishers and labels find the need to connect their largesse of intellectual properties with the rise of audio-visual outlets more important than they had in the recent past. To be sure, publishers have long had an interest in connecting with film and television producers. In some cases this meant selling their properties directly to studios. The practice of "selling" a song directly is called "song plugging." While the practice never completely disappeared, it did diminish substantially with the rise of rock and other genres that emphasized a singer-songwriter ethic and aesthetic. In 1998, the CEO of Los Angeles-based publisher Bug Music, Dan Bourgeois, said, "In the early '90s, when film and TV became such an issue, the major publishers began sending in their creative experts; they had neglected active song-plugging. We've been there all along. Our deal is structured so that we earn more if we get a placement with an administrated client. Economically, we can't ignore that" (Henderson, 1998, p. 47). Writing for *Billboard* one year earlier in 1997, Mark Fried of the independent music publishing company Spirit Music penned an article titled "Time for Song Plugging's Second Wind." In the article Fried noted that almost 10 years earlier, as a *Billboard* columnist reporting on song placement, he noticed notice of the use of the term "song plugging", a term that had once "disappeared from the lexicon of contemporary music publishing":

> I hadn't thought much about that years' old reference until recently. As I've crisscrossed the country hawking Spirit's catalog, I've observed that industry professionals—from A&R staffers to film directors to advertising executives—are not only responsive but seem downright refreshed by a pitching style that emphasizes personal contact, marketing-drawn ideas, and a thorough knowledge of the music and the project being pitched for. It occurred to me that the warm welcome we've received (and our respectable success rate) is thanks in equal parts to old-fashioned song plugging and vast new windows of opportunity for both traditional and nontraditional placements. (Fried, 1997, p. 7)

In the form of advertising, film, television, and a "new tech sphere" of "Microsofts, American Onlines, and Broderbunds," these "new opportunities," Fried predicted, would allow the best song pluggers to "win their respective companies much more than bragging rights as the new age dawns" (Fried, 1997, p. 7).

The publisher's emphasis on "networking" as a specific skill is deceptive. As a term, networking has a tendency to flatten the complexities involved in dealing with intellectual and artistic properties. Combining the business pressures exerted by the many legal nuances that music and recording copyright present with the ability to understand the complex artistic demands of any given production and/or specific scene means that the role of the music supervisor must address each transaction as a unique negotiation between specific marketplace and artistic needs. Even calling the work of a music supervisor as an act of "liaising" runs the risk of reducing the complexities of music supervision to "social networking." Let's remind ourselves that the items music supervisors work with are thick with numerous financial, legal, social, and aesthetic consequences and potentials. Thinking about musical properties as "thick entities" allows us to understand them as the complex items that they are. The supervisor must treat music as an aesthetic and narrative entity that cannot simply be plopped into any film or television show. Even if the supervisor is convinced that the material he or she has selected is absolutely the best choice possible, if the director or producer choose otherwise then the supervisor has to find another selection that both serves the needs of the scene and is within his or her budget. Musical properties are also financial and legal entities whose attending obligations (i.e., songwriting credits, clearances, etc.) are neither clear nor simple. Songs and records are knotty propositions: they may seem to be discrete units but when one looks closely at the property it is often an object that is woven together by numerous stakeholders and even other properties, each of which demand legal and financial attention. In a sense, musical properties that are invested in capitalist systems of production and exchange are thick things that are invested in and invest themselves into multiple systems.[2]

When we start to think of songs and recordings as "thick things" we begin to understand how music supervisors see their job. It's also why it is so difficult to explain what they do to others, even those that are closest to them. Humorously, Randall Poster pointed out in 2007 that he was "65 films into my career, and my mother still ask[ed] me what I do for a living." Sporting a longtime working association with Wes Anderson, Todd Phillips, and Richard Linklater, Poster also noted that, "It can be a difficult job to explain to people outside or even inside the industry, because sometimes the best work you do as a music supervisor is the invisible work—it just supports the movie in a way that's so integrated people don't take particular notice of it" (Crisafulli, 2007). To quote Chuck Crisafulli of *The Hollywood Reporter*,

> The basic requirements of the music supervisor's job are to sit in on spotting sessions with directors or producers to see where licensed tracks are needed either for soundtrack or music within a scene, to come up with suggestions for what specific recordings might work, and then, after a greenlight from directors or producers, to negotiate licensing fees for

the desired music and to follow through on all required clearances for the music to be used. But the work is not always that straightforward.

Alexandra Patsavas is even more straightforward: "There has never been a typical work week for me" (Crisafulli, 2007).

Part of what makes the work so difficult to understand is that the job requires so much more than having a tasteful ear. In 2009, the managing director of Leap Music, Richard Kirstein, stated in an interview with *Music Week* that when they bring on a client who wants a set of songs the firm delivers "on a project by project basis" a protocol whereby they "approach all the leading rights owners with a clear, written brief and a set of required rights, timelines, costs and deliverables and ask them to pitch their work against them. Only tracks which fit both the creative and the commercial requirements get through." Music supervisors must also be part broker and part lawyer as they dedicate a substantial portion of their time to the complexities of intellectual property law and exchanges. Kirstein notes in the same interview that "knowledge of copyright law, the intricacies of public domain status and the importance of due diligence is of paramount importance. You have to be niche experts in these areas because if you get it wrong, clients can be faced with expensive and embarrassing lawsuits" (Anon., 2009, p. 15). So complex are these issues that once a supervisor establishes a somewhat clean and successful record of clearances they will have acquired perhaps their greatest capital asset: trust. With credits as a songwriter, editor, and sound and music supervisor, Skip Adams underlines that "trust and confidence mean everything in this business. Nobody wants a copyright problem gumming up the works, or perhaps even ruining the show, so most professionals turn to the following trusted sources when they look for music" (Adams, 2003, p. 8). Trust is also the reason that so many supervisors have significant histories in elements of the music industry, ranging from concert booker to disc jockey: it is assumed that they not only love and know music, but understand how the music industry works. For example, in a 2007 *Variety* profile about Jay Faires, the president of Lionsgate's music and publishing unit who also oversaw both music supervision and the organization of the existing catalogs, explained that his success as the owner and operator of independent label, Mammoth Records was a key reason for trusting him with a new four-year contract. In a joint statement made by Lionsgate CEO Jon Felltheimer and vice chairman Michael Burns, the two noted that, "As technology continues to change the way music gets to listeners, Jay's expertise will ensure that Lionsgate remains ahead of the curve in terms of reaching end users" (Gallo, 2007, p. 1).

Again, the importance of being in the loop for publishing is paramount to the discussion of music supervisors who must work closely with this segment. In 2007, BMG Music Publishing's then-director of global marketing, Steve Levy, underscored the importance of connecting with music supervisors as the clients that can place their properties. Levy noted that while the "quality of your [catalog's] songs matters," a publisher's business also depends on "how good your clearance and licensing team is too. If a client gets a smooth service then they'll come back for more" (Anon., 2007b, p. 20). The quality of the connection that the publisher has with the client is key and the stakes are high. Paul Rogers, a veteran music license revenue expert and founder of Fintage House, an independent global company devoted to the exploitation of film, television, music, fashion, and sport related rights, noted in 2004 that "the publishers are pushing this. Publishers are desperate to make money with the record industry dying" (Callaghan, 2004). This push is also symptomatic of the resiliency of music publishing. Longtime music publisher and co-owner of the independent Espy Music Group Ronda Espy noted in 2005 that "over the last 30 years we've reinvented ourselves several times" through many moments of music industry crisis. Indeed, connecting with music supervisors gave publishers like Espy Music their "first opportunity to look within our catalogs." For a publisher like Ronda Espy, "it's just more exposure for the catalog and it keeps us in the loop with others in the industry" (Butler, 2005, p. 14).

This "loop" is key. As a loose association of organizations and people who work in specific rhythms, being in "the loop" may seem vague, but to those who are in it or long to be in it, it is a very real and valued thing. Getting into that loop has long been the primary job for publishers who want the ear of music supervisors. In a 1998 *Billboard* article, Stacy Palm, the senior creative director of film and television music for Famous Music, had this piece of advice for publishers:

> Stay in touch with music supervisors and film and television studios. Try to find out what they need as early as possible and get appropriate music to them. Being enthusiastic about newer artists is the only way you'll get them in. If you are over the moon about the band, you can convince someone else that the music is worthy of consideration. (Henderson, 1998, p. 47)

Or as Carol Sue Baker, owner of Ocean Park Music publishing, put it, "Making a lot of phone calls; that's my primary function" (Henderson, 1998, p. 47). Indeed, connecting with music industry operators has been the primary function of music publishers for hundreds of years. So has been finding ways to reinvigorate the value of old catalogues. In 2006, the independent publisher Kobalt Music discovered one such case when '60s cult singer-songwriter Vashti Bunyan found her catalogue repopularized when her song "Diamond Day" wound up being licensed to T-Mobile for a 2006 commercial. As a result, Kobalt continued to pursue sync fees by placing songs from Saint Etienne in Pedro Almodovar's 2006 film, *Volver* (Anon., 2007b). Perhaps one of the most impressive syncs came in the placement of Eddie Grant's song "Electric Avenue." In 1983 the song reached the number two position of the charts in both the U.S. and UK, Warner Chappell looked at the 20-plus year property, shortened it, and made it the sound-track to television commercials for a UK electrical goods chain for well over 18 months in a 2006 to 2007 campaign (Anon., 2007b). Indeed, the search for sync revenue became so appealing to publishers that in some cases they began to sign deals with bands who had no label interest in their recordings simply because they exhibited "strong sync presences." Such was the case of Chrysalis Music's 2009 signing Los Angeles-based group and songwriting duo The Frequency to an exclusive, global publishing agreement. As an independent band with three album releases, the band had found that having their music licensed for a BlackBerry TV campaign made them attractive to publishers. "Even though there is no label involved at this stage there are certain things that we can develop," noted Chrysalis' A&R manager, Hugo Turquet, who admitted that the band's albums would be a catalogue worth refining for even more sync licensing opportunities (Clarke, 2009).

Publishers and labels who wish to connect with music supervisors must invest in quite a bit of prep work to get them in the loop. In 1997 Mark Fried advised in *Billboard* that publishers take three simple steps to plugging music as more and more new media opportunities increased sync income: (1) Listen closely to your clients as they provide you all the clues you need to make a "meaningful match" for their programs; (2) while it is tempting to embrace your most popular songwriters and titles, "know the breadth and depth of your catalog" as "your reputation and the company's bottom line will ultimately be served by your ability to pluck obscure gems from within the catalog and secure less than obvious placements"; (3) and finally "pitch with humanity":

> [We've] almost forgotten the importance of house calls. Our business remains one of relationships, and the young manager who takes the time to establish and maintain direct, face-to-face contact and ongoing, service-oriented relationships with industry professionals will score in many more instances than with inanimate pitching devices. (Fried, 1997, p. 7)

Thirteen years later the CEO of the music licensing company, Jingle Punks, Jared Gustadt, echoed Fried's emphasis on making relationships with as, "many independent music supervisors and supervisors at networks as possible. When you're sending along a package you should always make it easy for them to understand which type of show you feel your music would work well in." In the case of your potential clientele, you need to know what a producer's needs are by doing enough research to know that "'Project Runway' doesn't want death metal." In fact, you should do enough research to "know the format you're going after. When you watch 'Project Runway' or reality shows, you'll see that they don't want fully fleshed-out songs. They're after ideas that bring a vibe out of a scene. If you want placement in shows, you've got to stay current with trends" (Anon., 2010a).

For publishers perhaps the most vital trend beginning in the mid-1990s and forward was the almost unimaginable pace at which the media landscape metastasized from one of few channels and a mass orientation to one dominated by niche media and seemingly limitless amounts of spectrum. Of course, the technological force that most clearly disturbed the media landscape in the 1990s was the rise of the Internet. However, the Internet was hardly the lone technological culprit. At the beginning of the 1990s, while the typical North American household may have begun its migration to compact discs, the influx of new communication technologies that this household would have to choose to adopt within a 10-year period was simply unprecedented. While many households subscribed to cable, many others were beginning to consider satellite television services. At the beginning of the 1990s, the average U.S. household might have access to a VHS player and a membership at an accompanying video store. Yet, by the end of the decade the same household would begin to consider DVD technologies and the prospect of replacing cassettes with discs. And while the video game industry had collapsed in the late-1980s, it would find its legs once again in the 1990s and mature to become a dominant media industry in the 2000s. Finally, at the beginning of the 1990s while few North American household members could claim to own a personal computer and fewer still a mobile phone by the late-1990s these households would claim a computer, mobile phones, and consider purchasing a laptop, a tablet or both. At this same time that households were acquiring more televisions, they saw their cable and satellite channels multiply as telecommunication companies began to make their first broadband Internet offerings to residencies.

The previous paragraph may seem monotonous, yet it is important to recognize that each of these numerous objects and services brought with it its own cultural, political, and economic agenda. For those members of the popular music ecosystem, whether they be musicians, publishers, or label workers, the consequences of these technological and cultural shifts meant that the market would have more licensing opportunities just as the sales of recordings quickly dwindled. As media channels grew so did the need for programming that demanded music. Early in the 2000s it became apparent that the demand for music on new channels and new media would stretch into new artistic territories. As *Electronic Musician* noted in 2003:

> You've heard the rumors. Like never before, unknown bands and singer-songwriters are getting their music into films and on TV shows. From the Travel Channel to network prime time, from small indie flicks to major studio releases, personal-studio denizens are making their marks and cashing in.

For *Electronic Magazine*, the "rumors" of this change was "due largely to a timely convergence of three major factors." These included the "low cost of high-quality recording equipment," "limited music budgets," and, most importantly, "the explosion of cable TV, which has created huge demand for content to fill the programming hours" (Adams, 2003, p. 8). The result would be a growing, systematic demand for adequate music supervision to make music popular. In this new ecosystem the quality music supervisor supplies a rare set of skills that includes issues of tasteful discrimination, negotiating business deals, working with creative personnel from two or more distinct production cultures, and understanding the knotty terrain of licensing. In other words the person who could dig deep and find the best tracks in a library company, speak with independent publishers and artists alike, and provide the quality that television and film producers demanded became a prized commodity that was relatively new.[3]

Also new was the competition for licensing fees as the value of music for films and television continued to grow. As early as 2000, *Billboard* would report that a number of music composers and soundtrack writers believed that, "Music budgets for films and television [were] still generally inadequate" and that "music [was] the undervalued component" of these productions (Hunter, 2000). With film and television producers thinking of music as a secondary issue at best, record companies had seen little use in exploiting their sync rights on television. Soon everything changed. *Advertising Age* pointed out in 2003 that "not so long ago, the record industry couldn't have cared less about Madison Avenue":

> Freelance music producer Rob Kaplan remembers being on staff at Messner five years ago and getting nothing but the cold shoulder when he approached record companies about licensing original tunes. "Virtually no major label gave me support," he recalls. "I got a lot of, 'Here's a choice of one artist, and you can pay a lot of money and maybe we'll let you use him, maybe we won't.'"

However, five years later it became clear that the "landscape" had shifted as television and film producers started to rethink the value of music and perceived a new way to interact with the recording industry. According to one television producer, so desperate were major labels to gain any exposure on television that a couple of them called and "offered to do things simply for a chyron in the lower left hand corner of the screen, literally not charging us anything" (Diaz, 2003, p. 26). As one 2005 *Billboard* magazine cover announced, "TV is the New Radio" (Anon., 2005).

No doubt the attention the music industry began to pay television was due to the fact that increasingly record executives believed that television exposure led to better CD sales. Programs such as *The O.C.* and *The Sopranos* had found success including music in their episodes that not only sold the show's soundtracks but the records of the artists featured (Crisafulli, 2003). *The O.C.* in particular generated significant sales of the program's soundtrack. By 2007 the program could claim having produced six separate volumes of "Music From *The O.C.*" that moved more than a million units worldwide. Supervised by Alexandra Patsavas, she also helped produce albums for *Grey's Anatomy*, including "*Grey's Anatomy* Volume 2," a disc that would be nominated for a Grammy (very rare for a television-related soundtrack) and go on to sell over 350,000 albums (Garrity, 2007a, p. 3). Along with others, Patsavas' work as a music supervisor helped change the attitude of record companies about placing their music on television. In a 2006 interview with *Billboard*, Patsavas stated "that the record business is having to change the ways bands reach their fans," and, "The music industry needs to be more adventuresome, and bands want to be part of it":

> In the past, bands were much more reluctant to license to TV because they maybe thought it didn't lend anything to their credibility. Now, it's different. They're making more money and broadening their audience, finding some new fans because their song was heard [in a television show or film]. The only issues bands have had with associating their music with a television show is when it's about content, like some bands aren't about violence and don't want to be paired with violent imagery (Hasty, 2006, p. 20).

Television continued to evolve as more advanced video game platforms crept into the consciousness of more and more households. And at the same time so did the emphasis on placing music in these video games by both publishers and the record industry. In his dissertation Ben Aslinger relates how the intellectual property manager for Xbox games, Brendan Adams, noted that when the 2003 North American snowboarding game *Amped 2* was being developed his department received 1,000 songs for consideration in the game's soundtrack. For *Amped 3*, a sequel released two years later, the same department considered 5,000 songs submissions (Aslinger, 2008, pp. 38–39). Aslinger explains that one of the reasons that this enthusiasm grew so quickly and with such exponential power was an early-2003 report that was talked about widely in the trade press stating "consumer research done by ElectricArtists found that video game soundtracks had a positive effect on CD sales, with hard core gamers saying they were 40% more likely to buy CDs of music they had heard during game play" (Aslinger, 2008, p. 38). Of course probabilities do not always translate into actions. Still exposure in video games and commercials increases an artist's visibility. And, of course, there is the substantial benefit of the license fee. In short, landing a spot on a popular video game title could inject significant value into an artist's career. Such was the case with James D'Agostino, aka DJ Green Lantern, whose mix tapes caught the attention of Rockstar Games' *Grand Theft Auto* (*GTA*) franchise. Contacted to create a "radio station" for *GTA IV*, the DJ stated that getting involved was a "no brainer." The size of the platform and the fact that the game would be set in a "New York-type of setting" would allow him to leverage his "artist relationships and go make songs for this particular mood that I'm trying to achieve." But if DJ Green Lantern hoped to employ his skills as a unique disc jockey who both plays and makes music for the *GTA IV* soundtrack, his employment would serve double duty as a music supervisor who could breaks artists, even those whom he had signed. For Lantern it was clear that this was "about stepping into the world of music supervision and doing something for arguably the biggest title of the game world and see what else I can do next. The next step would probably be me being hands-on and either developing something for a game or just developing a game period. We'll see what comes along. I've got a few offers I'm feeling out just from the publicity I've received from this" (Bruno, 2008).

The line between disc jockey and music supervisor is thin enough that more than one DJ has stepped out from behind the board and into this line of work. Like music supervisors, the disc jockey is an intermediary that works to connect with the public through his or her curatorial abilities. Arguably no radio station has seen more of its DJs become music supervisors than Santa Monica, California's KCRW. As a community service station of Santa Monica College, KCRW is a public radio station that serves Los Angeles and Orange Counties with its FM signals. Unlike a commercial broadcaster, the station is able to place more ambitious and adventurous fare on its airwaves. For example, KCRW's music director throughout most of the 2000s, Nic Harcourt, claims that the station was "among the first, if not the first, to play Coldplay, Norah Jones, Sigur Ros, Damien Rice, [and] David Gray" (Morris, 2004, p. 78). The station's influence rests in the fact that its audience is "filled with entertainment-industry ears." In 2001, Harcourt pointed out that whereas commercial radio is composed of tight playlists, rigid formats, and research, he doesn't "impose anything on [my DJs]" and allows them to play what they like (Bloom, 2001). While the typical music director interacts with record companies and determines what should get played and how often, KCRW's Harcourt has taken a more "block programming" strategy that builds the station around selecting specific DJs who offer individual, unique shows rather than a genre-driven format. Harcourt himself hosted the very influential three-hour AM block, *Morning Becomes Eclectic*, from 1998–2008, while also acting as a consultant and music supervisor on a number of films and television shows. Indeed, a number of KCRW disc jockeys, including Liza Richardson, Tricia Halloran, Anne Litt, Gary Calamar, and Dan Wilcox, have all worked as music supervisors on significant film and/or television projects. For example, in 2002 the KCRW DJ Liza Richardson could not only claim 11 years on the air, but the title of head of the music supervision and research division for Stimmung, a Santa Monica shop specializing in music for commercials. According to a *Variety* report, Richardson planned to "work with ad agency creatives and broadcast producers seeking to find, license and remix music tracks for their programming, continue her KCRW show, 'The Drop,' and do music supervision on films" (Bloom, 2002a). Richardson's supervising skills were displayed on the eclectic, bilingual soundtrack for *Y Tu Mama Tambien* (Cuarón, 2001) and a series of Pixar iMac commercials (Burlingame, 2002, p. 4). Hired in 2002 by the music director of Sub-Zero, a Santa Monica consulting company that offers advice to ad agencies about music for their spots, Tricia Halloran's specific background as an industrial intermediary was notably cited as the reason for her tenure. SubZero's founder, Jeff Koz, stated, "We're incredibly fortunate to have Tricia on board. Her background as a producer and DJ at KCRW, L.A.'s most cutting-edge radio station, puts her, us and our clients ahead of the curve" (Bloom, 2002b).

This movement of DJs into music supervision positions is part of a structural demand for a new legion of intermediaries. It's important that we look again at the work of Antoine Hennion and understand that he argues that "the intermediary is not at the interface of two known worlds: he or she is the one who constructs these worlds by trying to bring them into relation" (Hennion, 1989, p. 406). Hennion's work on record producers transposes well to the issue of the music supervisor because, like the producer, what the music supervisor provides "the possibility of using channels that already exist: techniques whose effects are known, professional guarantees, a network of relationships, a technical circuit, a mass of savoir faire, publics already constructed." The jobs of both the music supervisor and the producer "string together concrete mediations" (Hennion, 1989, pp. 414–415). The "string of concrete mediations" creates a chain that allows an appropriate exchange to take place. As mentioned earlier regarding the guild, as sync licensing became more important so did the need for quality music supervision. The growing rush to license old catalogues of recordings and songs has effectively demanded a layer of brokers who can catalyze a market in both taste and clearance issues.

As music supervisors have become much more important, so have music libraries and other firms that are created to assist supervisors in finding their placements. In a sense, these are middlemen who help middlemen. The continued demand for musical content caused Ant Music founder Anthony Vanger to note that "it's just insane how many music houses have started up." The collapsing costs of quality recording equipment has allowed all types of music boutiques to compete for business (Weiss, 2005, p. 139). These boutique music companies work with musicians, labels, and publishers to place music in video games and television programs by connecting directly with music supervisors. For example, then-NBC director of music supervision Alicen Schneider explained to *Billboard* in 2003 that the sheer number of recording labels and publishers that these firms worked with meant that they could provide television programmers with a deep and flexible source of music on a one-stop basis. For Schneider, "If you only have one hour to find a song [which is often the case with fast-paced TV production], you know that they will have something. And with all the problems the labels have been having, they can bring us small indies out of Sweden [when today, a label strapped for resources might not]" (Ault, 2003, p. 47). Indeed, such was the intent behind the merger of Evergreen Copyrights and Hunnypot Unlimited. *Billboard* reported that the music publisher and the placement/marketing firm merged as an expression of synergy, and the maneuver was

> seemingly a win-win deal for both companies. EverGreen, which has the catalogs of Tupac Shakur, MC Hammer and Rykomusic/Warlock Music, among 80,000 other copyrights, can now rely upon Hunnypot's contacts in the music supervision world to get these artists placements in film and TV shows. And Hunnypot, long-known for its tastemaker parties and online radio show, can tap into EverGreen's established administrative backbone. (Donahue, 2008a, p. 6)

Evergreen would be led by both John Anderson, a former VP of film, television, and creative at Windswept Music Publishing, and PJ Bloom, a music supervisor with extensive placement credits. This combination, Bloom argued, is what made this merger unique, as they would bring "a relationship with the placement and the synch world" in house (Donahue, 2008a, p. 6).

   Providing clearances to television, film, video games, and web programming is one form of market expansion, but these aren't the only spaces for possible music placement. One of the more interesting experiments came from a 2010 initiative called "Home Grown Music." While national grocery and coffee chains such as Whole Foods and Starbucks have been closely associated with music sales throughout the 2000s, the 2010 music licensing program associated with the New Seasons Market, a regional grocery chain based out of Portland, Oregon, rested on the premise that customers would not only pay attention to what is played in the aisles as they shopped, but that it could benefit regional musicians as a discovery force. Developed by the Portland-based ad agency Overland, the service received music supervision from Steve Berlin of the rock band Los Lobos, and Oregon Public Broadcasting radio host and program producer Jeremy Petersen. The goal was to get the "Home Grown Music" initiative off the ground and into 10 New Seasons outlets in the Portland area. Curating and compiling a database containing about 2,500 songs by more than 350 artists from Oregon, Washington and British Columbia, Berlin and Petersen's efforts would be available to each store through a "player" that would allow each location to "create playlists based on a certain area of the Northwest or on a tempo or mood." Taking advantage of audio identification technologies and smartphones "an accompanying iPhone app will tell customers what song is playing, and [that] they can purchase the track on iTunes" (Harding, 2010b). If the presence of recorded music wasn't enough, by November 2010 New Seasons announced that the bands on the playlist would occasionally perform in their Portland stores (McCollum, 2010).

Perhaps the most interesting experiment to occur in music supervision occurred at the end of the 1990s and the beginning of the 21st century: the release of Moby's *Play*, which may be one of the most important records in pop history. Released in 1999, the CD came on the heels of a number of critically-acclaimed but low-selling releases by Moby. However, the release of *Play*, while selling well initially, would go on to blockbuster status and eventually move over 10 million albums (Bishop, 2002). Thoroughly unexpected, *Play* became one of the bigger music stories of 2000. Part of this story was the fact that each of *Play*'s 18 tracks found placement in commercials. As Bethany Klein notes,

> Snippets turned up in films and television shows, and, for a period of time, in what seemed like every other commercial spot in markets around the world. *Play* tracks were licensed to Nissan, Rolling Rock, Maxwell House, Volkswagen, Nordstrom and American Express, among others. The licensing orgy around *Play* ultimately led to radio airplay that almost certainly would not have been conceivable otherwise, and record sales in the millions. Moby's success validated advertising as a launching pad for lesser-known or new musicians in both the independent and major label music worlds, where suddenly licensing became seen as not simply an extra source of revenue, but a way to break an artist. (Klein, 2008, p. 463)

Klein explained that *Play*'s embrace of licensing was a reactionary tactic that responded to a newly deregulated atmosphere of U.S. radio where formats became tighter and more standardized, thus making it even more difficult for artists and labels able to break into playlists (Klein, 2008, p. 467). While Moby himself claimed that this licensing "involved no strategy," Ethan Smith, writing for *Wired*, explained that Moby's managers, Marcus Weber and Barry Taylor, had an entirely different account:

> Even before the release of *Play*, with its record-setting run of commercially licensed songs, Weber says the strategy was core to the Organization. In 1996, for instance, they received reports that Moby's atmospheric "God Moving Over the Face of the Waters," which sustained the climactic scene in Michael Mann's *Heat*, had made an enormous impression on the film-music community. So during that year's Slamdance film festival, Weber and Taylor "invited every music supervisor in Hollywood" to a party to increase their client's visibility. "We put on this free show, big dinner, all that." Certainly sounds like a strategic soiree. Indeed, when it came to selling Moby's music

to soundtracks, Weber adds, the event "was a breaking point." (E. Smith, 2000)

Three years later Moby's management initiated a licensing strategy with *Play* precisely because they had seen Moby's first three albums ignored by radio and he had left his major label partner, Elektra. Signing in 1999 with V2, Richard Branson's then-independent label that he founded after selling Virgin records, *Play*'s embrace of the licensing strategy was, as Barry Taylor put it, "a conscious effort to create a marketing plan that had nothing to do with radio" (E. Smith, 2000). What the story of *Play* represents is a record that had found another distributive path, one that exploited another media who needed to attract prospective viewers and listeners. By 2004 the impact of *Play* was clear: the record had brought to the attention of many in the industry a new way to market music and artists as traditional revenue and promotional paths dried up. For musicians and labels alike this meant looking at licensing as a means to replace income lost from album and CD sales. For techno artists such as Moby, the preferred sales medium throughout the '80s and '90s was the 12-inch, 45 rpm single. The increase in licensing revenue income after *Play* was not only impactful for a techno artist like Moby but others in genres that had historically low-income expectations for music sales. As DJ Dave Audé, an artist whose music has appeared in ads for Nike and Coca-Cola, explained in a 2004 *Billboard* article, "Of course it helps an artist. Because there is no longer a lot of money in 12-inch vinyl sales, such musical placement helps an artist earn a living." Between the television ads, the "flat fee" of $5,000 per-track sync license for video games such as "Grand Tourismo," and producing music for the occasional film, Audé, like other artists, has begun to produce music in a way that treats syncs as primary income sources (Paoletta, 2004b, p. 1).

The combined constriction of radio and the rise of licensing opportunities would have made most musicians rethink how they reach their audiences. However, Moby's *Play* was unique as it came at the beginning of a period of popular filesharing and the demise of the physical object. *Play*'s sale of 10 million units would not be equaled by any of Moby's subsequent releases and his sales would slowly depreciate despite maintaining his star status. Of course, his depreciation of sales parallel the overall depreciation of recorded music objects. This combination of factors not only led artists like Moby to look for new ways of reaching audiences and funding their career, but led others to discuss how the industry is undergoing a paradigm change. In 2009 *Variety* reporter Melinda Newman labeled a new web series, *Rockville, CA*, as a signal that a new paradigm was emerging. Created by *Gossip Girl* and *The O.C.* creator Josh Schwartz and music supervisor Alexandra Patsavas, two hour-per-episode series were short narratives packed with multiple recordings. The

WB.com commissioned 20 of these webisodes, each of which averaged around four minutes in length and revolved around live music and clubbing. While licensing songs from many of the acts she placed into other shows she supervised, Patsavas applied a different set of rules to *Rockville, CA* by focusing on songs and live performances that were "compelling and diverse" rather than recordings that enhance the "drama in a scene, main title or montage" (Newman, 2009, p. A3).

If *Rockville, CA* challenged the rules of music supervision by placing music that made narrative subservient to the needs of a musical performance, then it should be noted that this was not a new model. Instead, it was one of many practices that were being positioned as experiments. This includes creating music supervisor firms that, like Patsavas' aforementioned Chop Shop, are a hybrid between music houses, publishers, labels, and supervising services. As reported in *Mix*, a trade magazine devoted to recording arts, in 2009 an annex that combines houses like Shout It Out Loud Music (SIOLM) and Sugarbox Studios would attempt to provide all of these services under one roof in an experiment in flexibility. Combining the leadership talents of SIOLM's experienced music supervisor and composer Francis Garcia and the Sugarbox Studios' composer-founder Andrew Hollander, the two work together, "as a team whenever it suits them, and separately as the projects demand." Because the projects the two work on do not follow into any set of limits "[the] creative boundaries are set up by the project, but the idea is that we'll work on whatever we think is inspiring and right for the project on an ongoing basis" (Weiss, 2009, p. 20). Bringing together experiences of composers, music supervisors, and licensing allows a person like Garcia to serve and A&R capacity. As a result, Garcia actively pursues and "signs bands worldwide for licensing representation, giving him a wide network of varied catalogs to offer to films and commercials, as well as the capability to record new material from those bands if a sync project calls for it" (Weiss, 2009, p. 20). As Garcia points out:

> People want to get their music heard, and they're very open about how to get it out into the world. What we do here is emblematic of all the different ways that music is branching out—it's part of the business plan for any band to integrate TV, film or ad music into their whole agenda. Music licensing has become a new model in terms of artist promotion, and we're helping to facilitate that. (Weiss, 2009, p. 20)

Or as Rene Arsenault, Onda Productions' cofounder, noted about his firm that specialized in both production and music supervision: "Everything that we do evolves into something else. The best part of it is that we're not reacting to what's going on. We're simply doing what we've always done. We are the new music business model" (Paoletta, 2004a).

For a moment let us focus on Onda Productions' use of evolution as a metaphor to help us understand how Arsenault's firm embraced a brand new slew of opportunities. As the industry adapts to a new environment it doesn't mean that physical sales or radio airplay are no longer useful or sought after. Rather the industry felt the need to develop new income streams was imperative. Take the example of Koop. A Swedish electronic-jazz duo that in 2007 would find their cuts licensed to the FX television program *Nip/Tuck* and the trailer for the video game *Saboteur*. As much as the band credits these placements for helping them move downloads, they still long for radio airplay. Koop band member Oscar Simonsson told *Billboard*, "[Radio plays] the whole song, without any disturbance, and that's the best way to discover Koop." The band's manager, Guy Trezise, reiterated the point while getting a track into the promo of *Grey's Anatomy*. A show like *Grey's Anatomy* "garners interest, opening millions of ears to Koop's music," however Tresize hoped that some of those ears would belong to radio program directors: "Hopefully, mainstream TV will help build a story at mainstream radio" (Paoletta, 2007b, p. 17). Of course the question is to what end? Given that the sale of recorded music has continually plummeted it is difficult for artists to pin their hopes on sales. So deep and swift was the downturn that by 2004 the then-BMI VP of film and television music, Doreen Ringer-Ross, could tell *The Hollywood Reporter*, "The way (recording artists) become solvent today isn't the record industry; they're looking at an increasingly diverse array of approaches to staying solvent, and licensing is definitely one of them" (Callaghan, 2004).

From the perspective of the music industry sales slumps are problems whose solutions have often existed in finding new musical trends or technologies that would continue to bolster recording sales. Even as multimedia corporations that emphasized the exploitation of a property in a synergistic manner swallowed up major record companies in the 1980s and 1990s, part of the goal of this synergy was to sell more records. Given the example of an artist such as Moby, the initial response from labels in 2000s was predictable: search for ways to get sync income that could also promote the sales of records. An initial success such as 2000's release of the *O Brother, Where Art Thou?* soundtrack CD of "bluegrass" and "acoustic based" country music (over 7 million copies sold in the U.S.) was exceptional, however it sparked an industrywide conversation about how to create soundtracks that would sell (Kipnis, 2002). Still as the sales of CDs continued to diminish, increasingly labels slowly began to take a more sophisticated look at licensing. Licensing would not simply focus on plugging music into programs to promote discs, but be used to address the more social aspect of an act's existence, i.e., the lifestyle and branding demands of programs and products alike. For example, New York-based E-magine Entertainment, home of acts such as Danzig and Samhain, began to explore the world of music supervision by partnering directly with clothing and skin care companies in 2003. For the label it was a move of financial necessity.

E-Magine CEO Christoph Rucker explained that, "In such tough times, you must always consider new revenue streams. As a music supervisor, you can offer businesses a non-standardized service that tailors music to fit their branding. In the process, an additional way to market your artists presents itself" (Paoletta, 2003, p. 34). Providing services that discovered, compiled, and packaged the correct music as well as offering the proper payments to performance rights organizations, E-Magine aimed to expand throughout the U.S. and internationally (Paoletta, 2003). Another independent label, Quango, reported that by 2008 its revenues were "split pretty evenly" from three distinct sources: record sales, licensing, and branding partnerships. None of this occurred overnight for Quango. Based in Los Angeles and founded in 1993 by DJ Bruno Guez, the label had actively curried relationships with branding partners, finding placement opportunities for 15 years. As Guez notes, "I still want to sell records, but the future is in licensing. My goal is to use my curatorial skills to build both my label as a brand and build a reputation as someone who can create a soundtrack for a brand" (Harding, 2008).

Making a soundtrack for a brand is what the Deustch Ad Agency decided to do in 2005 when it took on its latest client, Bon Jovi. As a band, Bon Jovi had been in the recording business for over 20 years and had consistently been a multimillion unit selling artist even into the late-1990s. However, by the 2000s the band was seeing a steady decline in record sales. Although the band's 2000 release *Crush* would sell close to five million copies worldwide it paled when compared with its 1995 predecessor, *These Days*, which sold 11 million units worldwide. By 2002 the trend was clear. Although Bon Jovi's *Bounce* would debut at No. 2 in the U.S., the disc failed to achieve platinum status, the only one of their albums unable to fulfill this goal. In 2005 Bon Jovi attempted to revive their flagging careers with their ninth full-length record of songs, *Have a Nice Day*, by working with the agency to produce an album and image that would be fully integrated into merchandising opportunities. Using what the agency described as a "pissed-off smiley face" for the cover of the CD, the design was picked to help resuscitate the band's commercial status in a "bigger way by tapping into and connecting with the almighty, much-coveted youth market—while not losing sight of its longtime fans." Designing the logo, the agency hoped to cut through the clutter, blurring "the lines between marketing and entertainment" by "marketing messages into larger forms of entertainment." The implications of this tactic, as Joseph Jaffe, president of the new media consulting company Jaffe, pointed out would be that "any band—brand—could then go to an agency and have it produce a fully integrated campaign for them" and provide "new revenue streams for agencies" while validating "the power and importance of long-form content" (Paoletta, 2005, p. 20). By 2007 the importance of Bon Jovi's brand had been effectively coordinated with that of Major League Baseball (MLB). With the release of the band's 10th long-play release, *Lost Highway*, Bon Jovi released a 2 minute and 30-second video for its song "I Love This Town." The video was created to look like a standard music video that promoted both Bon Jovi and TBS' post-season coverage of MLB. But both the song and the video were positioned to be a module that could stand alone as a spot and be played in over 6,000 movie screens in theatrical pre-show programs or be cut up for interstitial use. Finally, the song and the video were produced so that they could be edited in a way so that the love of any particular town could be applied to whatever team was appearing in the ballparks. And this was not the only song to be licensed off of *Lost Highway*. Prior to the album's June release, "We Got It Going On" and the title track were licensed to ESPN ("Arena Football") and the film *Wild Hogs* respectively (Paoletta, 2007a, p. 22).

This integration clearly worked in terms of landing placements, but it also helped the band move albums. *Have a Nice Day Sales* would sell over 1.5 million units and *Lost Highway* over 1.2 million. Still, perhaps the most important indication that band's brand had been somewhat rejuvenated came in the 2009 release of Bon Jovi's 11th studio release, *The Circle*. Upon the record's release the band's lead singer, Jon Bon Jovi, would be named NBC's first "artist in residence." Coinciding with the Christmas shopping season of the CD's early November release, Mr. Bon Jovi would be contracted to appear multiple times in various NBC programs over a two-month period. This tenure included standard live appearances where Bon Jovi he would perform with his band on *Today* and *Saturday Night Live*. But Jon Bon Jovi would also lend his persona to cameos on programs such the situation-comedy *30 Rock*, as well as interviews on *NBC Nightly News* and *Inside the Actor's Studio*. While *Actor's Studio* typically focuses on the lives of stage and screen actors, the program on the NBC-owned Bravo network would "cover the history of his band as performers and some of Mr. Bon Jovi's film work." Reportedly, Jon Bon Jovi brought the idea to NBC's CEO Jeff Zucker, after Bon Jovi's manager, Jack Rover, suggested it. According to *The New York Times*, Bon Jovi explained, "Of course you usually try to be out there everywhere, when a new album is coming out. So we have to sacrifice certain shows and relationships. We hope this doesn't jeopardize any of them. But in a shrinking media environment, you have to kind of reinvent the wheel." Jon Bon Jovi pointed out that his manager said, "'Forget about Top 40 radio; how about Top 40 TV?'" (Carter, 2009, p. C2).

Both Jeff Zucker and Bon Jovi were responding to similar pressures of shrinking media shares and budgets in an ever-increasing landscape of channels, gadgets, and competition. Executive producer of the 2003–2006 Nickelodeon series *Romeo!*, Tom Lynch, echoed this concern about shrinking media playlists, particularly radio, when speaking about why more artists were seeking more television placement. Working with music stars such as Master P and Master P's son Romeo in acting roles, Lynch noted that musicians are turning to television because it is much more flexible in accommodating musicians when compared to FM radio (Newman & Paoletta, 2006b). As Jennifer Czeisler, VP of licensing for Sub Pop records, put it in 2005, "When you can only get so much radio airplay—which is mainly taken over by major labels—[TV] helps with a critical-mass kind of approach" (Whitmire, 2005, p. 33). While the collaboration between television and established artists may net large-scale exposure for artists and their brands, television executives such as Jeff Zucker are in search of musical acts who bring a specific sound that can assist in quickly establishing a program's brand in a climate of tightening production budgets. Oddly enough, a solution has been partially provided via a budget climate in which television producers have placed an emphasis on hiring younger staff to produce their programs. Along with the lower salaries this younger staff also brings with them more of an interest in popular music than most of their older, better paid peers. The effect of this hiring trend did not go unnoticed. Alexandra Patsavas noted in a 2006 interview that because people running television shows today are younger than ever they understand the manner in which pop music works because "music is part of their daily lives" (Newman & Paoletta, 2006b, p. 32). Although the risk of hiring such a young workforce means working with talent who may not have adequate skillsets remained, this staff was not only more interested in music but more "in touch" with a set of actors who are able to work with more obscure sources of popular culture such as independent labels and acts that often provide less costly wares.

This connection with independent labels is important. More often than not independent labels provide acts that are on the forefront of popular music cultures. Because most independents operate with smaller staffs who are part of distinct musical niches, they are quicker to mobilize their resources to engage both emerging trends in popular music and business operations. For example, as one of the first labels to leverage the Internet to make his label's wares instantly available for preview and discovery, Bruno Guez of Quango asserted he was able to take a proactive stance "in turning synchs into digital marking opportunities." While his label did not have a specific division dedicated to nothing but syncs, he had Quango create "a custom [online] landing page for each synch" the label manages that was optimized so that these titles appear at the top of searches for potential customers to see. To hear the title the label demands an email address in exchange for "a 30-second clip of the song." The reason for the email address, Guez explained, was that the label would "then have their info to create a one-on-one relationship going forward" (Harding, 2008). The importance of these one-on-one relationships is that many television and advertising clients view independent music as a significant licensing value. Because independents typically sign and record acts that are much less popular than those at major labels, their fees tend to be much lower for the purposes of sync licensing. Yet this isn't the only appeal of independent music. As senior producer of music and integration for Chicago-based advertising giant DDB, Gabe McDonough understood the power of independent rock and pop. Joining the firm in 2004 after working as promotions director at Chicago's famous independent music venue The Empty Bottle, and in sales, licensing, and touring at the independent label Thrill Jockey Records, McDonough explained that, "[Indie] music works for advertising on a lot of levels; obviously, pricewise, but also because it's a lot more interesting instrumentally than some other genres. Even if you pull the vocal out of an indie rock song, there is still a lot going on musically" (Harding, 2010a). The advantage is that a well-placed, inexpensive purchase could bestow an audible distinctiveness to whatever programming it graced. Matt Wishnow, president of the marketing company Insound/Drill Team, explained that while working with the Peterson Milla Hooks ad agency in 2005 to put together a series of webisodes for the Target chain he chose to pepper the spots with independent rock acts to go after coeds. Using the sounds of Bloc Party, the 22–20s, the Hold Steady, British Sea Power, and others, Wishnow wanted bands that were "new and emerging, as well as relevant to college students" (Paoletta & Walsh, 2005, p. 10).

This emphasis on the unique audible branding of a production or a program has become more of the norm. In 2007 Touchstone formed a music department and turned to veteran music supervisor Dawn Soler. Charged not only with supervising the development of temporary scores and searching for original and licensed music, Soler received another mission from her direct supervisor, executive VP of television production Barry Jossen. Jossen explained that, "Soler's depth of knowledge of music in television and film will expand Touchstone's reputation as a trendsetting leader in the television music industry. She will be an integral part in shaping the future of the studio's music identity" (Andreeva, 2007, p. 1). Part of the appeal of popular music for programmers, particularly "independent music," is that it leverages an ideological investment in "authenticity" as a source of product differentiation. Nicole Dionne, who leads the licensing boutique Primal Scream, explained to *Advertising Age* in 2003 that she didn't find that agency creatives are as drawn to traditional composers anymore. People are tapped-in enough to demand something genuine. They don't want leftovers, they want the entree" (Diaz, 2003, p. 26). Television's desire for a sort of quality and authentic musical earmark dovetails nicely with the aims of Man Made Music, a music supervision company that specializes in "sonic branding." While specializing in television, the company also works with other media to create "tiny identity-building mnemonics—short but memorable brand 'logos'—to promos, themes and entire soundtracks." With the aim to put a "sonic signature" on products and programs, Man Made created short pieces that would be "instantly memorable" (Harvey, 2006, p. 57). Concurring with this assessment, the television composer famous for his themes for *The West Wing* and *thirtysomething*, W.G. Snuffy Walden, stated that one of the reasons that programs like *CSI: Crime Scene Investigation* paid a purported six-figure licensing fee to use The Who's "Who Are You" as its theme is that, "Everything in the industry moves so fast now, (and) people are looking for every advantage to make a quick impression" (Callaghan, 2004). Walden and his peers had reason to pay attention to this trend. In 2004 NBC alone licensed Elvis Presley's "A Little Less Conversation," Electric Light Orchestra's "Mr. Blue Sky," and the Long Beach Dub Allstars tune "Sunny Hours" to theme *Las Vegas*, *LAX* ,and the *Friends* spinoff *Joey*, respectively. Echoing Walden, Mark Mothersbaugh, member of the rock band Devo and claimant of multiple film and television composing credits, noted that trend stemmed from a struggle for instant impact: "There are no new 'Andy Griffith' themes today because they're looking for something that's already established as opposed to waiting for something to germinate. When you're fighting to see if your show will be on next week, you need something that works right away" (Callaghan, 2004).

For some networks the need to sonically brand television extends beyond the confines of commercials and narrative programming. Perhaps the most salient example of this exists in NBC's investment in the Olympic Games. As the exclusive broadcaster in the United States for Winter and Summer games until 2020, NBC's investment in the these biannual events has been an ambitious attempt to leverage the Olympic Games across the entirety of its broadcast, cablecast, and webcasting assets. The importance of this event would appear in NBC's efforts to produce the events with particular attention to music supervision. The vast nature of the Winter and Summer Olympic Games means procuring numerous licenses needed to keep the events feeling fresh over more than two-week periods of time and a variety of competitions, ceremonies, and athletic teams; it is nothing less than a massive undertaking. In 2000, the many coaches, competitors, families, and nations that brought with them their many colors, costumes, and backstories also brought with them an unstated demand for a significant musical infrastructure. Scott Elias, president and CEO at Elias Arts, spent months working to orchestrate and compile all the pieces played on NBC during the games. As an *Advertising Age* article explained,

> Though this is the second Olympics the company has handled, the job just keeps getting bigger, even as the ratings shrink. There are more than 7,000 spots where music is used in the broadcasts—everything from Australian Aboriginal sounds to hip-hop—and all of it is categorized in a database, sometimes arranged by thematic concept, like Victory, Defeat, Inspiration and Determination. There are also a number of name acts involved in the show, including Santana, the Goo Goo Dolls, the Backstreet Boys and Colin Hay of Men at Work, who offered a remix of "Down Under," the most Aussie-awesome song after "Waltzing Matilda." (TK, 2000, p. 24)

Billboard explained in 2006 that, "NBC uses music in four ways for the Olympics: network campaigns in advance of the Games; co-branding opportunities; features and interstitial footage broadcast during the athletic events; and the nightly concerts" (Newman & Paoletta, 2006a, p. 22). Furthermore, "by using hip, under-the-radar acts" NBC openly hoped to land the "much-coveted youth demo" of 18-to 34-year-old viewers (Ibid.). As NBC baited younger viewers with music, labels and artists saw the games as a means to promote their releases. *Billboard* reported that in 2002, John Williams, Sting, Train, Dixie Chicks, and Barenaked Ladies all witnessed at least a 25% increase in the sales of their recordings after appearing at the 2002 Winter Olympics in Salt Lake City (Newman & Paoletta, 2006a). So impressive was the effect on sales that the Cherrytree/Interscope hip-hop group Flipsyde used their placement in the 2006 Winter Olympics to relaunch their album *We the People*. Originally released in July 2005, *We The People* was rereleased in December with one more additional track in to coincide with the hip-hop group's song "Someday," named as the "theme song of [NBC's] Winter Olympics coverage." The track was played and identified in spots promoting the games beginning in December 2005 through to late-February 2006 when the Winter Games ended. For NBC, "Someday" allowed the network to find a way to audibly market the games with an "edgy song filled with hope and achievement" (Paoletta, 2006, p. 14). In return the group saw its sales increase substantially. Selling only 500 units for the final week of the 2005 Christmas shopping season, the disc doubled its sales one week later for the week ending January 1, 2006. By January 14, 2006, *We the People* had sold 2,000 units, almost a full month before the Winter Olympics' opening ceremonies (Paoletta, 2006).

The combined emphasis on the branding and sales partially explains the rise of numerous music and dance-oriented television projects that emerged on U.S. television in the 2000s. While music-oriented programs of the last 12 years such as *American Idol, The X Factor, America's Got Talent, Dancing with the Stars,* and others are often spoken as a hybrid of reality and game show program genres, the fact is that all of these programs have substantial musical components. Although the licensing issues for such programs are substantial, these reality/competition programs are still substantially cheaper to produce when compared to scripted television programming.[4] The objectives behind these kinds of talent programs for the music and television industries are clear: networks get a relatively cheap source of programming that includes an interesting mix of amateur and professional performers who integrate a high-profile music catalogue into their performances, while performers and songwriters are able to publicize their work, receive licensing fees and residual income.

However the term "economic efficiency" does not necessarily apply to the 2009 appearance of the music-driven dramatic comedy series *Glee*.

Moved into the 2009 Fox television schedule as a midseason replacement, *Glee* was given a significant budget of $3 million per hour episode. Part of this cost, *The New York Times* reported, was attributable to the "fees paid for music rights." Unlike other scripted narratives and advertisers who went for the low-cost option of independent music, *Glee*'s producers went for name songs from significant artists. The pilot included a variety of songs such as Amy Winehouse's "Rehab" and the 1960s folk standard "Leaving on a Jet Plane." Producer Ryan Murphy explained that he felt that one key to the show about a high school choral group "is to do songs that people know and interpret them in a different and unusual way." No doubt *Glee*'s embrace of mainstream hits and the dramatic portrayal of amateur performance was directly inspired by Fox's megahit of the decade, *American Idol*. Indeed, the first episode of *Glee* received its launch with the 2009 season finale of *Idol* as its lead in, drawing from the episode's more than 27 million viewers (Wyatt, 2009).

However, what makes *Glee* so exceptional in modern U.S. television is that the program harkens back to the business designs of Broadway and film musicals. To lower some of the show's substantial production costs, including some the costs coming from *Glee*'s music licensing, Ryan Murphy pointed out that the program "had seven companies bidding for the soundtrack rights" and that they intended to "release several soundtracks a year" (Wyatt, 2009). Those labels bidding to gain the soundtrack rights were also excited by what *Billboard* reported "as a rare bright spot in the TV networks' annual upfront presentations." Overseeing this relationship between the show and labels was P.J. Bloom. Music consultant for a number of HBO Films and music supervisor for CBS' *CSI: Miami* and FX's *Nip/Tuck*, Bloom explained to *Billboard* that *Glee* involved numerous pre-production efforts essential to creating a set of placements that would be "instantly recognizable":

> We must front-load the creative, business and production elements of our soundtrack well in advance of our shoot days. Our music team is in loop much earlier than traditional television shows where 90% of the music needs are addressed in postproduction. On *Glee*, we have concept meetings, receive acts and scripts as they're written and even work from Ryan's stream of consciousness. The latter keeps us all on our toes, but it's a creative process we've come to appreciate and why it's so critical we work as a team.

Furthermore,

> Budgeting for "Glee" has been an intensive, complicated process. Most television shows only deal in traditional music licensing and even that is an afterthought often addressed in postproduction. On this show, in addition to the common clearance and licensing issues,

we deal with prerecords, studio sessions, on-camera song production, musician and vocalist contracting, choreography, [Screen Actors Guild] and [American Federation of Musicians] union interaction, auditions, demo-ing and a variety of other financial issues that come up on a daily basis. In order to budget appropriately, we spent many hours with the Fox team during the development of this show to plot exactly how we were going to execute this series. (Donahue, 2009, p. 17).

Bloom pointed out that he felt that the pilot was "a bear" to supervise and while his team had months to produce it, future episodes would be equally as dense with music placements (Donahue, 2009, p. 17).

Like *American Idol*, Fox's *Glee* found a convenient partnership in Sony music on the soundtrack side (Donahue, 2009). However, the program hardly limited itself to record sales. The American music book publisher Hal Leonard published a number of *Glee* piano and vocal songbooks marketed toward high school and junior high school music departments for practices and recitals. There were even discussions of a Broadway show and a "Glee on Ice" (Wyatt, 2009). In late spring of 2011, *The Los Angeles Times* pointed out that the program, just like *American Idol*, was being franchised into a tour among other items:

The "Glee" machine has generated a Chevy commercial that redefined product placement (the commercial was part of an episode and ran after the Super Bowl), fashion deals with Macy's and Claire's, a series of "Glee" books and an upcoming 3-D concert movie. There's "Glee" bedding and pajama pants, an official "Glee" journal, a "Glee" board game and a "Glee"-tastic microphone. There was even, as apparently required by the Disney handbook of mass-marketing young people, a controversial GQ photo shoot. (McNamara, 2011)

By 2011 the franchise that had convinced teens and 20-year-olds to put Fleetwood Mac songs on their iPods had metastasized to "Vegas-sized proportions" much to the delight of its fans (McNamara, 2011). Of course *Glee*'s rapid boundless growth was nothing new for seasoned music supervisors. Speaking to *Billboard* in 2004 about the nature of her craft, Rene Arsenault noted that his work was something that always "evolves into something else." A music supervisor who has assembled a client roster of Gucci, Old Navy, Hugo Boss, Ikea, and others, Arsenault has built a music supervision firm focused on the creation and remixing of music for television ads and fashion shows. Arsenault explained to *Billboard* that, "The best part of [my job] is that we're not reacting to what's going on. We're simply doing what we've always done. We are the new music business model" (Paoletta, 2004a, p. 6).

BIBLIOGRAPHY

Adams, S. (2003, July 1). Reel Money. *Electronic Musician, 8*.

Alder, K. (2007). Introduction. *Isis, 98*(1), 80–83.

Andreeva, N. (2007, January 6). Touchstone TV Playing Music With Soler. *The Hollywood Reporter*, 1.

Anon. (2005, October 8). TV Is the New Radio: Prime-Time Dramas Champion New Artists. *Billboard*, Cover.

Anon. (2007a, October 20). Home Front: 360 Degrees of Billboard. *Billboard*.

Anon. (2007b, January 20). Publishers: Sync When You're Winning. *Music Week*, 20.

Anon. (2009, August 1). Syncing: From Brief to Broadcast. *Music Week*, 15.

Anon. (2010a, February 20). Project Runway. *Billboard*.

Anon. (2010b, December 11). Women in Music 2010: Top 30 Women in the Music Business. *Billboard*.

Arkoff, V. (1995, September 8). Basic Instinct: More Filmers Entice Artists As Supervisors. *Daily Variety*.

Ashton, R. (2010, March 27). SYNC: Sony Secures Services of Veteran Music Supervisor. *Music Week*, 4.

Aslinger, B. S. (2008). *Aural Appearances: Popular Music, Televisuality, and Technology*. Doctoral Dissertation, University of Wisconsin–Madison, Madison, Wisconsin.

Ault, S. (2003, May 3). Licensing Liaisons Serve As Middlemen For Labels, Acts. *Billboard*, 47.

Bishop, B. (2002). Moby Didn't Feel Pressure to Follow Up 'Play,' '18' Bows At Number Four. *Yahoo! Music*. Retrieved from http://new.music.yahoo.com/moby/news/moby-didnt-feel-pressure-to-follow-up-play-18-bows-at-number-four—12054910

Bloom, D. (2001, November 26). Pubcaster Launches New Events, Musical Careers. *Variety*.

Bloom, D. (2002a, January 22). Deejay Tops Stimmung. *Variety*.

Bloom, D. (2002b, June 3). Halloran Adds Subzero. *Daily Variety*.

Bruno, A. (2008, May 3). 6 Questions With DJ Green Lantern. *Billboard*.

Burlingame, J. (2002, July 29). Spinmeister Richardson Lives For Moment. *Variety*, 4.

Burlingame, J. (2006, July 28). Alexandra Patsavas, Music Supervisor. *Daily Variety*, A18.

Butler, S. (2005, November 19). The Publishers' Place: Indie Resilience. *Billboard*, 14.

Callaghan, D. (2004, November 16). From the Universally Recognizable. . . . *The Hollywood Reporter*.

Carter, B. (2006, May 29). Reality TV, Ripening In the Heat of Summer. *The New York Times*.

Carter, B. (2009, October 15). NBC Names Jon Bon Jovi 'Artist in Residence.' *The New York Times*. Retrieved from http://www.nytimes.com/2009/10/15/arts/television/15bonjovi.html?emc=eta1

Clarke, S. (2009, February 21). Publishing: What's The Frequency, Hugo? *Music Week*, 14.

Coates, N. (2002). *It's a Man's, Man's World: Television and the Masculinazation of Rock Discourse and Culture*. Doctoral Dissertation, University of Wisconsin–Madison, Madison, Wisconsin.

Crisafulli, C. (2003, November 21). New Program: 'TV Is the Way to Sell Records.' *The Hollywood Reporter*. Retrieved from http://www.allbusiness.com/services/motion-pictures/4883338-1.html

Crisafulli, C. (2007, November 1). Music Supervision Starts With Passion For the Form. *The Hollywood Reporter*. Retrieved from http://www.hollywoodreporter.com/news/music-supervision-starts-passion-form-153986

Crowe, M. (2011). About—Guild of Music Supervisors. Retrieved August 1, 2011, from http://www.guildofmusicsupervisors.com/about/

Cuarón, A. (Writer). (2001). Y Tu Mamá También. Mexico.

Diamant, L. (1987, August 3). 'In-House' TV Production? *Advertising Age*.

Diaz, A.-C. (2003, July 1). Them Changes; Commercials Music Licensing Mania and a Horde of Bands That Can't Wait to Do What Used to Be Called Selling Out Have Presented Ad Music Houses With a Simple Darwinian Truth: Adapt and Survive. Herein, a Survey of Music Mutations. *Advertising Age's Creativity*, 26.

Donahue, A. (2008a, March 1). How Sweet It Is: Evergreen and Hunnypot. *Billboard*, 6.

Donahue, A. (2008b, April 26). Republic Tigers Burning Bright. *Billboard*.

Donahue, A. (2009, May 30). The Billboard Q&A: P. J. Bloom, Neophonic Partner. *Billboard*, 17.

Forman, M. (2002). 'One Night on TV Is Worth Weeks at the Paramount': Musicians and Opportunity in Early Television, 1948–1955. *Popular Music*, 21(3), 249–276. doi: 10.1017/S0261143003002179

Fried, M. (1997, May 24). Time For Song Plugging's Second Wind. *Billboard*, 7.

Frith, S. (1988). Picking Up The Pieces. In S. Frith (Ed.), *Facing the Music* (pp. 88–130). New York: Pantheon.

Frith, S. (2002). Look! Hear! The Uneasy Relationship of Music and Television. *Popular Music*, 21(3), 277–290.

Gallo, P. (2007, February 14). Lionsgate Has Its Conductor. *Daily Variety*, 1.

Garrity, B. (2006, October 7). Stars Select Shows' Songs. *Billboard*, 8.

Garrity, B. (2007a, March 27). Music Supervisor Patsavas Forms Record Label. *The Hollywood Reporter*, 3.

Garrity, B. (2007b, March 31). TV on the Radio? *Billboard*, 9.

Guerin, A. (2006, January 10). Supervision. *The Hollywood Reporter*.

Harding, C. (2008, May 3). The Indies: Driving Licenses for Quango Records. *Billboard*.

Harding, C. (2010a, September 4). 6 Questions: Gabe McDonough. *Billboard*.

Harding, C. (2010b, November 27). Northwest Orient: Grocery Chain Artists. *Billboard*.

Harvey, S. (2006, September 1). This Sonic Branding Is Man Made. *Pro Sound News*, 57.

Hasty, K. (2006, November 18). Q&A: Alexandra Patsavas. *Billboard*, 20.

Henderson, R. (1998, December 19). Independent Music Publishing: Media Exposure—Indie Pubs Find the Ticket to Getting Into the Movies and TV. *Billboard*, 47.

Hennion, A. (1989). An Intermediary Between Production and Consumption: The Producer of Popular Music. *Science, Technology, & Human Values*, 14(4), 400–424.

Hunter, N. (2000, May 20). Rodford Champions Movie Scorers: Air-Edel Exec Seeks Exposure For Rookies, Protection of Rights. *Billboard*.

Jenkins, H. (2006). *Convergence Culture: Where Old and New Media Collide*. New York: New York University Press.

Kasdan, L. (Writer). (1983). The Big Chill. In L. Kasdan & M. Nasatir (Producers).

Kipnis, J. (2002, October 26). Film & TV Confab Addresses Visual Path to Musical Exposure. *Billboard*.

Klein, B. (2008). 'The New Radio': Music Licensing As a Response to Industry Woe. *Media Culture Society*, 30(4), 463–478. doi: 10.1177/0163443708091177

Kot, G. (2009). *Ripped: How the Wired Generation Revolutionized Music*. New York: Scribner.

McCollum, S. (2010). New Seasons Markets to Get Local Live Music For Shoppers. *Portland Home & Living Examiner*. Retrieved from http://www.examiner.com/home-living-in-portland/new-seasons-markets-to-get-local-live-music-for-shoppers

McNamara, M. (2011, May 23). Critic's Notebook: The 'Glee' Machine. *The Los Angeles Times*. Retrieved from latimes.com/entertainment/news/tv/la-et-glee-franchise-20110523,0,4471492.story

Mitchell, G. (2010, April 17). 6 Questions with Joel C. High. *Billboard*, 35.

Morris, C. (2004, August 21). A Q&A With Nic Harcourt. *Billboard, 78*.

Newman, M. (2009, July 7). New Kids on Net. *Daily Variety, A3*.

Newman, M., & Paoletta, M. (2006a, February 4). Good Sports: Artists on Fast Track for Wide Exposure at Winter Olympics. *Billboard*, 22.

Newman, M., & Paoletta, M. (2006b, May 13). TV: Seen + Heard. *Billboard*, 31–32.

Paoletta, M. (2003, May 10). Beat Box. *Billboard*, 34

Paoletta, M. (2004a, March 27). Onda Expands Production Role Beyond TV, Fashion. *Billboard*, 6.

Paoletta, M. (2004b, March 6). The Beats Go On. *Billboard*, 1.

Paoletta, M. (2005, September 20). Making The Brand: Turning Bands Into Brands. *Billboard*, 20.

Paoletta, M. (2006, January 14). Making the Brand: Rocking the Winter Games. *Billboard*, 14.

Paoletta, M. (2007a, September 15). Making The Brand: Bon Jovi's Designated Hit. *Billboard, 22*.

Paoletta, M. (2007b, October 6). Making the Brand: Helping Koop Recoup. *Billboard*, 17.

Paoletta, M. (2007c, September 22). One Man, One Soundtrack. *Billboard*, 32–33.

Paoletta, M., & Walsh, C. M. (2005, August 13). Kmart and Target Ads Get Hip With Under-The-Radar Acts. *Billboard*, 10.

Scott, T. (Writer). (1986). Top Gun. In J. Bruckheimer & D. Simpson (Producers).

Smith, E. (2000). Organization Moby: Tech-Smart, Self-Effacing, and Supremely Market-Savvy, Electronica Superstar Moby Isn't a Cog in the Machine. He Is the Machine. *Wired*. Retrieved from http://www.wired.com/wired/archive/10.05/moby_pr.html

Smith, J. (2001). Taking Music Supervisors Seriously. In P. Brophy (Ed.), *Cinesonic: Experiencing the Soundtrack* (pp. 125–146). North Ryde NSW, Australia: Southwest Press Pty Ltd.

TK. (2000, October 1). Going For Music Gold. *Advertising Age's Creativity*, 24.

Trakin, R. (2006, May 15). Alexandra Patsavas, Music Supervisor; Indie-Music Fans Are All Ears For Uncanny Touch of Patsavas With Soundtracks Almost As Popular As Hit Show. *Advertising Age*, S9.

Weiss, D. (2005, January 1). New York Metro. *Mix, 139*.

Weiss, D. (2009, August 1). New York Metro. *Mix*, 20.

Whitmire, M. (2005, October 8). TV Tunes: Partners in Crime. *Billboard*, 32–33.

Wood, M. (2008, September 13). One-Stop (Chop) Shopping. *Billboard*, p. 59

Wyatt, E. (2009, May 17). Not That High School Musical. *The New York Times*, AR26. Retrieved from http://www.nytimes.com/2009/05/17/arts/television/17wyat.html

6 In a Land of 360 Deals 1,000 True Fans Can't Be Wrong

Financing the Social Musician and Online Relationships

In 2006 and 2008 Lupe Fiasco, one of hip-hop's most interesting artists released two of the more critically-lauded albums of the genre in *Food & Liquor* and *The Cool* (Fiasco, 2006, 2008). Both *Food & Liquor* and *The Cool* reached top ten positions on *Billboard*'s "Hot 100" chart, and received nominations and positive reviews. One of those rare artists that receives both critical praise and laudable sales numbers, Fiasco seemed positioned for a lengthy career of regular releases and tours as he finished his third album that was slated to be released in 2009. Yet 2009 passed and there was no new Fiasco release. 2010 came and went with no new Fiasco record delivered to retailers. It wasn't because Fiasco hadn't created new material. In fact, Lupe Fiasco began performing songs from what was to be a new release and had turned in a new album of material to his label, Atlantic Records, in late-2009. In 2010 Fiasco claimed that Atlantic's delay was due to a perceived lack of "hit singles." Even though he had been offered a number of what the label thought would be hit recordings by producers and writers, Fiasco turned them down noting that if he had agreed to the terms offered, he would not own any of the publishing rights. Fiasco's complaint was not an unusual one. Disputes between musicians and the producers about what should and should not be on an album are not unusual. What was unusual was the emergence of an online petition assembled by Fiasco's fans demanding the label release the album for retail (Reid, 2010). Fiasco explained he was delighted with this display of fan power: "It was dope to see that. I didn't fall back on them to do that, they did that themselves and protested in the streets to get my record released. It was also humbling, because it makes me think about my responsibility when I go to make records" (Carroll, 2011, p. 6). Fiasco's third record was finally released almost two years after its recording. The release was partially attributable to the power and dedication of Fiasco's fans. The deep connection he had with his fans, his willingness to reach out and communicate with them online, and their ability to communicate with him and each other made Fiasco too attractive to ignore. However, this fan devotion cut two ways. Fiasco discovered that his fans' loyalty was so coveted by his label that it would become a source of significant dispute. The initial problem, that his album lacked singles, had quietly receded into the background and Fiasco's dispute with Atlantic now turned on his resistance to a new set of contractual terms. Fiasco's initial deal was a variation on what the industry used to call a "standard deal." However, the deal was made in the mid-2000s when these standard deals started to lose favor with labels. Instead, Atlantic wanted to renegotiate Fiasco's contract and have him sign what has become known as a "360 deal" (Carroll, 2011). Without this new type of contract in hand Atlantic had one leverage point left and effectively shelved any new product he could release. As Fiasco put it, "I don't have a 360 deal, so that put me in a different priority list" (Koha, 2011, p. 7).

Fiasco's problems were not unique. Artists and labels alike had come to a new understanding about what was of value and it was no longer record sales. Instead, it was the social capital that artists and acts cultivated and maintained, a capital that allowed them to better license themselves, sell merchandise, bring crowds to concerts, and, perhaps, sell records and downloads. To understand this change is to understand a new system where entities are financing musician and music as social entities who can enable exchanges at multiple sites as opposed to the primary site of recording. In this case, the combination of a rapidly changing music industry and Fiasco's intense and committed fan base provides a significant example of how the arrival of a user-based economy has altered the music industry. The "fan uproar" that Fiasco identified as "a revolutionary moment'" was the kind of activity that had forced the industry to rethink its investment agenda. The decline of record sales and the rise of the user has not only altered the culture of consumption but the nature of patronage, a change which involves actors from sectors not typically associated with artist investment. These actors are experimenting with practices in a search for profitable financial models. This chapter places these emergent practices of the "360 deal" and the "crowdsourcing of finance capital" into this context. Although there is no dominant model, what dominates each is an emphasis on being social to connect with, cultivate, and quantify the types of relationships with fan communities. Indeed, the outcome of crowdsourced capital and an ascendant embrace of online analytics have resulted in an emphasis on cultivating sets of evangelical fans who will both purchase and promote your work. The most formalized version of this strategy centers on the creation of "1,000 True Fans" through which artists attempt to generate a set of niche-oriented income streams to achieve middle-class status.

To be sure, the difference between a standard deal and a 360 deal is not one of measure but rather one of mode. Fiasco's initial problem with the record company demanding that he produce some ready-for-radio-airplay records was about how much of an aesthetic and promotional compromise each party would make. This compromise was made within the context of a specific kind of record contract that emphasized the sale of recorded music objects. In the mode of the standard contract the single was both a tactical source of sales and promotion for compact discs, long-play records, pre-recorded cassettes, etc. The so-called "standard contract" typically included an advance or set of advances that the artist(s) would accept. Depending on the terms of the contract, the artist would be obliged to exclusively record and produce a number albums or songs within a set period of time for the label. The label would receive the master tapes and own the recordings and their copyright. After the advances were paid back in a process known as "royalty recoupment," the label would then dispense royalties to the artists in rates that could vary dependent on the number of conditions. By exchanging these assets artists shifted the financial risks incurred in professional recording on to the label. In turn the label would be incentivized to make marketing decisions that would best beget profits. The classic standard contract was an arrangement that many artists and managers understood and felt comfortable negotiating. Thus, management could direct aspiring recording artists onto career paths designed with these contracts in mind. Recording artists worked for years with these kinds of contracts and while returns on records could be relatively insubstantial, the label's investment rarely extended beyond the recording. As a result, artists could look to other areas such as live performance and the sale of merchandise to create additional outside streams. However, as the sale of recordings precipitously waned so did the ability for labels to find profitability in the standard contract. By the mid-2000s music industry financiers were forced to go beyond merely tweaking one standard contract after another. What the music industry began to generate was a financial practice known as a "multiple rights deal," eventually known as a "360 deal." While the standard contract invested primarily in the recording, the 360 deal is an investment that attempts to recoup from every aspect of the artist's career. Unlike the standard contract, the 360 contract invests in most artists as a brand proposition whose income may come from any variety of sources. The recoupment from this investment includes taking substantial percentages from publishing, live appearances, merchandise, and television and film careers, as well as from artists' recordings.

Given the circumstances of the early- and mid-2000s, it would be hard to fault Atlantic and other labels to search for ways to place their artists into new financial agreements. The changes that an ecosystem of digitally networked filesharing users ushered in have demanded a substantial renegotiation in what Frith identifies as the three terrains that modern popular music systems must negotiate: the economic, the technological, and the cultural (Frith, 1988, p. 11–23). Accordingly, the shift from an industry based on the sale of objects to audiences forced financiers to experiment. Arguably one of the most important acts to quickly realize the necessity of experimenting financially was the English pop superstar Robbie Williams. As a singer, musician, and sometimes actor, Williams had spent the first half of the 1990s in the boy band Take That. Leaving the group in 1995,

Williams worked with Tim Clark and David Enthoven of the management firm IE Music. Throughout the second half of the 1990s the team worked with EMI Music to make Williams into a global star. After Williams' contract expired in 2001, the 28-year-old artist was able to negotiate a celebrated four album £80 million deal with EMI in 2002 that included a commitment to break him in the United States (Anon., 2002). The substantial price tag caught the eye of the worldwide press. Less understood at the time was the structure of the deal. Working with Patrick McKenna, chair of the Ingenious Media Group, Clark, Enthoven and Williams were able to forge a new kind of recording contract. Forming what would become a "joint venture" between Williams and EMI, EMI would receive a minority stake in Williams' recordings but receive income from every other aspect of his career, including concerts, record sales, acting, merchandising, sponsorships, and so on. Although EMI was initially criticized, by 2008 the label claimed that it had gone well into the black on this deal. Furthermore, other labels were looking to duplicate their success (Rosso, 2008).

By 2007 the 360 deal had become an industry wide buzzword (Bruno, 2007). Most interestingly it became clear that labels were not the only actors interested in this mode of finance. Among the more heralded 360 signings was Madonna who committed to Live Nation in October 2007. A company that had never released a record for national or international release, Live Nation is most famous for controlling and promoting large live performance venues. But in late 2007, Live Nation's CEO and president, Michael Rapino, explained that his company was signing Madonna to a 10-year $120 million deal as the founding artist for the company's new Artist Nation division. Their reason was simple: Live Nation boasted that its company, not a traditional label, was best prepared to grow her career:

> The real story here is while everyone's talking 360 [degree deals], we were quietly building the services to do it right. We have spent a considerable amount of resources building this Artist Nation division first and then going after artists second. Madonna would not have done a 360 deal with us just because of our touring capability. We had to prove to her and others that we have been working on and built a very good execution capacity at Artist Nation. (Caufield, 2007)

Rapino further explained that Live Nation had "been consistent for two years talking about taking our global concert business of 10,000 shows and 1,000 artists [annually] and extending them to the fan through our online ticketing, and [forming] longer and deeper relationships with the artist" (Caufield, 2007). For companies such as Live Nation and others attending *Billboard*'s 2007 Touring Conference & Awards event, the 360 deal seemed to offer the live music sector of the industry a newfound possibility to compete with labels and sign musical talent. In explaining Live Nation's 2007 signing of Madonna the company's chair of music, Arthur Fogel, offered a reason that hinted at future acquisitions: "We're all looking at the same picture. It's just a natural evolution. For us, it's not that radical of a departure, but a logical extension" (Bruno, 2007). Live Nation would continue to recruit and sign other heavyweight acts like Jay Z, Nickelback, and U2 to its roster with various forms of 360 deals. At the same time Live Nation acquired Front Line Management Group, the talent agency headed by former label executive and longtime personal manager Irving Azoff. Part of the confidence that the live music sector exuded came from the fact that it had already made significant investments in a successful digital infrastructure. For example, after merging with the leading ticketing service in the U.S., Ticketmaster, Live Nation could point to the fact that 80% of their service's sales were conducted online. Furthermore, Ticketmaster was riding a wave of growth as worldwide ticket sales increased "35% from 2002 to 2006" (Bruno, 2007). Vendors such as Ticketmaster recognized that unlike selling recordings, "selling tickets or making concerts available online brings in additional revenue to promoters, venues and artists, without cannibalizing the original product—the concert itself" (Bruno, 2007). Comparing revenues made from the live music sector with those made from the sale of digital music one can see why in 2007 Live Nation would be emboldened. As *Billboard* explained, if you included all the income from "full-song downloads, ringtones and music subscription services" you would get roughly 20% of the bottom line for every major label. The scenario for the music industry seemed like Woodstock in reverse. As Vans Warped tour promoter Kevin Lyman said at the *Billboard* conference, "Touring can't be free. Music will be, but touring can't" (Bruno, 2007).

As Live Nation restructured itself to better manage talent, so did the labels in their exploration of the 360 deal. This meant restructuring areas such as artist and repertoire (A&R) divisions. While A&R devotes itself to managing some aspects of an artist's career, these divisions have long been devoted to service the needs of publishers and record companies. As *The New York Times* reported in 2007, the 360 deal would likely begin to alter the way the A&R divisions operated as they would have to scout and cultivate talent differently in light of the demands of multiple rights deals. Craig Kallman, chair of Atlantic Records, explained that within the context of the 360 deal the label's staff "could take a really holistic approach to the development of an artist brand" (Leeds, 2007, p. 1). To be sure, as Atlantic and other labels began to sign acts to 360 deals, the transition to an effective set of 360 deals would prove to be more difficult than writing up a new type of contract. It meant running and staffing a new type of organization. As Kallman pointed out, if Atlantic signed more artists to multiple rights deals and thereby spread its capital resources into new terrain, the label would have to increase services and resources to a less expansive roster. By acquiring talent managers, merchandisers, touring operations, promoters, and publishers, labels had, in Kallman's words, "doubled and tripled down on everything" (Leeds, 2007, p. 1). Such a transition not only included investments in new areas, but for majors these investments needed to be made at a global scale and in such a way that connects with local markets. This was the reason why the Australian division of Sony BMG Music purchased a 50% stake in the artist management company Calpice Management. As part of Sony BMG's global strategy, the purchase of the Australian company was part of a wholesale reconfiguration that would entail purchasing yet another artist management company (a company that would remain a separate entity), a television production division, and a "business enterprise department" that would work to set up promotions and sponsorships for artists and recordings with other companies. The CEO of Sony BMG, Dennis Handlin, explained that his company's moves into artist management and tours were "logical steps," as "the deals we have with artists these days are much broader than recording deals, covering areas such as brand alliances, events, corporate gigs, sponsorships and so on" (Shoebridge, 2007, p. 50). What areas would be developed could vary from contract to contract and in many cases it would take some time before it became apparent. As one longtime major label A&R executive admitted, it would take at least "a couple of years" after signing an act to a 360 deal to determine whether a particular "group's ancillary income can offset the continuing slide in album sales." As such, Atlantic disclosed how one recent signing of an undisclosed act was an example of how it could arrange a deal. At its base, Atlantic's signing appeared like a standard record deal: upon signing the label would provide a conventional cash advance and the artist would receive royalties after the advances and expenses were recouped. However, Atlantic's contract included an option that could kick in as early as the release of an artist's first album whereby the label could "pay an additional $200,000 in exchange for 30 percent of the net income from all touring, merchandise, endorsements and fan-club fees" (Leeds, 2007, p. 1). Furthermore, Atlantic reserved "the right to approve the act's tour schedule, and the salaries of certain tour and merchandise sales employees hired by the artist." Finally, the deal would oblige the artist to "a 30 percent cut of the label's album profits" (Leeds, 2007, p. 1). Of course, 30% is a significant improvement over the typical cut of 12–15% of an album's profits in the standard deal. Still, this improvement would only be seen if the album actually made a profit, something that record labels in their heyday could never claim for a majority of their releases.

As 360 deals began to emphasize what *The New York Times* called in a headline, "The New Deal: Band as Brand," new and old business practices became apparent. While new signees' decisions would develop to sell records and build their fan bases, for older artists this meant revitalizing their catalogue to produce fresh income streams through strategic brand development and innovative licensing activities. Although catalogue artists are not necessarily subject to 360 deals, those recordings and songs that labels and publishers already own have long been subject to similar treatment. It is within this context we begin to understand how the Beatles' catalogue was marketed in 2009 and 2010 to engage a multiple-rights strategy that repositioned the Beatles' brand. Although this catalogue had been reissued, repackaged, and remarketed by EMI-Capitol multiple times (and no doubt it will be again), what distinguished this particular 2009–2010 multiple-rights process is that the Beatles' catalogue is the most revered in rock history. As such, all Beatles' licensing opportunities are closely reviewed and involve considerations far beyond immediate renumeration. Such was the case in the summer of 2009 when MTV's game subsidiary Harmonix released *The Beatles: Rock Band*. The video game included 45 Beatles' recordings, the largest number of songs in the history of the *Rock Band* franchise. The popular music-based video game franchise licensed well-known records and songs so players and individuals can work together to "play" them using controllers that come in the shapes of guitars and drum sets. The elaborate amount of licensing involved in the project meant that EMI, Sony/ATV, Paul McCartney, Ringo Starr, and the families of George Harrison and John Lennon were all included as parties in developing the property. For Paul DeGooyer, senior VP of electronic games and music for MTV Networks Music Group, getting all the parties with vested interests in *The Beatles: Rock Band* to work together was important because "when you have that many rights holders involved in a catalog, it's not obvious that their interests align at all points." DeGooyer's interest was not mere exploitation, but to create "a new way to play with the Beatles' music" and produce something more than "a new 'Rock Band' game" (Bruno, 2009). For DeGooyer, "If we did our jobs right, it is an authentic piece of the Beatles' catalog of work, and that sounds kind of crazy because it's a videogame" (Bruno, 2009). To make the experience even more notable, for $90 more the gamer could purchase a deluxe version of the game that included plastic controllers designed to replicate McCartney's Hofner bass guitar and Starr's Ludwig drums. For $200 more an avid fan could complete the quartet of instruments by purchasing replicas of George Harrison's Gretsch Duo Jet and John Lennon's Rickenbacker. Martin Bandier of Sony/ATV explained that the importance of the combined efforts from artists to developers in producing the game was that his would be "a significant event in bringing the Beatles into the 21st century" (Bruno, 2009).

The efforts to extend licensing of The Beatles did not end with the video game. In conjunction with the release of *The Beatles: Rock Band*, the group and label would release newly-remastered CD sets. Steve Glasenk, the VP of licensing at Live Nation Merchandise, explained that September 9, 2009 was "going to be a huge day, no doubt about it, and lead to a huge few weeks of sales" and carry over into the Christmas buying season. Apple Corps had been working with Live Nation Merchandise to release "a special Beatles edition of Trivial Pursuit, new apparel, guitar straps, journals, address books, key chains—even a baby stroller." Michael Krassner, Live Nation Merchandise's executive VP of retail licensing worldwide, stated that the licensing possibilities for The Beatles would result from ideas offered by many and working with Apple Corps would be "only constrained by their idea to have quality product" (Peters, 2009). For Apple that meant that the Beatles brand would not be used to license alcohol or cigarettes. Nevertheless, the licensing opportunities in 2009 were numerous enough to stock 500-plus Borders' stores with front-of-store merchandise setups and enough high-end stylish goods to fill spaces dedicated to The Beatles in Restoration Hardware stores across North America. In the latter case, Restoration Hardware offered a Beatles-oriented CD storage unit for $89.99 in conjunction with the remastered rerelease of the Beatles catalogue on compact disc (Peters, 2009). The products rolled out in 2009 set the stage for licensing the Beatles catalogue once again, this time to Apple so that the company could finally include it as digital downloads in its iTunes music store. Released in 2010, the Beatles debut on iTunes was escorted into the marketplace by a prominent media blitz in late November, just in time for the Christmas shopping season. The brief but intense blitz of commercials would establish that rock's most esteemed catalogue was finally available as legal digital downloads, a key part of the EMI's strategy. EMI Group CEO Roger Faxon explained that "each new offering, format and approach expands [The Beatles' fan base] and the way they enjoy music." Martin Bandier, the chair and CEO of Sony/ATV Music Publishing, the group that controls the Beatles' song catalogue, made it clear that the seeds planted in the last two years were part of a long-term strategy that would "reap long-term benefits": "This is not a sprint, it's a marathon" (Christman, 2010). As part of planning for the long run, Bandier led the company to become more proactive in its licensing efforts and convert itself "from a sleepy, little profitable place to an extremely profitable, wide-awake place, always circling and looking for new opportunities." As *Billboard* reported, one month before the release of *The Beatles: Rock Band*, Sony/ATV had invested in an important piece of licensing infrastructure and built a new, state-of-the-art web-based royalty and licensing system. Sony/ATV's chief information officer, Bill Stark, pointed out that, "Most other publishers are using the AS400 IBM hardware, but we went with a newer technology that gives us more flexibility and scalability. It was very hard for the old system to track new streams of revenue. We can handle large amounts of data coming in quickly" (Christman, 2009, p. 23).[1]

Catalogue entities such as The Beatles, Elvis, Bob Marley, Michael Jackson, and others may occasionally undergo comprehensive analyses of their brand position by publishers and labels. Of course, these artists and their estates are able to do so because the parties involved understand the importance of these holdings and are willing to provide the resources necessary for their maintenance. Yet as significant legacy acts have received these services, when these kinds of branding services are offered to new artists as part of their multiple-rights deals they come with rather large grains of salt. What seems a simple proposition, to develop a new band's brand rather than concentrate solely on the sale of records

would quickly run into questions posed by those actors who have historically been involved in brand development. For example, significant concerns were voiced by Phil Tripp when Sony BMG announced that it was
entering the world of artist management. Wary of this arrangement, the
longtime Australian music consultant complained that Sony BMG's move
created "a conflict of interest" and asked "how does the record company
represent the artist as its manager in an adversarial position when negotiating deals with other entities that are part of the record company" (Shoebridge, 2007, p. 50). Tripp was hardly the only talent manager to find
360 deals problematic. A number of critics saw these contracts as simply
"money grabs" by labels who viewed T-shirts and concerts as new income
streams from bands who saw little from their record sales. A greater problem arises when one compares the different work practices that a personal
manager delivers with those of a standard record company and it becomes
clear how these complaints were not simply the sour grapes of agents
losing their fees. Personal managers are hired to build long-term relationships with artists and work with their clients on an ongoing basis. Record
companies may sign long-term contracts, however labels' work patterns
are significantly different from those demanded for personal management. Unlike personal managers, labels tend to center their efforts around
specific projects, i.e., "releases." Historically, building a promotional and
sales strategy for each release dictates the work rhythms of a company
with each release receiving a specific amount of the company's staff and
their focus. When the release can no longer significantly affect the label's
promotional efforts for the better, the label no longer "works" the record
and leaves it without promotional support to fend for itself in the marketplace. It is because of this history that Bruce Flohr, the talent executive
of Dave Matthews' label ATO Records, expressed his skepticism about a
major label's willingness to patiently develop an artist's career when the
record isn't selling. As Flohr told *The New York Times* in 2007, a major
label's claim that it would calmly persist over the long term to develop an
artist's career was "a hard speech for many people to buy into. You can
[tell] me that you're going to work a record for 18 months. You're going to
work a record for 18 months when it's selling 420 copies six months from
now? Come on—really?" (Leeds, 2007, p. 1).

This skepticism over the ability and willingness to develop an artist's
brand was the reason Lupe Fiasco balked at signing a 360 deal. Fiasco
explained that "record labels now want to be like Disney," placing their
signees on TV shows, on radio, in films, on tours, and, of course, records.
Yet Fiasco understood that the difference between Atlantic and Disney was
more than significant and that it would be "one thing to want it and it's
another to be like Disney where you have the infrastructure to do that.
They own the radio stations and TV stations and the factory which makes
the clothes. All the record label does is make records, and they send everything else out to individual vendors." Furthermore,

I told the label I'd sign a 360 deal if they brought the facilities and experts in to the building. I'm not going to sign a deal to do TV shows if you don't have an accomplished TV producer working for you. The AR man can't do TV shows just because he went to school. Just because you're a master at moving records doesn't mean you're a master at everything else. They need to spend more time working out those deals instead of trying to cheat the system and get things on the cheap. (Carroll, 2011, p. 6)

A panel of artist managers echoed Fiasco's concerns at the 2008 International Live Music Conference in London noting that 360 deals brought with them numerous problems. Carl Leighton-Pope of The Leighton-Pope Organisation, a UK-based performing artists management company, complained that the "the problem with 360 deals is that people are bringing in people who aren't experts to look after each area." Sony BMG A&R development vice president Mark Pinder agreed: "We don't believe 360 works for those very reasons because we don't have the in-house expertise to deal with them" (Goldie & Barrett, 2008, p. 10). Pinder stated that 90% of Sony BMG deals were ancillary rights deals where, if Sony BMG asked for live or publishing rights, the company would "put money on the table for them." Marc Marot, the head of the UK-based Terra Firma Artist Management company, and whose resume includes signing a wide variety of artists at Island Records, working U2's catalogue, and guiding the band throughout the 1990s, summed up that his largest concern with multiple-rights deals would be the widespread lack of unified strategies. For Marot, "unless there is a controlling mind at the top of the company making sure the passion for the artist is felt by everyone in the company—including the manager, publisher, merchandise—it won't work" (Goldie & Barrett, 2008, p. 10).

Soon, the simmering concerns about 360 deals had matured into outright disgust. In 2009 Tori Amos told a *Billboard* reporter that she had refused to sign a 360 deal with Universal Music Group. It was a luxury that she could afford as she had secured a loyal fan base and already owned publishing and merchandising companies, which provided Amos with enough clout to demand different terms than others were offered by her label. Amos also explained that there was little upside to such a deal unless it was "$100 million." Even then Amos would "have to give half of it in tax, and a huge percent to my attorney." Worse yet, "someone else owns songs I haven't even written" (Titus, 2009). When asked her opinion about 360 deals during a 2010 Oxford Union speech, longtime frontwoman of Hole, Courtney Love, was more forthright: "friends don't let friends do 360 deals" (Anon., 2010). Less curt but just as emphatic, entertainment contracts lawyer Bob Donnelly underscored in a *Billboard* opinion piece that the most basic problem with these deals was that they forced artists "to subsidize executive compensation packages worthy of Wall Street" (Donnelly, 2010). Donnelly explained that it was nothing new for labels to place the problem of lost revenues on the shoulders of artists when a new mode of business enters the fray. For example, when the compact disc replaced the long-play vinyl record as a dominant format, labels passed the costs of new manufacturing onto artists "in the form of royalty reductions" that they claimed were necessary for "research and development." The difference for Donnelly was that this was an even more insidious "power grab" as it involved "taking a portion of income from categories that have always belonged exclusively to the artist." Worse, many of these deals demanded that record company income come out of "gross revenue" despite the fact that personal managers and artists are never paid on gross (Donnelly, 2010). The 360 deal had become such a strain that in 2010 *Music Week* reported these deals were having a significant impact on lawyers who represented musical acts. Cliff Fluet of the UK-based law firm Lewis Silkin explained that to adapt to a reality of 360 degree signings, "What we have effectively had to do is grow a whole bunch of new, very commercial skills" (Woods, 2010, p. 22).

Because these deals was that it had forced numerous intermediaries to develop new skills many more actors were now that equipped with the skills necessary to advise their clients to a "DIY path to success" and how to piece together parts of the puzzle consisting of "web deals, mobile deals, sponsorships and brand partnerships" (Woods, 2010, p. 22). As labels, publishers, lawyers, musicians, and management engaged in 360 deals they have slowly restructured themselves around some basic ideas of brand development and licensing opportunities. Furthermore, other capital formations with no historical investment in music have decided to enter into the music business. Because an act's brand position is a dominant concern in 360 deals, the answer to the question of who could best develop their value no longer rested solely in the realm of labels. In this atmosphere any agency or intermediary that could best develop an act's social capital had become much more important. For example, in 2008 the Spanish Broadcasting System (SBS), a powerful Spanish-language radio network with a number of television stations and website holdings, announced it would begin operating a music publishing division. The aim for SBS would be to integrate its entertainment divisions to provide artists with numerous "promotional platforms" and "branding opportunities via its relationships with advertising agencies and major sponsors." SBS had often cross-promoted programs between websites and stations. But with this new reorganization there was the addition of a new division that would take on an A&R function and "specifically seek out deals with established and up-and-coming artists and their labels" (Cobo, 2008). In effect, like Live Nation, SBS had begun to take on some of the functions of a label while devaluing those that were no longer as important in a post-object economy. In another example of a nontraditional entity taking on some of the functions of a label, the global spirits brand Bacardi signed the dance act Groove Armada to a multiple-rights deal in 2008 that included the "integrated marketing deal encompasses recordings, touring and audiovisual content" (Brandle, 2008). According to the Bacardi global experiential manager Sarah Tinsley, "essentially we are taking over the role of a record label—producing the music, promoting new music, and the artist is playing at our events." However, unlike most contracts with record companies, Bacardi's contract with Groove Armada involved only signing for a year, during which the liquor company would underwrite the production of an EP and "consider the music for its own global advertising campaigns" (Brandle, 2008). After the group finished its five-year deal with Sony BMG's Jive Records in 2007, Groove Armada's manager Dan O'Neil explained that they were seeking a deal with an entity "outside of the traditional music business" (Brandle, 2008). As O'Neil explained, "We see this deal as giving us an increased opportunity to take our recorded and live music to new parts of the globe and to new potential markets. Frankly, we haven't found that [to be] easy with a major label" (Brandle, 2008). Obligated to play a number of Bacardi live events, Groove Armada worked with the brand to produce "audiovisual footage" that could be given to "third parties" such as broadcasters. Nevertheless, Groove Armada would retain control of the masters and copyrights they generated during the contract, regardless of how they are used by Bacardi. Although neither party would divulge the financial details of the contract, it was clear that this was an unorthodox deal even by 360 deal standards. According to O'Neil, "Bacardi doesn't see this as something that they want to earn money from, which is, quite rightly, something a label has to do. [Instead,] they are looking at it from a point of view of association, and they're getting access to a license to use the music to implement their strategy worldwide" (Brandle, 2008). Without an advance, the group's members were paid a salary with separate budgets kicking in to different programs on an as-needed basis. For O'Neil this arrangement was an experiment dedicated to "creating a 360-style model where the artist is getting all the benefits, with the expertise of the brand reaching a large number of people with their product. It's all the upside potential of the 360-degree deal, without the artist having to give loads away" (Brandle, 2008). For Bacardi, Tinsley noted, "We want to prove the mutual benefit of a relationship like this, to prove to ourselves and the record industry that this is a viable model. If we do that, we'd want bands approaching us" (Brandle, 2008). An industry player such as Steve Stoute who had spent time in both music and advertising could see that with the 360 deal on the rise the lines were blurring enough that his talents could allow him to consider running a label, almost. When asked by *Billboard* if he would begin a label at his Translation Advertising agency, Stoute responded that although he had considered it, he was sitting on the fence "because the music business still hasn't figured out its core model yet" (High, 2009).

At least one major label threw its weight behind making the 360 deal the standard. In *Music Week*'s interview with Fred Goodman about his latest book on Warner Music Group's CEO Edgar Bronfman, Jr., the magazine revealed that by 2007 the company had been able to sign half of the acts on its label to 360 deals (Barrett, 2010). One year later *Music Week* reported that Christian Tattersfield, Warner Music's UK CEO, had become the industry's "chief advocate" of the 360 deal and refused to take on any talent who would not sign one. Although this meant missing out on some significant signings, it was worth the risk for Tattersfield. As he told the reporter, "Warner will only sign people to so-called 360 deals because I want to be involved in every aspect of an artist's career. The music industry is an industry that runs on basic economics. Physical recorded music is in decline and digital sales are not making up the loss" (Cardew, 2011, p. 4). Reorienting the label around this approach meant that instead of signing 20 acts with the hope that one would get big, Tattersfield and Warner Brothers would "sign five acts and hope they all get big" (Cardew, 2011, p. 4). In Tattersfield's view, Warner Brothers would be part of the music industry for a long time and for him those "People who don't do these deals, I think they don't believe they are going to be around for a long time. At Warner, though, we care about the future" (Cardew, 2011, p. 4). Warner continued to invest in multiple-rights deals and by 2012 the company had more than 70% of its active global roster committed to this kind of financial arrangement. Still, Warner Music continued to lose market share and book significant losses and in 2102 Bronfman Jr. stepped down from his position as the transnational CEO. With its resources devoted to these financial arrangements many wondered if Warner Music was involved in a temporary transitional phase or if its slide would continue with no end in sight. As one Warner staffer told *Variety*, "We used to be one of the biggest cogs in the business—we used to be the biggest cog. And now we're not. It's one thing to be in transition when business is great. Everything has been exacerbated by business conditions" (Morris, 2012, p. 1).

As labels and other investors experimented with 360 models an entire ecosystem of third parties has emerged to provide artists many of the services that labels historically provided. These third parties included the distribution of content to digital and physical retailers, as well as streaming services. Many of these services had developed a set of widgets that enable end users to share with their social network. On the back end a number of these services provide musicians and management spaces where they can collect various forms of data such as who is sharing their wares and with whom, who has directly purchased their wares, and they can collect emails from fans who have provided them. As a result, these business-to-business platforms such as ReverbNation, Bandcamp, CD Baby, TuneCore, and others are building lists of listeners that can be used by acts and management to directly connect with fans through email and an emergent social media infrastructure. The result is that these connections have substantially altered the manner through which musicians and fans can create both business opportunities and community. One interesting and unexpected outcome of this new infrastructure is how it has allowed entrepreneurs to generate modes of financing that leverage an artist's online social capital. Third party sites such as Kickstarter, Pledge Music, Sellaband, and Indiegogo have been formed to create crowdsourcing campaigns that finance the creation and initial distribution of a product.

The status of these third parties is dependent on the quality of the connections they can generate between fans and artists. In a 2010 *Billboard* opinion piece Adam Blumenthal of the Asheville, North Carolina-based brand strategy and interactive marketing firm Curious Sense called for the industry to generate a "360 deal for fans." Explaining that customers are willing to purchase their goods, Blumenthal made it clear that this would require a 360-degree concept as it exists in advertising, where the concept "describes the multichannel communications ecosystem where you connect with your audience" (Blumenthal, 2010). According to Blumenthal, "the idea is to start a conversation with the consumer in any one channel and continue it across all the channels where the consumer encounters your product. Then move from having a conversation with a consumer to building a relationship" (Blumenthal, 2010). It is the relationship between fan and act that is key to this paradigm and one that allows band and management to "integrate new types of products, like music videogames or online virtual concerts" (Blumenthal, 2010). Blumenthal claims that if you offer "consumers new ways to interact with the music they love, [then] they'll have a new reason to pay for it." In other words, once you have established this relationship you can create a new business model and generate new revenue sources (Blumenthal, 2010).

For Adam Blumenthal this "new business model" meant networking with brands to become brands (Blumenthal, 2010). Indeed, part of any business model is how to create and leverage specific social networks.[2] As more users share and listen to files and streaming stations, the power of networking has been distributed throughout the Internet and its importance has been amplified. Such is the lesson of Jonathan Coulton, who in the early-2000s decided to leave his job as a computer programmer to pursue a life as a musician while dealing with new industry models. What Coulton decided to do was experiment with a way to produce, record, and distribute through a social media infrastructure a song a week for a year. Both as a way to force himself into productivity and a means to connect with a growing fan base, between September 2005 and September 2006 Coulton engaged in a "thing-a-week" experiment that caught the attention of a number fans and, eventually, the industry itself. Coulton had hit what one reporter labeled as a "perfect zeitgeisty moment with the rise of stuff like Boing Boing and YouTube and ScreenHead, and blogs in particular, where [one has] this entire sort of rapid fire network by which these things can be shared with people" (Plume, 2006). By 2007 his career had blossomed and he claimed that he was finally making more money than he did in his last year as a programmer (Laporte, 2008).

This "zeitgeisty moment" of the mid-2000s was the moment of Web 2.0, that moment when the Internet had finally developed enough tools that the everyday user was finally able to produce, post, share, and discuss content through a "natural language." The numerous social networking sites and practices that comprise Web 2.0 altered the demands and practices of artists and management. A significant portion of Coulton's ability to connect with fans is well-documented as a wiki on his own website. Under the heading of "Fan Projects—JoCopedia, The Jonathan Coulton Wiki," the site documents projects of multiple lengths and scale that employ Coulton's works or have been "inspired by them." They include fan-inspired and fan-directed T-shirt design contests, video contests, cover song tributes, playlists, a Jonathan Coulton musical, an "Internet cover band" titled "The Mandelbrot Set," and others (Coulton). Coulton explained that others who decided to use many of the new tools and platforms that had emerged on the web in the last decade could forge these two-way connections between artists and fans. Coulton suggests that artists could "start a blog" where they can write, and offer samples or even entire projects online. After an artist begins this process, Coulton advises that artists should begin to go to places online where they think their fans may be and get your music in "any one of the million different places where people come to discover new music." For Coulton, artists have to build an online presence and play a game of "pretend":

> [You have to] pretend the audience is there, even if you think it's zero. The truth is, your friends will come and read it. And then it'll be your friends and some guy who lives in Cleveland who you never met. Just keep talking and putting stuff out there. My thing has always been to talk about what I'm doing as a musician and why I'm doing it. "Hey, I quit my day job, wonder if this will work," and, "Hey, I posted a new song and nobody liked it. Oh, well." All this stuff is interesting to the people who care about you, whether they're your friends or your rapidly growing fan base. If you're consistent, word of mouth will grow your audience. (Feehan & Chertkow, 2009)

Once the plan is engaged, Coulton notes, the artists better be ready to monetize because one never knows when a song or record will hit. Coulton had learned this lesson the hard way. When Coulton's cover of Sir Mix-a-Lot's "Baby Got Back" was released and hit Coulton did not have a store attached to his site. The result was Coulton could not take advantage of the site's rapidly increasing traffic and lost sales. Coulton eventually built a "digital store" and even though the great majority of the site's visitors opted for Coulton's free content, more users began to purchase MP3s and CDs. As the traffic grows, so do the responsibilities that the artist has to engage. Describing the manner in which he curried his audience, Coulton noted that,

> At the height of it, I would spend five hours a day on the non-music stuff. I would head to the coffee shop, sit at the laptop, answer e-mails, read and post blog comments, and work on my site. It was intense and

not glamorous. But I treated it as my job. But I was also so thrilled to be receiving comments on my music. So I would spend my day responding. (Feehan & Chertkow, 2009)

Listening to the demand of his fans through his blog and other networking sites allowed Coulton to cater more efficiently to their needs. For Coulton, "It's one of those ideas that makes you wonder how we did it the other way for so long. It's the only way I have been able to tour—by finding the places where I actually could make money" (Feehan & Chertkow, 2009). Coulton emphasized that *these* social practices were the key to his success: "I honestly don't believe I could have made this thing happen under the old [music business] system. So to me, the internet is everything—it changed my life, it saved me, it continues to sustain me today" (Coulton, 2012).

These connections and conversations created between users and artists would be part of the aforementioned "360 deal for fans." As labels decided to adjust what and how they would make their investments in recording artists, musicians now had to learn how to create new relationships. This has meant that artists and acts have had to experiment with opening themselves and their work online so that users could make them topics around which connections could be formed. The proposition to the fan is that an act's online presence, the work, and the activities can be used as a source through which community can be formed and explored. The online aspect of this particular practice is important as it quickens community formation. Artists and fans once hindered by the limitations of local geographies could now find fans using a set of global networking tools that had sprung up in the 2000s. Forms of community have always played important roles in music scenes and fandom. Indeed, one could consider the social aspect of music making and listening as the lifeblood of any musical event. Christopher Small has noted that musical events often forge connections among strangers: "Strangers they may be to one another, and yet in certain respects not strangers at all. Those taking part in any musical event are to some extent self-selected in terms of their sense of who they are or of who they feel themselves to be, and this event is no exception" (Small, 1998, p. 41). The social component of music is not a byproduct of music, but it is an absolutely essential component of the experience of music. Simon Frith reminds us that "in terms of live performance [music] is certainly experienced both as collective participation, our movements tied in with those of other people, and as musical participation, our response (as in the classic African call-and-response tradition) a necessary part of the music itself" (Frith, 1996, p. 142). For example, "the club"—both in terms of "fan clubs" and the practice of "clubbing"—has long been vital for popular music audiences and fan experiences. The contact that artists have with these associations often plants the seeds from which careers grow. What is more important, clubs promise their associates richer social and aesthetic experiences of art and artists. What digital social networking technologies have done is amplify nascent sets of social desires. Fans who for whatever reasons have little or no access to clubs and concerts can connect with other fans as well artists both asynchronously and in "real time." Just as blogs have taken the place of many music oriented publications, Twitter, Facebook, and other social networks provide an infrastructure for a new type of digital "word-of-mouth" so essential to music discovery. For example, by the late-2000s hip-hop star Kanye West had embraced blogging, Twitter, and the user-based video streaming platforms of U-Stream and YouTube with such gusto that he no longer felt the need to offer himself to music magazines to promote his releases. West explained his problem with the press on one of his YouTube videos stating that "you say what you say and then you get paraphrased. I wanna get approval over the shit" (Vanhemert, 2010). These new platforms allow artists unfettered, unedited, open access to fans and critics to share their voice, opinions, and experiences as they occur. As users have been able to quickly develop and stitch together these online networking practices musicians have had to adapt. Those like West and Coulton who are comfortable behind a keyboard and a screen have been able to discover and leverage their opportunities to connect.

Nancy Baym has pointed out that these connections "may entail a shift away from seeing the audience as revenue streams toward seeing them as relation partners engaged in a shared enterprise" (Baym, 2011, p. 25). Indeed, Eamonn Forde of *Music Week* reported that the global research firm The NPD Group had surveyed listeners in the UK and U.S. in 2007 and 2008 with the results indicating "that music is a key component of social networking activity and digital is central to their discovery of music and artists" (Forde, 2009, p. 9). Furthermore, the difference between the fourth quarters in 2007 and 2008 made it clear that social networks were quickly becoming important forces in this new digital ecosystem. In Q4 of 2007 15% of listeners listened to music on social network and by Q4 2008 the figure had grown to 19%, an almost 27% percent increase. But most alarming were the percentages and growth rates of college students listening on social networks. In Q4 of 2007 NPD Group reported that 30% of college students had listened to music on social networks. By Q4 2008 that number had grown by almost 36% to 41% of college students (Forde, 2009). The value of social networks has become even more important as they become increasingly integrated with streaming services such as Spotify, Rdio, and Pandora. As discussed in earlier chapters, the integration of these streaming services allowed each side to leverage the other's assets, thus clarifying the importance that "sharing" plays in digital music economies.

The development of legal, cloud-based streaming systems, social networks, and a stockpile of users has created an economic imperative where media's value is developed through their continual circulation and transformation. This is the user-based model I describe in Chapter 1. It is a model where media find their value through sharing and association. Whatever it is labeled, the emphasis is on making media that are designed to be significantly altered through their rapid, continual exchange by users has also displaced a number of organizing principles that musicians and producers relied on for decades. To even those that embraced these changes it has been a source of consternation. Such was the case of Ok Go. Despite a successful run with their label where both band and label worked to be much more online and social, in the spring of 2010 the band decided to end their 10-year relationship with Capitol/EMI to start their own label, Paracadute. The relationship between Capitol/EMI and Ok Go soured when the two parties could no longer agree on how to place the band's creations online. Ok Go had become more reliant on generating easily-shared, spreadable viral content as their key means of promotion.[3] So successful were these videos that Ok Go were able to gain enough notoriety to tour five continents, win a Grammy, and bring to Capitol/EMI's ledger a "black number in our column." However, this rare "everyone wins" tactic quickly morphed into a problem when the band went to release an album in early-2010 and discovered that their latest videos, while posted on YouTube, could no longer be shared onto other sites. Because of the popularity of the videos Capitol/EMI had decided to disable the embedding capabilities of users and force viewers to YouTube where the label could benefit from the service's reported $.004 to $.008 per stream royalty. In search of new income streams, Capitol/EMI found a trickle in YouTube. Still, no matter how minimal, for a label that had lost so much in the 2000s, this income stream, no matter how minor, could no longer be discounted. The effect of this disabling, Kulash claimed, was that views of their famous "treadmill video" dropped from an average of 10,000 a day to 1,000. In effect, EMI/Capitol had decided to exchange 10 times the exposure for just under $3,000 gross from one year's worth of the video's streaming (Kulash Jr., 2010). Tim Nordwind, the band's bassist and singer, explained that the "no embed" policy left the band at odds with the label, which would culminate into a "pretty amicable" split (Ohanesian, 2010).

As Ok Go and others found ways to connect with audiences online and somehow create virality, the importance of this kind of distribution system has only continued to grow as digital social networks have become more commonplace. Perhaps the most impressive example to date came in the example of "The Harlem Shake." Released in May 2012 by the American disc jockey Baauer, "The Harlem Shake" did not receive any significant radio airplay nor did it begin to show significant sales until February 2013 when the record had become the basis of a 30-second video meme. Baauer's moment arrived at the same time that *Billboard* began to incorporate the number of YouTube streams into its charts, thus counting the well over 100,000-plus Harlem Shake user-generated videos. The result was the first meme-based No. 1 single in the history of the Hot 100 chart. Both Baauer and Ok Go may provide examples of virality, yet they were singular and could not provide a standardize path to virality. Still, both Baauer and Ok Go's examples made one thing clear: if you want your work to be shared you need to make your work sharable. As John Jurgensen reported for *The Wall Street Journal*, "that's one reason why the indie record label that released Baauer's song, Mad Decent, gives fans free rein to use its releases in their YouTube videos." The label's manager was much more succinct, "If we hadn't allowed that to happen, we wouldn't even be talking about this right now." As Tim Hwang, founder of ROFLCon, a conference devoted to Internet memes explained, "The new mechanism at work is that everybody is primed to jump in [on a breaking meme] and run with it, companies in particular. It's not just the usual Internet geeks and fraternity bros in college doing it" (Jurgensen, 2013).

Despite the prominent examples of Ok Go and Baauer, the importance of making one's work more "open" and "shareable" has taken some time for artists and labels to understand. To reconceive one's work as imminently shareable has meant that one of the standard practices that has organized musical production since the mid-20th century, the album, may no longer claim dominance. Such is the argument made in a 2009 blog posted on the Hypebot-managed site *Music Think Tank* by Dave Allen of the post-punk group Gang of Four. In the post he argues that the much-publicized pricing and distribution experiments of Radiohead and Nine Inch Nails laid the groundwork for ending the album as "the organizing principle." Allen explained that, in an era of MP3 players, streaming Internet radio, web apps, cloud-based music collections, and the ability to "shuffle your entire digital music collection," he believed that the album "has no place in a digital future" (Allen, 2009). Because digital music is offered under the umbrella of "ubiquitous access," "music fans are no longer patiently waiting for their favorite bands to deliver new music according to the old customary cycle—album, press release, video, radio, tour" (Allen, 2009). Instead, Allen explains than an act must simply become more social than before as "the fan base has to be regularly and consistently engaged" (Allen, 2009). This means openly communicating with your fans, really listening to them to build a "two way interaction with them" in order to build goodwill. Most importantly it meant that musicians should forget everything they knew about the "business" and to "start to monetize the experience around your music" (Allen, 2009). By 2010 this philosophy of fan engagement had become embraced by some as the year of "direct-to-consumer," where musicians and businesses now had to work hard to rearrange their finance and marketing priorities into a set of relationships with users. This would be no easy task. Russel Coultart, the CEO and founder of Digital Stores, a UK-based online service that runs digital storefronts for acts such as The Beatles and Queen, warned, "It's very hard to make [direct-to-consumer] work. You have to be prepared to go the extra mile. You always have to put yourself in the position of the fan and understand what it is they want. It is not about `pile 'em high, sell 'em cheap'; it's about engaging properly with the fan. And a lot of people just don't understand that." To be sure, as Coultart noted, "the artists that understand it's about being everywhere are the ones who are going to succeed" (Forde, 2010, p. 18).

Arguably the most successful artist to directly connect with her fans is Amanda Palmer. Before embracing her solo career, Palmer experienced success in connecting with her fans in her band from the early-2000s, The Dresden Dolls. The Dresden Dolls purchased a number of records from their label, Roadrunner, and repackaged them as part of a "Christmas package." Well before social networks and direct-to-fan platforms had developed, the band announced the offer on the band's site and through the email lists that the band had developed through years of touring and were able to generate a few thousand orders. Palmer continued to explore ways to connect with her fans as a solo act, including the maintenance of an active blog, online fan forums, and a variety of platforms that allow her to experiment with ways to directly connect to her fans and provide them with a variety of experiential goods. This continual practice and dedication to connect directly with her fans earned her the label of "social musician" and has allowed her to part ways with her label in 2009 after a significant dispute and continue to reap significant returns.[4] Her continual engagement with social media allowed her to achieve a striking, unexpected success using the crowd-funding platform Kickstarter. Beginning in spring 2012 Palmer worked with Kickstarter setting an initial goal of $100,000 in pledges and donations to fund the production and distribution of what would be her latest album. Offering her fans tiered premiums and her willingness to connect online, she surprised everyone, including herself, upon finishing her campaign with almost $1.2 million in donations. After Kickstarter's 10% take, Palmer would claim nearly $1 million net and with no record label involvement she would retain the full ownership of her master recordings and publishing as she produced and distributed directly to buyers. If she so wished, Palmer also had the option of setting up a licensing deal with a label (Robinson, 2012). In other words, for Palmer Kickstarter acted as a kind of "benevolent middleman" that allowed her to generate a near $1 million advance that she would not have to repay and a list of donors she could contact in the future (Robinson, 2012).

Like other musicians who are steeped in the social aspect of their careers, Palmer noted that these connections came with a significant downside: social networking tools for many musicians had become secondary only to the instruments they use in studio and onstage. For Palmer this became clear to her when she admitted to an anxiety about blogging when she took a trip to China in 2009 where she would also take a week off from her computer. Palmer worried that "I will pay for those seven days in China by working 18-hour days at home, where my fingers will rarely come off my computer keys and my piano." Reporting about Palmer for *The Washington Times*, Andrew Leahy noted that "Twitter updates, e-mail correspondence and blog entries are a daily part of the songwriter's life. [Palmer] views them as indispensable tools, as central to the process of promoting her music as a full-time publicist. They effectively cut out the middleman, giving Miss Palmer direct access to her fans and—much to her audience's delight—ensuring something of a reciprocal relationship" (Leahy, 2009, p. B3). While this may seem to be, to quote Palmer, "a huge blessing," it comes with the responsibility of being "always on" (Leahy, 2009, p. B3). Or as Jonathan Coulton told *The New York Times Magazine* in 2007 as he sipped his coffee and typed on his computer keyboard, '"People always think that when you're a musician you're sitting around strumming your guitar, and that's your job. But this, this is my job" (Thompson, 2007).

As musicians began to understand the need to become more social, another anxiety arose: it was one thing to have no model to follow, it is another to have no goal. In the United States a large number of the discussions about how artists should connect, with whom, and how many connections should be made have been centered on the identification and development of "1,000 True Fans." One part theoretical construct and one part collective experiment, the conept revolves around whether developing 1,000 True Fans is a viable means of financing an artist's career. The 1,000 True Fans proposition emerged from Kevin Kelley's 2008 essay/blog "1,000 True Fans," which was written as a reply to Chris Anderson's "Long Tail Economic" model (Kelly, 2008). Both Kelly and Anderson have held the title of editor of the popular technology and culture magazine *Wired*, a publication that has followed the growth of online culture and personal computing since 1993. Furthermore, both Kelly and Anderson come armed with an interest in market economics. While Anderson spent considerable time covering the Internet while working for *The Economist*, Kelly is a former publisher and editor of countercultural *The Whole Earth Catalog* (1988). While not professional economists, Anderson and Kelly have explored the economic effects of rapidly improving digital storage and retrieval systems combined with a system of ubiquitous networks. Anderson's most important contribution to understanding these changes is the 2006 publication of his book *The Long Tail: Why the Future of Business is Selling Less of More* (Anderson, 2006). As mentioned earlier, Anderson argues that unlike past eras where limits of space, manufacturing, and product placement demanded significant and reoccurring capital investments, digital and networking technologies have not only released media industries from these limits but introduced new actors and practices. For Anderson the key to these digital media formations is an infrastructure of databases, computer servers, and reliable broadband networks that drive new media services such as Amazon, iTunes, and Spotify. Unlike physical retailers, digital retailers and services can avoid the issues such as inventory limits, shop hours, and the physical transportation of goods, thereby making investments under a radically different set of circumstances. Following the logic of the "Pareto Principle," physical retailers understood well that roughly 80% of their stores' sales came from 20% of their sales and stocked accordingly. Thus, low selling, unpopular records were, at best, stocked in significantly lower numbers and given little promotion by distributors and retailers alike. Without the aforementioned limits of space and distribution, digital retailers are only limited by their ability to secure their digital wares. What wasn't predictable was the effect this would have on sales. With stock no longer chosen based on the considerations of space and transportation costs, digital retailers soon began to see considerable sales coming from "less popular" holdings. Because of the less popular stock in the "long tail," these digital services can explore an "economics of abundance," a "shift from hits to niches," which is "what happens when the bottlenecks that stand between supply and demand in our culture start to disappear and everything becomes available to everyone" (Anderson, 2005). The result for music is that digital retailers and streaming services are incentivized to embrace both the storage and promotion of "unpopular" popular music. The strategy involved for online retailers has been twofold: first, those with the means and position to do so embrace a "stock everything that is possible" strategy. For retailers and services such as Amazon, iTunes, eMusic, Spotify, Rdio, Rhapsody, etc., this has meant acquiring material in new ways. These include but are not limited to direct acquisitions from artists, working with labels, and third parties that provide business-to-business services to connect artists with retailers and other music services. Second, retailers and artists alike have had to open up their wares and services in such a manner that purchasing opportunities can be shared online through an ever expanding, decentralized set of connections. Thus, both retailers and musicians have had to turn to their fans, specifically their most engaged end users, as key to the processes that explore the long tail of unpopular products. Thus, the figure of the fan plays a specific and necessary role in this niche economy. Without the fan who can use and contribute to long-tail media formations, the social capital necessary to lubricate the exchange of experiential goods cannot be adequately generated.

Finding fans is not simply the same as finding an audience to purchase your tickets for your concerts and downloads. Instead, networking with audiences has always been the key for a musician to completely articulate musical creativity. The question is "just how many and what type of fans are needed to be effective agents in bringing music in a post-object age of experiential goods?" Kevin Kelly begins to address this in his March 2008 post on his personal blog *The Technium*, with an essay titled "1,000 True Fans." The post quickly became one of his most popular musings and opens with the announcement that, "The long tail is famously good news for two classes of people; a few lucky aggregators, such as Amazon and Netflix, and 6 billion consumers. Of those two, I think consumers earn the greater reward from the wealth hidden in infinite niches" (Kelly, 2008). However, Kelly warns artists that the long tail brings with it a "mixed blessing" because this new economic model "does not raise the sales of creators much" and, at the same time, adds "massive competition and endless downward pressure on prices." In short, for the individual artist, "the long tail offers no path out of the quiet doldrums of minuscule sales." But it is in these minuscule sales that Kelly believes that there is an achievable solution that "is worth trying to formalize": finding "1,000 True Fans." The key to this is Kelly's definition of the "True Fan":

> A True Fan is defined as someone who will purchase anything and everything you produce. They will drive 200 miles to see you sing. They will buy the super deluxe re-issued hi-res box set of your stuff even though they have the low-res version. They have a Google Alert set for your name. They bookmark the eBay page where your out-of-print editions show up. They come to your openings. They have you sign their copies. They buy the T-shirt, and the mug, and the hat. They can't wait till you issue your next work. They are true fans. (Kelly, 2008).

Kelly provides a conservative estimate that the true fan spends upwards of a $100 a year on his or her artist of choice. Basing his calculation on the premise that the true fan will spend "one day's wages per year in support of what you do" what this means is that if artists could find 1,000 of these fans they would have base pre-tax gross income of $100,000 (Kelly, 2008). Yet Kelly argues that the power of true fans does not lie solely in their willingness to consume more than the average fan. Rather, the idea of currying 1,000 true fans is that artists directly connecting to their fans could leverage fan enthusiasm and use them to create a network effect. The idea is that surrounding every true fan are "concentric circles of Lesser Fans" and that will help you nurture Lesser Fans. In essence, true fans distinguish themselves because they amplify your message, acting as an evangelical force that recruit those who may only purchase one download or come to a concert, but not necessarily both. Kelly offers a few caveats. First, that this strategy is cut out mainly for the solo artist and that once your artistic project involves others you will need more true fans. Second, not every artist will be willing to engage this strategy and they may need a third party like a manager or an agent to help them connect. Third, the more fans that are in direct contact with the artist, the better. The artists must be able to secure direct payment from them as anything resembling a third party that takes a cut of their payment means that the number of true fans needed to make a living grows substantially. Because true fans take much more time to cultivate there exists a distinct incentive to eliminate as many third-party entities as possible. And finally, the number of direct fans may vary depending on the material needs of the artist. As Kelly explains, "in fact the actual number is not critical, because it cannot be determined except by attempting it. Once you are in that mode, the actual number will become evident. That will be the True Fan number that works for you" (Kelly, 2008).

Kelly's blog post was quickly seized upon by many and continues to be a popular topic for discussion with reporters, on-the-ground Internet consultants, artists, and online business gurus. As of spring 2013 a simple Google search of the term revealed that close to 64,500 blogs use the term "1,000 True Fans," with over 16,000 of these entries coming in 2012 alone. Writing almost two months after Kelly's blog post, the CEO of the technological "insight company" Floor64 and the operator of the tech blog *Techdirt* since 1999, Mike Masnick pointed out that for all of the Internet chatter debating Kelly's assertions, "the key point that Kelly makes stands: if you connect with fans in a real and meaningful way, it may take time, but you can start to put together business models that will allow you to support yourself, without having to go the traditional route where only the top of the top can actually make a living." For Masnick the importance of this is it underscored just how different the world was "just a short while ago" (Masnick, 2008). For most authors the patience to connect and "focus on long-term relationships and lifetime value" could allow any business to move from finding customers for its products to "find[ing] products for your customers" (Godin, 2009). In 2010 career advice author Emily Bennington explained, along with Malcolm Gladwell's "10,000-hour rule," the concept of 1,000 True Fans was a breakthrough idea "that changed my life." Bennington claimed that once she had read about the idea she "got this concept immediately and put it into practice." As a result, Bennington switched from trying to address as many "faceless buyers as possible" and "instead turned to building a defined community of engaged followers" (Bennington, 2010). Furthermore, Kelly's concept made it clear that if entrepreneurs could not find 1,000 people who would be willing to purchase goods and content using the tools of social media then their products were "probably not very good in the first place" (Bennington, 2010).

Nowhere has the applicability of the 1,000 True Fans concept been more debated than among the independent music industry. In search of a viable economic and financial path, independent labels, musicians, and consultants have held up and criticized 1,000 True Fans as a means to middle-class achievement. Kevin Kelly's blog was posted on March 4, 2008 and one day later on March 5 Alec Saunders, VP of developer relations for Research in Motion, blogged that Kevin Kelly's was one of two posts he had read the day before that addressed the viability of making a living in the music industry, and that Kelly's post was "wonderful" because it applied to so many different artistic endeavors (Saunders, 2008). By March 6, Kelly's concept was being mentioned in the pages of *The Guardian* as a way that musicians could make money in a long-tail economy (Dowling, 2008). In little more than a month the concept popped up in *Globe and Mail*. It discussed not only the theory, but publicized another Kelly post where he describes how he received a letter from musician Robert Rich, who specializes in the genre of "ambient music." According to Kelly, Rich claimed that he has "been able to support himself by marketing to loyal fans—but just barely," and "If it weren't for the expansion of the Internet and new means of distribution and promotion, I would have given up a long time ago." By fall 2008, the idea had found its way to the panel rooms of CMJ's Music Marathon, the most important annual conference of college radio and New York City's largest music event, when independent musicians, artists, and the editor of the *Village Voice* came together to discuss the state of the industry. One panelist, repeatedly returned to the phrase "1,000 True Fans" as a means for defining success for independent music. Until then he had always thought of the term "independent music" "as a metaphor for 'commercially unsuccessful'" (Hendrickson, 2008).

While a few artists and bloggers began to speak about and analyze Kelly's theoretical insights as they resonated with their own experiences, at least a few elements of the music industry began to openly experiment with this model to generate enough social capital to be sustainable. By 2009 PepsiCo announced the introduction of a Mountain Dew music label, Green Label Sound, that would work with independent musicians. The label would begin as an explicitly "singles-only label that attempts to strengthen artists' bonds with their '1,000 true fans' and to expand that social bond to potential fans." While not based completely on the theory—the investors justified their experiments with the claim that music economies had previous examples of "social tools" such as jukeboxes and top 40 radio—the label would explore how to create social currency with digital tools and artists willing to experiment. The label would not charge for the singles and worked with acts such as The Cool Kids, Flosstradamus, and Caroline Polachek, who had experimented with the creation of gift economies to develop and deepen relationships "with existing fans." These musicians and the label would work together tweaking this model where music would serve "as a catalyst for expanding the social bond" and make money from income streams other than their recordings (Cooper III, 2009, p. 9).

Key to this is the employment of gifts as to generate collective obligations and establishing a long-term social commitment in which exchanges happen on a continual basis. As the professional bassist and voracious blogger Steve Lawson explained in April 2008, Kelly's piece was inspiring because it allowed him to get away from talking about "numbers" and rather talk about the process of "connecting and relating to 'true fans,'" or as he likes to call them "friends." Throughout the Lawson's post he explains that he truly likes most of his fans, and not because they pay for his music and come to his gigs. Rather, it is because they are the kind of people that he would want to "hang out with." These fans are important because they propagate a musician's music as a around the world in such a way that the artist acquires social capital. The reason that a fan's enthusiasm is key is that "in our culture of attention, people need peer approval to find where the cool shit is on line." The key for this is to find and give "the people who like what I do but don't think like marketers a space to explore how they can help me out" (Lawson, 2008).

Because fans come in many different forms and intensities, the question is not only discovering those who would be willing to help, but converting less intense fans into those who are "more willing." With the goal of making more loyal, true fans there was now a need to measure and better understand the value of specific fans. Indeed, understanding their behaviors and labeling those users who are more influential than others has been a longstanding issue for many new media enterprises. The new media user is constantly monitored and analyzed. Understanding traffic patterns and the power of linkages dovetails with the discussion of superfans who are willing to purchase and evangelize more than others. It is also something that is conveniently represented by the visual metaphor of a "fan funnel." As explained by Jed Carlson, the president and cofounder of ReverbNation, a business-to-business venture that connects musicians of independent labels with digital retailers and services, while also providing those same creative entities their own digital storefronts and spaces to house their music for streaming, downloading, embeddable shares, etc., the discussions surrounding "1,000 True Fans" and developing more valued fans reminded him of the "fan funnel" metaphor that his business employs.[5] For his company the visual metaphor of the fan funnel is essential and it has been used to help musicians and their business associates conceptualize fans and their relative value. At the top one has larger fans but they exert less intensity and follow into the funnel in an inverse relationship. As one goes further down the funnel the differences between fans begin to appear with some willing to purchase more and promote more than others. In this concept Carlson claims "many Artists have an untapped base of extremely loyal fans who have never been engaged to actively help them grow their popularity," and that, "This is a wasted marketing asset." Furthermore, ReverbNation has "seen the power of this [conceptual] tool for even the newest Artists, and it is POWERFUL. Remember, artists with smaller followings often have a familiar relationship with their fans (read: friends and family) where established Artists only have an affinity relationship. It is often the case that these close relationships can be the seed crystal that these Artists need to grow from obscurity to local recognition in their area" (Carlson, 2008). Finally, ReverbNation provides "Fan Funnel Stats" directly to the artists who use their sites. Like other business-to-business ventures, ReverbNation provides metrics that are "based on the empirical evidence we have around the things that make a 'successful' artist. Soon we will be able to incorporate the actual sales data that come back from digital retailers like iTunes, closing the loop on how the activities of the 'FAN FUNNEL' impact real business objectives like selling music" (Carlson, 2008).

Access to and understanding these metrics do not solve a band or artist's problems, although it does provide a musician with information that is far more nuanced than units sold. Once unthinkable, these kinds of metrics have become ubiquitous in the past few years. The combination of social networks and business-to-business operations such as Bandcamp, TopSpin, Nimbit, and others provide analytics about those fans using their materials directly to musicians and their management in a manner that was once simply unimaginable. Indeed, musicians who understood their careers solely as artists are now expected to interact online and understand how their interactions best generate brand equity as they analyze refined sets of information about their fans. Henry Jenkins has pointed out that this movement toward a more refined understanding of fan qualities through quantitative analytics is something that numerous entities including both consumers and producers have wanted as part of an emergent discourse of "affective economics" (Jenkins, 2006). In this framework the practices of the end user must be constantly measured and repeatedly engaged. As Dorothy Hui, vice president of marketing and sales for the tinyOGRE Entertainment label, stated at a 2011 CMJ panel in New York that another factor, the emergence of legal streaming services, means that the relationship with the fan that once ended at the cash register once a record had been sold had changed to an economy based on "driving fans to listen to things over and over again, not just once." The share-ability of these services across social networks now turns Spotify, Pandora, and Rdio into a "marketing and taste-making tool" of the best kind. Dalton Sim, artist manager at Nettwerk Management of the Nettwerk Music Group, explains the advantage simply: "No marketing in the world trumps peer-to-peer, friends telling friends that they love a band." Sim furthered emphasized the importance of understanding how fans, whether they number in the 100s or the 1,000s, want to consume music since "consumers will decide how they want to consume music, whether it's streaming, mp3s, vinyl, or touring. Our job is to give them options" (Rys, 2011).

In the United States there has been no louder voice in investigating and connecting artists to social networking tools and practices that will help musicians achieve their 1,000 True Fan goals than Ariel Hyatt. Founder and CEO of CyperPR Music, Hyatt is the author of trade books that aim to make musicians better able to negotiate social media platforms. Beginning in 2011, Hyatt started to offer a CyberPR Class at Middle Tennessee State University, one of the United States' preeminent music business programs (Anon., 2013). Part of the appeal of the 1,000 True Fan Model for Hyatt is that it reminded her of her entry into the music business in the late-1990s. Living in Boulder, Colorado in 1996 she opened her first PR firm, a boutique venture called Ariel Publicity, and began to represent acts that had been local and regional staples. These acts "made fantastic livings touring and selling their independent releases from coast to coast" and did it "with no label, no distribution, and no major marketing budgets: just a manager, a tour manager, and me." Furthermore, she also represented a number of independent bands during the third-wave ska movement of the late-1990s, all of whom "had a core group of fans that supported them by seeing several shows a year, buying merch and albums" and were able to make "full time livings from playing and touring." Beginning a series of blog posts in 2009 that have covered a number of years (and continue to grow) titled "In Defense Of 1,000 True Fans," Hyatt explains that, "Plenty of artists are getting to 1,000 True Fans, but it's going to take some time for them to prove the model because it takes time to build true fans in today's two-way conversation economy" (Hyatt, 2009a). Throughout her columns and books, the marketing and PR educator draws attention to issues such as understanding how your fan base is composed of multiple communities; how to engage them; tips on how to build rapport rather than simply sell to them; what social media tools an artist should use, and how and why; asking artists to identify their social media bases and gaining a complete understanding of their product line; offering examples of superfans; and providing interviews with musicians who are able to speak with specificity about how many true fans they have, as well as who they are, how these fans affect their bottom line, and just how problematic the process of this goal has posed for their lives. Perhaps even more important is how these posts resonate with the readers who are allowed and encouraged to leave celebration and criticism alike in the comments section (Hyatt, 2009a, 2009b, 2009c, 2010a, 2010b, 2010c, 2011, 2012) . But ultimately Hyatt admits that becoming more social and achieving 1,000 True Fans may be painful and feel unfair as much of this contact rests on the backs of musicians themselves (Hyatt, 2009a). In a world with so much music, so much clutter, so much noise, Hyatt makes no bones about the need for musicians to effectively engage their audience. It is an engagement that "starts with understanding your audience" and that what people want is "to feel connected." It is about communicating with and not talking to your fans. As Hyatt explains, "if you're just speaking at people and you're not speaking with people, they'll go elsewhere for that connection" (Bethune, 2011).

BIBLIOGRAPHY

Allen, D. (2009, April 1). The End of the Music Album As The Organizing Principle. Retrieved from http://www.musicthinktank.com/blog/the-end-of-the-music-album-as-the-organizing-principle.html

Anderson, C. (2005). Definitions: Final Round! Retrieved from http://www.long-tail.com/the_long_tail/2005/01/definitions_fin.html?cid=3407617#comment-6a00d8341bfb6353ef00d8346f2eb069e2

Anderson, C. (2006). *The Long Tail: Why the Future of Business of Selling Less Is More*. New York: Hyperion.

Anon. (2002). Robbie Signs '£80m' Deal. *BBC News*. Retrieved from http://news.bbc.co.uk/2/hi/entertainment/2291605.stm

Anon. (2008, November 22). Fuck Roadrunner. Retrieved from http://www.the-shadowbox.net/forum/index.php?topic=6054.0

Anon. (2009, December 19). Agenda Items. *Billboard*.

Anon. (2010). Courtney Love Blasts UK Music Scene and Slags Off 'America's Sweetheart' During Oxford Union Speech. *New Music Express*. Retrieved from http://www.nme.com/news/hole/49737

Anon. (2013, March 3). Meet The Team. Cyber PR Music. Retrieved March 3, 2013 from http://cyberprmusic.com/about/meet-the-team/#ariel

Barrett, C. (2010, July 17). Interview: Fool's Gold for Warner? *Music Week*, 13.

Baym, N. (2011). The Swedish Model: Balancing Markets and Gifts in the Music Industry. *Popular Communication, 9*(1), 22–38.

Bennington, E. (2010). Two Breakthrough Ideas That Changed My Life. Retrieved from http://www.personalbrandingblog.com/two-breakthrough-ideas-that-changed-my-life/

Bethune, A. (2011). Interview With Ariel Hyatt, Founder of Ariel Publicity (a Social Media PR Firm) and Author of "Music Success in Nine Weeks." Retrieved from http://playitloudmusic.wordpress.com/2011/01/05/interview-with-ariel-hyatt-founder-of-ariel-publicity-a-social-media-pr-firm-and-author-of-music-success-in-nine-weeks/

Blumenthal, A. (2010). 360 Deals for Fans: Ad Agencies Provide Lessons on Connecting With Consumers. *Billboard.* Retrieved from http://www.billboard.biz/bbbiz/content_display/magazine/opinion/e3ib75f76acc2901e26001dece6a12275bc

Brandle, L. (2008). Bacardi Gets Into the "Armada" Groove. *Billboard.* Retrieved from http://www.billboard.biz/bbbiz/others/bacardi-gets-into-the-armada-groove-1003782117.story

Bruno, A. (2007). Digital Entertainment: Full Circle. *Billboard.* Retrieved from http://www.billboard.biz/bbbiz/others/digital-entertainment-full-circle-1003679387.story

Bruno, A. (2009). Games Beatles Play. *Billboard.* Retrieved from http://www.billboard.biz/bbbiz/others/games-beatles-play-1004009310.story

Cardew, B. (2011, February 9). Christian Tattersfield: Tattersfield's Long-Term Vision For Warner Music. *Music Week, 4.*

Carlson, J. (2008). From Exposure to Conversion—'How to Create a Real Fan'—Part One. Retrieved from http://www.musicthinktank.com/blog/from-exposure-to-conversion-how-to-create-a-real-fan-part-on.html

Carroll, J. (2011, March 4). On the Line. *The Irish Times, 6.*

Caufield, K. (2007). Update: Madonna Confirms Deal With Live Nation. *Billboard.* Retrieved from http://www.billboard.com/news/update-madonna-confirms-deal-with-live-nation-1003658914.story#/news/update-madonna-confirms-deal-with-live-nation-1003658914.story

Christman, E. (2009, August 15). Don't Stop 'Til You Get Enough. *Billboard,* 22–23.

Christman, E. (2010). Beatles for Sale. *Billboard.* Retrieved from http://www.billboard.biz/bbbiz/others/beatles-for-sale-1004132620.story

Cobo, L. (2008). Billboard Exclusive: SBS Casting a Wide Network. *Billboard.* Retrieved from http://www.billboard.biz/bbbiz/others/billboard-exclusive-sbs-casting-a-wide-network-1003714055.story

Cooper III, F. (2009, September 12). With The Brand. *Billboard, 9.*

Coulton, J. Fan Projects—JoCopedia, The Jonathan Coulton wiki. Retrieved February 16, 2013 from http://www.jonathancoulton.com/wiki/Fan_Projects

Coulton, J. (2012). Emily and David. Retrieved from http://www.jonathancoulton.com/2012/06/20/emily-and-david/

Dannen, F. (1991). *Hit Men: Power Brokers and Fast Money Inside the Music Business.* New York: Vintage Books.

Devine, R. (2009). Stomach For a Fight, *The Sunday Times, 12–13.*

Donnelly, B. (2010). Buyer Beware: Why Artists Should Do a 180 on "360" Deals. *Billboard.* Retrieved from http://www.billboard.biz/bbbiz/others/buyer-beware-why-artists-should-do-a-180–1004077523.story

Dowling, T. (2008, March 6). G2: Shortcuts: Are Just 1,000 Fans the Key to Success? *The Guardian, 3.*

Feehan, J., & Chertkow, R. (2009). Industry Insider: Jonathan Coulton. *Electronic Musician.* Retrieved from http://www.emusician.com/career/0983/industry-insider-jonathan-coulton/137474

Fiasco, L. (2006). Food & Liquor.

Fiasco, L. (2008). *The Cool.*

Forde, E. (2009, March 28). Digital: Music at the Core of Social Networking, Survey Reveals. *Music Week, 9.*

Forde, E. (2010, January 23). Midem 2010: Monetisation: The Reckoning. *Music Week,* 18.

Frith, S. (1988). *Music For Pleasure: Essays in the Sociology of Pop.* New York: Pantheon.

Frith, S. (1996). *Performing Rites: On the Value of Popular Music.* Cambridge, MA: Harvard University Press.

Godin, S. (2009). First, Organize 1,000. Retrieved from http://sethgodin.typepad.com/seths_blog/2009/12/first-organize-1000.html

Goldie, A., & Barrett, C. (2008, March 22). ILMC 2008 Agrees to Disagree. *Music Week,* 10.

Hendrickson, J. (2008, October 24). Indie's Dying Breath. *University Wire.*

High, K. (2009). The Billboard Q&A: Steve Stoute. *Billboard.* Retrieved from http://www.billboard.biz/bbbiz/others/the-billboard-q-a-steve-stoute-1003943222.story

Hyatt, A. (2009a). In Defense of 1,000 True Fans—Part I—The Mountain Goats1. Retrieved from http://www.musicthinktank.com/blog/in-defense-of-1000-true-fans-part-i-the-mountain-goatsl.html

Hyatt, A. (2009b). In Defense of 1,000 True Fans—Part III—Amber Rubarth. Retrieved from http://www.musicthinktank.com/blog/in-defense-of-1000-true-fans-part-iii-amber-rubarth.html

Hyatt, A. (2009c). In Defense of 1,000 True Fans—Part IV—Kelly Richey. Retrieved from http://www.musicthinktank.com/blog/in-defense-of-1000-true-fans-part-iv-kelly-richey.html

Hyatt, A. (2010a). Get Paid in 2010: Want to Increase Your Bottom Line? Focus on Your Fans! Retrieved from http://www.musicthinktank.com/blog/get-paid-in-2010-want-to-increase-your-bottom-line-focus-on.html

Hyatt, A. (2010b). I Fight Dragons: 1 Band, 1 Year, & 10,000 New Fans—In Defense of 1,000 True Fans—Part V. Retrieved from http://www.musicthinktank.com/blog/i-fight-dragons-1-band-1-year-10000-new-fans-in-defense-of-1.html

Hyatt, A. (2010c). Your Three Communities. Retrieved from http://www.musicthinktank.com/blog/your-three-communities-part-1.html

Hyatt, A. (2011). In Defense of 1,000 True Fans Part XI—Marian Call Leveraged Twitter to Tour 50 States & Returned w/Money in Her Pocket. Retrieved from http://www.musicthinktank.com/blog/in-defense-of-1000-true-fans-part-xi-marian-call-leveraged-t.html

Hyatt, A. (2012). Ariel Hyatt's Social Media Food Pyramid. Retrieved from http://www.musicthinktank.com/blog/ariel-hyatts-social-media-food-pyramid.html

Jenkins, H. (2006) *Convergence Culture: Where Old and New Media Collide.* New York, NY: New York University Press.

Jurgensen, J. (2013). Why the Harlem Shake Matters. *The Wall Street Journal.* Retrieved from http://online.wsj.com/article/SB10001424127887324503204578318180356471240.html?mod=e2fb

Kelly, K. (2008, June 15). 1,000 True Fans. Retrieved from http://www.kk.org/thetechnium/archives/2008/03/1000_true_fans.php

Koha, N. T. (2011, January 16). Fans Cause a Revolution. *The Sunday Mail,* 7.

Kulash Jr., D. (2010, February 19). WhoseTube?, Op-Ed. *New York Times,* A17. Retrieved from http://www.nytimes.com/2010/02/20/opinion/20kulash.html

Laporte, L. (2008). This Week in Tech: Jonathan Coulton—Functional and Elegant (Vol. 133). Retrieved from http://twit.tv/show/this-week-in-tech/133

Lawson, S. (2008). One True Fan—Thoughts on Street Teams. Retrieved from http://www.stevelawson.net/2008/04/one_true_fan_th/

Leahy, A. (2009, November 13). Riffs: Money For Nothin'; Amanda Palmer Pays Her Own Wages. *The Washington Times*, B3.

Leeds, J. (2007, November 11). The New Deal: Band As Brand. *The New York Times*, 1.

Masnick, M. (2008). Does the Math on 1,000 True Fans Add Up? Retrieved from http://www.techdirt.com/articles/20080312/095631518.shtml

Morris, C. (2012, January 27). Tempo Changes For Warner Music; Shrinking Major Frets Over Next Step. *Variety*, 1.

Ohanesian, L. (2010, June 16). Synthful: EXCLUSIVE Interview: OK Go's Tim Nordwind on Why the Band Left EMI. Retrieved from http://blogs.laweekly.com/westcoastsound/synthful/ok-go-leaves-emi-interview/

Palmer, A. (2008, December 2). The Rebellyon. The Deal With Roadrunner Records. Retrieved from http://blog.amandapalmer.net/post/62721071/the-rebellyon-the-deal-with-roadrunner-records

Palmer, A. (2010, April 6). FREE AT LAST, FREE AT LAST (DEAR ROAD-RUNNER RECORDS . . .). Retrieved from http://blog.amandapalmer.net/post/501070649/free-at-last-free-at-last-dear-roadrunner-records

Peters, M. (2009). Baby You're a Rich Band. *Billboard*. Retrieved from http://www.billboard.biz/bbbiz/others/baby-you-re-a-rich-band-1004009314.story

Plume, K. (2006). Interview: Jonathan Coulton. Retrieved from http://www.asite-calledfred.com/2006/09/28/quick-stop-interview-jonathan-coulton/

Reid, S. (2010). Lupe Fiasco Talks Fan Petition, *Lasers* Being In Limbo. Retrieved from http://www.mtv.com/news/articles/1644559/lupe-fiasco-talks-fan-petition-lasers-being-limboi-love-see-this-petition-it-brought.jhtml

Robinson, T. (2012). Interview: Amanda Palmer on Being a "Social Musician" in the Crowd-Sourcing Era. *The A.V. Club*. Retrieved from http://www.avclub.com/articles/amanda-palmer-on-being-a-social-musician-in-the-cr,84702/

Rosso, W. (2008). Perspective: Recording Industry Should Brace For More Bad News. *CNET News*. Retrieved from http://news.cnet.com/Recording-industry-should-brace-for-more-bad-news/2010-1027_3-6226487.html

Rys, D. (2011). CMJ 2011 'Make It Work and Make It Pay' Panel Looks at New Money-Making Methods As Technology Shifts. *Billboard*. Retrieved from http://www.billboard.biz/bbbiz/industry/retail/cmj-2011-make-it-work-and-make-it-pay-panel-1005427472.story

Saunders, A. (2008). Squawk Box March 5—Digital Music and Free Speech. Retrieved from http://www.saunderslog.com/2008/03/05/squawk-box-march-5-digital-music-and-free-speech/

Shoebridge, N. (2007, December 10). Sony BMG Gets Into Management, Goes on Tour. *Australian Financial Review*, 50.

Small, C. (1998). *Musicking: The Meanings of Performing and Listening*. Hanover, NH: Wesleyan University Press.

The Whole Earth Catalog: Signal Communication Tools for the Information Age (1988) K. Kelly (Ed.). Harmony.

Thompson, C. (2007). Sex, Drugs and Updating Your Blog. *The New York Times Magazine*. Retrieved from http://www.nytimes.com/2007/05/13/magazine/13audience-t.html?pagewanted=all&_r=0

Titus, C. (2009). Tori Amos: She's Got the Power. *Billboard*. Retrieved from http://www.billboard.biz/bbbiz/others/tori-amos-she-s-got-the-power-1003963423.story

Vanhemert, K. (2010, August 25). Does Kanye's Twitter Mark the Death of Music Magazines? Retrieved from http://gizmodo.com/5622087/does-kanyes-twitter-mark-the-death-of-music-magazines

Woods, A. (2010, October 16). Legal: The Changing Law of the Band. *Music Week*, 22.

Conclusion

Niels Bohr, the famous Danish physicist who is often attributed with the foundational contributions to developing quantum mechanics, is also credited with saying that "Prediction is very difficult, especially about the future." In the past seven years that I have been dedicated to this topic no quote seems more appropriate. Music services, models, and technologies have come and gone with a pace and promises unfulfilled. Indeed, researching this book has been something of a Heraclitian dream, where a subject examined not only changes the day after one sees it, but sometimes as one is studying it. In some corners it might be fashionable to say that this constant change will remain and that there may never be another period of relative stability. The problem with this is that it somehow ignores the fact that people and societies demand relative stability, even if that means understanding that a period of constant change would be a kind of stability. In this world musicians and investors alike could embrace an ecosystem of "perpetual beta" and adaptation. This world of technological updates and new formats may, on the face of it, feel difficult. However, musicians and investors have long existed in a world where technologies change and formats quickly come of age. What has changed is that these new formats and technologies, while essential, have offered no clear path to profits for those invested in music production.

What is becoming clearer is that the stress on things "social" in a landscape of ubiquitous networks is that the music industry has fully morphed into a service economy where the most profitable industries understand their customers as users. Like other service economies, the threats to a middle class existence come from numerous sources and have affected workers whose skills that once insured them a chance at significant gains have quickly been devalued. As one musician at 2013 Northern California technology and music conference complained, "We used to sell an album to every kid at college, now we sell one album to one kid and everyone at the college gets a copy from that kid" (Foremski, 2013). What is worse are the skills that are needed to succeed are not clear. The questions surrounding cloud-based music services and where musicians fit in this order may be becoming clearer, but straightforward answers are far from coming.

This book has spent its time considering what answers seem to be emerging in the form of services, middlemen, and practices that a decade and a half ago either did not exist or were so marginal that their existence was not taken seriously. Indeed, the issues of time and space have conspired to limit any attempt to speak to areas such as business-to-business models and the concerns surrounding metadata that every modern musician who hopes to access the marketplace must address. There will be time enough for these in future scholarship, both mine and others. Perhaps the most concerning issue for my research is that it could never be completed: we may be able to discern trends, but the future remains as elusive as it has always been. Worse, in a world that is composed of technologies that promised a utopia of always-accessible libraries of music, art, and literature, a world where these works have seemed to be more valued than ever as capital is ever more dedicated to creative innovations, it seems that too many musicians, authors, and artists have yet to adequately capitalize on their creations. To quote Yogi Berra, another wise voice concerned with predictions, "the future ain't what it used to be."

Thus, there remains an even greater threat: even if this new service-oriented music industry does generate answers, there is little to no assurance that it will lead to a world where musicians find an equitable place at the table. Yes, musicians may indeed have to become more social. Yes, music-oriented services will have to better engage their users. However, like so many aspects of a service economy, this new music industry may simply be rife with wage inequity as income gaps become ever wider. Despite the examples of success presented, for every anecdote about investors who are finding moments of success, there is no reason to believe that a new digital order of music will by itself establish a strong middle class with equal opportunity. Indeed, new technologies of capital never simply provide this. What provides strong class mobility are laborers who understand the importance of policy and the collective actions that it takes to affect policy. While I am not convinced that we are even close to a unionized movement by musicians and other elements of the industry, discontent exists and its expression may become formalized as business practices begin to solidify. However much the future may seem to rest in the hands of emerging entrepreneurs, even entrepreneurs need assurances that their lives and the lives of their families will have some basis in stability. It's fashionable to demand that creatives become more like independent businesspeople, actors whose designs must consistently encounter market opportunities. This may be the case. Yet it is one thing to say to a musician go hunt for your money. It is quite another to say go hunt but not provide a target. As those interested in a fair marketplace it is our responsibility to identify those targets and demand that they are worth the hunt.

BIBLIOGRAPHY

Foremski, T. (2013, February 21) Sfmusictech Summit: Musicians and Geeks Searching for New
Business Models. *ZDNet*. Retrieved from http://www.zdnet.com/sfmusictech-summit-musicians-and-geeks-search-for-sustainable-business-models-7000011592/

Notes

NOTES TO THE INTRODUCTION

1. As the 21st century began, the largest record companies, the "major labels," could claim six members: Warner Music Group, EMI, Sony Music, Poly-Gram, MCA, and BMG. By 2010 the number decreased by a third as BMG Music Publishing, PolyGram, and MCA were merged under the banner of Universal Music Group, a subsidiary of Vivendi, and BMG Music Group, a rights management and label group distinct from BMG's Music Publishing assets, was acquired by Sony to eventually become Sony Music Entertainment, a 100% wholly owned entity by Sony Corporation of America.
2. Four days before Tower's regional manager wondered aloud about the room for retail, *The Washington Post* reported that the "proverbial thinning of the pie" could be seen in the case of one notable local chain. Having operated 33 stores in the DC Metro area, Kemp Mill Music announced the need to close seven of them. Then-executive vice president Howard Appelbaum claimed that the stores fell victim to the rise of competitors and the low prices that these box-store retailers could place on their best sellers to use as popular "loss leaders" (Webb Pressler, 1995a, p. C01).

NOTES TO CHAPTER 1

1. According to Raymond R. Panko, "The American Productivity and Quality Center defines the term knowledge management as the 'broad process of locating, organizing, transferring, and using the information and expertise within an organization.'" Panko quotes O'Dell and Grayson's book *If We Only Knew What We Know*, to explain that "knowledge management is a conscious strategy of getting the right knowledge to the right people at the right time and helping people share and put information into action in ways that strive to improve organizational performance." See, Raymond R. Panko, *End User Computing: Management, Applications, and Technology* (New York, John Wiley & Sons, 1988), p. 163.
2. Again, it is instructive to remind ourselves that although Kuhn's work has been widely adapted to the world of researchers beyond the "natural sciences," the utility of the term "paradigm change" is located in its flexibility. Thus, while Kuhn spends the majority of his work discussing how "abnormal situations" are discovered through "extraordinary measurement" that slowly alter in the paradigmatic theoretical core of Astronomy, Physics, etc., Kuhn suggests that while this move to paradigmatic reformation can come through

other means, however the recognition of the abnormality is very important: "I suggest, therefore, that though a crisis or an 'abnormal situation' is only one of the routes to *discovery* in the natural sciences, it is prerequisite to *fundamental inventions of theory*" (1977, p. 208).

3. Deleuze and Guattari argue that this extends far beyond digital composition to writing in general: "writing has nothing to do with signifying. It has to do with surveying, mapping, even realms that are yet to come" (Deleuze & Guattari, 1987, pp. 4–5).

4. To quote one blogger, "as D&G write, one never deterritorializes alone; there are always at least two terms, hand-use object, mouth-breast, face-landscape. So what is the reterritorializing pair for the projected identity? It would seem that the natural pairing for this is the database as the deterritorialized archive. The database, the list of the traces that make up the individual tendrils of our projected identities, is in a very literal sense, a deterritorialization of the physical, panoptic archive. The relationship between projected identity and database is much like that between hand and tool (use object). The tool exists for the hand, the hand exists for tools, just as the projected identity exists to be in a database (otherwise functionality of the specific applications would be lost) and the database exists to store projected identities. We now have our pair, the projected identity reterritorializes on the database.'" See, *Swarming Media: Projected Identity, The Database, and Deleuze & Guattari in Web 2.0*, 2009, 2006 [cited July 12, 2009]. Available from http://www.swarmingmedia.com/2006/02/projected_identity_the_databas.html

5. The importance of the textbook should not be ignored. Thomas Kuhn argues that the importance of a textbook is that along with lectures and laboratory exercises, textbooks help reveal a "community's paradigm": "By studying them and practicing with them, the members of the corresponding community learn their trade." Indeed, this kind of evidence is produced by "mature" communities of practice and allow their paradigms to "be determined with relative ease" (T. Kuhn, 1996, p. 43).

NOTES TO CHAPTER 2

1. Both Greg Kot and Frederic Dannen document how the use of independent record pluggers, "Hit Men" as Dannen dubs them, provided monetary gifts intended to populate radio playlists with major label records. This manipulation of the marketplace is the type of activity that has traditionally been held up not only as a rank form of corruption, but often offered as an explanation for the reason major labels effectively dominate radio. An arguably lesser form of manipulating the record marketplace comes in the form of gifting other aspects of the distribution chain such as retailers and critics to grease the sales process (see Dannen, 1991; Kot, 2009).

2. The practice of severe discounting was often used by large U.S. retailers such as Target, Walmart, and Best Buy in the 1990s and 2000s. So problematic was this employment, that large retailers and manufacturers felt the need to establish "minimum" prices as competing loss leaders drove price floors continually downward. So conspicuous was this practice that on September 30, 2001 then-Attorney General of New York State Eliot Spitzer filed a lawsuit against the "largest American distributors of recorded music—Bertelsmann Music Group, EMI Music Distribution, Warner-Elektra-Atlantic Corporation, Sony Music Entertainment, and Universal Music Group—and

three large music retailers (Trans World Entertainment, Tower Records, and Musicland Stores, a unit of Best Buy Co., Inc.)." Accusing these defendants of "price-fixing," "the suit charged that in attempting to combat 'loss leader' CD pricing by some large discount retailers, the defendants conspired to establish minimum prices for CDs (so-called "MAP," or minimum advertised prices) in violation of U.S. "fair trade" law." The defendants quickly settled and by October 2002 agreed to pay out $67.3 million in cash to the 28 states participating in the suit and donate close to $75.7 million in compact discs (around 5.5 million CDs) to "public entities and nonprofit organizations in each state to promote music programs" (see Willis, 2002). As the practice of loss leaders continued, it may have offered consumers lower prices but it received the criticism of independent retailers. As Jim Bland of Richmond, Virginia's Plan 9 Records put it in 2011, "We feel pretty good when we can sell a CD for $9.99. Then we look online and see Amazon is selling it for $5 as a loss leader. Best Buy sells CDs below cost hoping that someone will also buy a big-screen TV. The distributors are still making money, but ultimately it hurts [record retailing in general]" (See Mcelhinney, 2011).

3. As Anderson argues, "one of the reasons Free is often so hard to grasp is that it is not a thing, but rather the absence of a thing." A similar difficulty around the issue of "concepts of absence" occurred, according to Anderson, in 3000 B.C. in the area known as the Fertile Crescent, which includes much of present-day Iraq. Drawing from Charles Zeife's *Zero: The Biography of a Dangerous Idea,* Anderson explains that because Babylonians counted on an abacus and based their mathematics on a system of powers, they "needed a placeholder that represented nothing. They had to, in effect, invent zero. And so they created a new character with no value, to signify and empty column." By contrast, "The Greeks, meanwhile, explicitly rejected zero. Since their mathematical system was based on geometry, numbers had to represent space of one sort or another—length, angles, area, etc.—zero space didn't make sense (Anderson, 2009, pp. 35–36; see Zeife, 2000).

4. The singles sections for many U.S. record stores were part of a little understood promotional practice. As a rule, from the late-1960s through the late-1980s the 45 rpm single sold anywhere from $0.50 to $1 and was positioned as a loss-leader that promoted the much more expensive album that would retail for anywhere between 6 to 20 times the single's price tag. As a single was released to promote the LP, the single would be stocked in stores and marketed with the hope it would find its way onto radio playlists. If the single became a hit and sold, it could recoup its costs and even make a profit. However, it could not recoup with the same speed as albums as albums boasted far wider per-unit profit margins. Thus, retailers were often encouraged to devote space to stock singles by distributors who often offered them a 100% per unit return against future orders. The result is that stocking 50 copies of the latest singer or act that no one had ever heard of could be provided with minimal risk to retailer: The product could be shipped back to the distributor for more product than the retailer would invariably need in the future. In essence, single records in the U.S. were essentially promotional items for an album-oriented economy. Like most ad campaigns, singles often operated at a loss for manufacturers and distributors, both of whom took it on the chin for production, storage, and shipping costs, as a means of stimulating the market.

5. As music industry attorney Michael Guido explained in a 2004 documentary about the collapse of the recording industry, "I would submit to you that anybody that has talked to any kid that is a proponent of downloading will say in the first 30 seconds of his defense some kind of a story about how they

bought a CD because they liked a song, and they took it home—and they paid all this money, and they took it home, and when they got home, the rest of the album was junk. So why should they be forced to buy all this junk to get the one song? That's a result of creating a business that only cared about the, quote, 'hit' single" (Kirk, 2004).

6. Of course, Anderson's proposition has received substantial criticism. His most vocal critic, Malcolm Gladwell, notes that *Free*'s most radical ideas are "the kind of error that technological utopians make." Gladwell's complaint is that these utopians "assume that their particular scientific revolution will wipe away all traces of its predecessors—that if you change the fuel you change the whole system. [Lewis] Strauss [of the Atomic Energy Commission] went on to forecast 'an age of peace,' jumping from atoms to human hearts. 'As the world of chips and glass fibers and wireless waves goes, so goes the rest of the world' Kevin Kelly, another *Wired* visionary, proclaimed at the start of his 1998 digital manifesto, 'New Rules for the New Economy,' offering up the same non sequitur. And now comes Anderson. 'The more products are made of ideas, rather than stuff, the faster they can get cheap,' he writes, and we know what's coming next: 'However, this is not limited to digital products.'" Gladwell points out that *Free* conveniently forgets about the substantial infrastructural investments that go into producing the "unlimited shelf space," "the plants and the power lines," "the expensive part" of making intellectual properties and innovations. *Free* also forgets about the breakthrough work in engineering and pharmaceuticals, where the most costly expenses have "never been what happens in the laboratory. It's what happens after the laboratory, like the clinical testing, which can take years and cost hundreds of millions of dollars" (Gladwell, 2009). Henry Bodget begins his critique of *Free* by noting that "the first problem with the 'free' argument" lies in the "Cost of Goods Sold." Bodget argues that, "When you're a few guys in a band who can record a song for $10,000, you can afford to give the song away for free and live off the t-shirt sales. When you have to fork over hundreds of millions of dollars in bandwidth and licensing costs, however, it's a different story" (Bodget, 2009).

7. The rise of the business-to-business ecosystem includes a variety of services. In the United States this includes services such as ReverbNation, TuneCore, Bandcamp, etc. These services have been vital to a number of the more recent developments in maturing digital music economy. Most importantly, these services have replaced a number of the distributive functions that has been lost as CD sales have declined and physical retail has substantially contracted. They deserve their own dedicated analysis, however at this moment any such study will be bracketed to another space for the sake of time.

8. As mentioned earlier, the practice of the loss leaders is a form of direct cross-subsidization that has long been embraced by distributors and retailers alike. More commonly understood has been the construction and embrace of three-party markets. In these markets, the music industry has been able to supply its wares as content and exploit the triangulation between audience, broadcasters, and advertisers. In the case of U.S. commercial broadcasting, these three parties use free programming as bait. In exchange, audiences are exposed to broadcast messages that are paid for by advertisers (see Meehan, 1990; Webster, Lichty, & Phalen, 2008). Beginning in the late-1940s and early-1950s the record industry started to systematically supply radio stations with musical recordings that they could use as the cheap programming it needed. The result was that the record industry and radio formalized a set of practices that has produced a

symbiotic relationship between advertisers, audiences, and media services that persists as new online streaming services such as Pandora, Rdio, and Spotify emerge.

9. The reason for the new model, according to Pandora's FAQ page, is due to Pandora's payment structure. As Pandora explained on its own blog, "unlike traditional broadcast radio, Pandora pays music royalties for every single listener, on every song we play, so each additional listening hour adds to our costs. However, on the revenue side, the number of ads a listener will see or hear declines sharply after 40 hours, so it's difficult to cover these additional costs per listener with advertising alone." The shift in policy would allow Pandora to offer a significant amount of free music and "have the business side of things covered" (Anon.)

10. The manner in which Pandora and Spotify procure licenses varies drastically and they exact different business strategies as a result and I will discuss these differences in later chapters.

11. Pandora is able to access catalogue because it, unlike Spotify and other "on-demand" streaming services, can exercise compulsory licensing arrangements that are spelled out in the 1998 Digital Millennium Copyright Act (DMCA). These are terms and flat rates established by a copyright board in Washington, DC. In essence, the terms of business are nonnegotiable by all parties, which makes the marketplace much easier to engage.

12. As the same blog points out, "we don't know what period the royalty payment covered. Second, presumably Swedish collecting society STIM only pays out for Swedish plays of Gaga's music, and we don't know how much her music is played there, nor what she's getting from PRS for Spotify plays in the UK. Also, STIM may well be offering Spotify bargain basement rates to help them get off the ground. And the $167 may be Gaga's personal cut of a bigger pay out to the singer's publishing company. Plus she co-writes all her songs, so may only be receiving a small cut of the overall royalty paid on those songs, depending on the deal between her and her songwriting collaborators" (Anon., 2009b).

NOTES TO CHAPTER 3

1. Writing about music retail I am reminded of Thomas Kuhn's words on the perceived homogeneity of normal science practices: "What has been said so far [in my book] may have seemed to imply that normal science is a single monolithic and unified enterprise that must stand or fall with any one of its paradigms as well as with all of them together. But science is obviously seldom or never like that. Often, viewing all fields together, it seems instead a rather ramshackle structure with little coherence among its various parts" (Kuhn, 1996, p. 49).

2. Not every compact disc existed without copy protection. A number of labels attempted to install copy protection on their compact discs in the early-2000s, the most infamous example was Sony-BMG's XCP technology. The Electronic Frontier Foundation explained that once you inserted the disc into your Windows PC an "agree" window would pop up asking you to click on it. Once clicked, the disk would install "software that uses rootkit techniques to cloak itself from [the user]." Rootkits are forms of malware that deny the user certain abilities. In this case it denied the user the ability to play CDs on Windows computers. Although Sony-BMG released a "patch" that would reveal the XVP software, the patch created even more problems for the user.

Because the rootkit intentionally harmed the performance of the computers, Sony-BMG eventually recalled the product and became a defendant to suits from Texas and class-action suits from New York and California (Anon., 2005; Lohmann, 2005).

3. It is not completely clear that iTunes was the primary agency that persuaded the labels to give up DRM. However, if iTunes was able to make this the case then one way to think about this would be to conceive of DRM-less downloads as a widespread standard adopted to gain entry to a marketplace that has made a decision. There is precedence for this in the record industry as the search for a product that could lock a consumer into a media practice or ecosystem has been explored more than once. This has typically occurred through competing formats such as the competition between RCA's 45 rpm record versus Columbia's 33 1/3 rpm format in the late-1940s or Phillips' digital compact disc versus Sony's MiniDisc in the 1990s. These formats also promised their developers a form of incompatibility where if the consumer bought one disc format then they would have to own the proper hardware to play it. The aim was to lock the consumer into a hardware and licensing regime of standards. When "market forces" determined the eventual standard any resistance to the winning format would be nothing more than market suicide.

Still, there was at least one significant documented interest in DRM-like technologies that would limit the ability to copy recordings that took place well before digital. In Peter Doggett's book about The Beatles' breakup and post-breakup careers he notes that Apple had funded "Magic" Alexis Mardas to develop an electronic signal that could be added to a vinyl record, not to interfere with the sound of the music, but make it impossible to record. The recordable cassette tape had entered the market as fears abounded that it would do quite a bit of damage to the LP market. The thought was that, if successful, the investment in such an invention would have paid Apple back with royalties on every record pressed that used it. However, no such invention ever came to be (Doggett, 2009, p. 53).

4. Apple's lack of data transparency remains a source of substantial complaint and is a source of distrust. Writing for the entrepreneurial periodical *Fast Company*, in 2011 Steve Kehro explained that because iTunes was such a substantial force in the digital economy, controlling by some estimates more than 70% of online music sales "from an advertising perspective, Apple's lack of financial transparency is frustrating if not troubling. Any large market suffers when financial performance data is limited. And iTunes, especially for its size, is one of the least financially transparent markets out there. It has about as much transparency as a hedge fund" (Kehro, 2011).

5. The pay differential between Last.FM's radio service and an on-demand model is substantial. Last.FM may pay an artist $0.0005 for every stream, but in 2009 every time it plays a song in full on a "user's personalised radio service" in an "on-demand" fashion the same song "pays ten times as much— half a cent" (Anon., 2009).

6. As one market researcher put it, "the digital generation never learnt the habit of paying for music. There are fewer people buying fewer units, but there is more actual music being consumed than at any time in history. The problem is, very little of it is being paid for" (Anon., 2009).

7. In March 2012, reports surface that Spotify and Facebook would attempt to test German privacy law inscribed in the "Telemedia Act" by requiring Spotify users to establish a Facebook account. By June 2012 Spotify would update its services so that it would launch in Germany so that users would not need a Facebook account (Anon., 2012b, 2012c).

8. It is also worth noting that this is a reputation that stands in distinct contrast with Apple's rather notorious, relatively one-way relationship with business partners. However, it should be noted that unlike Facebook, Apple is not yet as invested in generating advertising as a quality revenue stream and has developed a distinctly different style of relationships as a result.

NOTES TO CHAPTER 4

1. The restrictions of the DMCA terminated the ability for sites that longed for noninteractive status where users could create "custom playlists, in effect creating free personal Web jukeboxes" (Haring, 2000). For a service like Live365.com, a service that in 2000 hosted several popular stations that the service would have to nix as they were noncompliant and devoted to nothing but playing music by a specific artist such as The Beach Boys, The Beatles, and The Grateful Dead, these restrictions were welcome (Fridman, 2000). Even with these new restrictions, the clarity that the legislation provided webcasters was worth the exchange. As John Jeffrey of Live365.com explained, "I'd rather have some restrictions that are clear and make it acceptable (to) the recording industry than go through the minefield of whether it's legal" (Haring, 2000).
2. It would be wrong to say that Pandora accepted the decision silently or without complaint. Pandora's blog explained that these revised royalties were still higher than other forms of radio and that the adjustment would mean limiting the hours of "free," aka "ad driven," listening to 40 hours a month. If a listener wanted more time, there would be a new fee structure (Ostrow, 2009).
3. As part of the micro-targeting strategy in 2011 Pandora began to program beyond music to find new listeners and added 10,000 comedy clips from over 700 different comedians to its catalogue. The company also noted that it would begin to look to sports and news talk as a way to possibly expand its content formats (Parr, 2011; Ha, 2011).

NOTES TO CHAPTER 5

1. Kot, G. (2009). *Ripped: How the Wired Generation Revolutionized Music*. New York: Scribner, p. 77.
2. The conception of a "thick" thing comes from the work of Ken Adler who draws from the work of Gaston Bachelard, Clifford Geertz, and Bruno Latour. Ken Alder explains his conception of a "thick" as opposed to a "thin" thing:

> The phrase "thick things" is meant to invoke two interrelated aspects of the artifactual life. The first is the brute challenge of shaping the material world by overcoming what one early modern engineer called the "resistance and obstinacy of matter." The second is the challenge of representing things in ways that at least partially and temporarily coordinate the diverse sets of human agents who design, make, and use them. The meaning I have in mind here is analogous to Clifford Geertz's contrast between the capacity of rich, "thick" ethnographic description to represent multiple (and divergent) human points of view and the reductive "thin" descriptions with which scientistic anthropologists once collapsed actions into a simplified matrix of functional behavior. In this respect, the thick-ness of both artifacts and their representations can be

contrasted with the "thinning" process described by Gaston Bachelard, in which the synthesizing explanatory power of the physical sciences—and the physical instruments that embody those theories—create those tractable objects that constitute legitimate objects of inquiry. (Alder, 2007, p. 82)

3. The emphasis on digging should be balanced by those sync licensing deals with big-name artists such as Aerosmith. In 2007 the American rock giant worked with the British-based company Stage Three Music publishing to wrangle a million dollar-plus sync license fee for Buick's use of "Dream On" for a 2007 campaign. However, these kinds of megadeals are the exception to the rule. The director of Stage Three Music, Steve Lewis, pointed out that "only a dozen or so deals of that size are done a year across the whole industry" (Anon., 2007b, p. 20).

4. Bill Carter of *The New York Times* pointed out in 2006 that although most reality series were no longer "dirt-cheap programming" and approach close to $1 million for an hour of production, this figure remained almost a "third less than a scripted hour" (Carter, 2006) .

NOTES TO CHAPTER 6

1. So determined were some music publishers to rethink their position, at least one head of a publisher suggested that, "Music publishers could start doing their own 360 deals." In 2009 Kathy Spanberger, president/COO of Peermusic, noted that some publishers "are already investing more in masters, have signed some artist and songwriters for management, and we have paid for video and promotion. If you own masters, do the publishing and run management, that's a 360 deal, although we don't do any merch stuff because we don't know that world" (Anon., 2009).

2. The importance of flexible, ad hoc networks in the history of popular music cannot be overstated. Indeed, there are numerous unwritten histories of the importance of DJ networks, rack jobbers, and fan clubs for the music industry. One exceptional history is Frederic Dannen's 1991 book about the music business, *Hit Men*. In it Dannen writes at length about an informal alliance of top independent promotion men who worked records into radio playlists titled "The Network." Allegedly formed in a 1978 summit meeting, as a term "the Network" first surfaced in a November 1980 *Billboard* article. Dannen explained that,

> though the term 'Network' conjured images of a powerful, secret society, it referred to the tendency of the promoters to work as a loosely knit team. Each member had a "territory," a group of stations over which he claimed influence. If a record company wanted national airplay for a new single, it could choose to hire one of the Network men, who would in turn subcontract the job to the other members of the alliance.

As Dannen explained, although "The Network" worked records onto radio playlists specializing in Top 40 and "urban" formats, the lessons of this distributed labor force remain pertinent despite the fact that radio, records, and audiences have so significantly changed (Dannen, 1991, p. 11).

3. The band's lead singer and guitarist, Damian Kulash, explained in a *New York Times* editorial that over time Ok Go was no longer famous for records but for making their own inventive music videos on modest budgets that were shared through social networking sites: "My band is famous for music videos. We direct them ourselves or with the help of friends, we shoot them on shoestring budgets and, like our songs, albums and concerts, we see them

as creative works and not as our record company's marketing tool." It is no surprise that the band was an early adopter of YouTube. Approximately one year after the establishment of the video service in 2005, Ok Go debuted a video consisting of one long shot where the four band members performed an elaborate and entertaining choreographed dance sequence on a set tread-mills. As Kulash explained, while the video quickly blossomed into a hit it also put the band "afoul of our contract, since we need our record company's approval to distribute copies of the songs that they finance." In addition, the video "also exposed YouTube to all sorts of liability for streaming an EMI recording across the globe." Nevertheless, EMI and the record labels contin-ued to view videos as a form of advertising and the band's efforts were seen as promotions that benefitted the label as well. As Ok Go's initiative was lauded, the band spawned other, more complex "homespun" videos to be shared with millions (Ohanesian, 2010).

4. Palmer's ability to connect through online tools is legendary and like Ok Go led to her leaving her label. In 2009 Palmer became embroiled in a dispute with her label, Roadrunner, when she released a video for the single "Leeds United" off of her debut solo album *Who Killed Amanda Palmer?* Upon the release, Roadrunner asked Palmer to re-edit the video "because her stom-ach wasn't flat enough" in it (Devine, 2009). Loathe to keep the argument between her and her label, Palmer took her prolific blogging skills and hab-its and posted her label's comments, including a synopsis she had with her A&R person at Roadrunner where she quoted him commenting about why she needed to heed his advice to edit the video because "i'm a guy, amanda. i understand what people like" (Palmer, 2008). Palmer's post reverberated throughout her longstanding online fan forum "The Shadowbox." Soon fans in this online space began to show their disaffection for Roadrunner's opin-ion by posting pictures of their own bellies (Anon., 2008). Other fans went as far as to send pictures of their bellies to Roadrunner in an act of solidarity. Eventually the dispute that became known as "ReBellyon" would be some-thing of a final straw for Palmer who began to blog demands that her record company let her out of her contract (Devine, 2009). On April 6, 2010 Palmer announced on her blog that her wish had been fulfilled and Roadrunner had released her from her contract. Her announcement came in a signature longwinded post where she proclaimed that "after endless legal bullshit, it's over, i've been DROPPED, RELEASED, LET GO, whatever you wanna call it. in other words: i am FREE AT LAST!!!!!! RAAHH!!" However, most importantly Palmer reached directly to her fans:

> as many of you know, i've been a very vocal advocate of artists being fearless in asking their audience and supporters for direct financial help. i come from a background of grassroots theater and street perfor-mance, and i think that artists should feel no shame while passing the hat around once they've entertained a crowd of people it's been a huge and obvious irony that i have been legally unable to ask for money for my music, since it's been verboten by my contract with roadrunner. now that i'm unshackled, i plan on doing a lot of really awesome and creative things with my songs and how people can pay for them—or, better yet, donate—now that i have control over my stuff. for right now & in cel-ebration of this great event, i am very pleased to be able to—for the first time since the year 2003—offer you this track from myhouse to yours. . . . legally and free of charge. if you should feel inclined to "donate" more than the bare minimum (ZERO/FREE), you can do that too. even if you only donate a symbolic dollar, i'll see every single cent of it (after paypal transaction fees, of course). this whole exercise may not seem

like a big deal to you (artists put up music for free all the time), but for years i have not legally been allowed to put a song on a website and say: I JUST DID THIS, GO DOWNLOAD IT. it's been illegal. i am so happy i can finally make music and just GIVE IT AWAY. SO GO TAKE IT, PLEASE. (Palmer, 2010)

5. Again, the rise of business-to-business opportunities has been rather remarkable in the four years I have been researching and writing this manuscript. Indeed, they are a vital part of the new music ecosystem. However, these entities fell out of the province of this work as I have attempted to focus on changes where some basic practices of the music industry were shaken into alteration. The business-to-business paradigm is a hybrid that mixes the logistical aspects of older distributors (storage, retailer connection, some very basic elements of promotion); retail (independent storefronts, some offer small-batch or even just-in-time production abilities); and digital metadata maintenance. Indeed, despite the limits of this project, their complexity will and should demand the attention of myself and other researchers in the future.

Index